Ethnographic Landscapes and Language Ideologies in the Spanish State

This book offers a multi-contributor view on the linguistic landscape research in Spain, focusing on both monolingual and bilingual regions of Spain with an interest in initiatives that promote social and linguistic justice without neglecting migrant and international languages in the territory. The agency of speakers is highlighted, as well as the processes of linguistic hybridization and identity claims that are created in Spain. This volume analyzes the semiotic meaning of different languages, varieties, and discursive practices in different Spanish contexts from an ethnographic, multimodal, and critical perspective. It observes how some languages, varieties, and repertoires are privileged in top-down institutional environments, whilst others respond to bottom-up initiatives that contemplate complex processes of identity construction in Spain, in order to decide whether or not a greater balance between majority and minority languages is achieved in different contexts and spaces nowadays.

Carla Amorós Negre is a PhD in Linguistics and Associate Professor at the University of Salamanca in the General Linguistics Area (Spanish Linguistics Department). Her main areas of scholarly interest include Sociolinguistics, Language Policy and Planning, Multilingualism, Anthropological Linguistics, and Applied Linguistics. She has been a visiting researcher at the University of Edinburgh and the University of Bremen.

Gabriela Prego Vázquez is Associate Professor of General Linguistics at the Universidade de Santiago de Compostela. She belongs to the MetalingüisTICa research group at the Universidade de Santiago de Compostela. Her fields of study are critical sociolinguistics, ethnography, and language education.

Routledge Studies in Language and Identity
Series Editor: Reem Bassiouney

The Routledge Studies in Language and Identity (RSLI) series aims to examine the intricate relationship between language and identity from different perspectives. The series straddles fields such as sociolinguistics, discourse analysis, applied linguistics historical linguistics and linguistic anthropology. It aims to study identity and language by utilising novel methods of analysis as well as ground breaking theoretical approaches.

Titles in Series:

Research Companion to Language and Country Branding
Edited by Irene Theodoropoulou and Johanna Tovar

Mixing and Unmixing Languages: Romani Multilingualism in Kosovo
Amelia Abercrombie

New Approaches to Language and Identity in Contexts in Migration and Disapora
Edited by Stuart Dunmore, Karolina Rosiak, and Charlotte Taylor

Multilingualism in Italian Migrant Settings
Luca Iezzi

Language and Identity in the Arab World
Edited by Fathiya Al Rashdi and Sandhya Rao Mehta

Ethnographic Landscapes and Language Ideologies in the Spanish State
Edited by Carla Amorós Negre and Gabriela Prego Vázquez

For more titles, please visit www.routledge.com/Routledge-Studies-in-Language-and-Identity/book-series/RSLI

Ethnographic Landscapes and Language Ideologies in the Spanish State

Edited by Carla Amorós Negre and
Gabriela Prego Vázquez

LONDON AND NEW YORK

First published 2025
by Routledge
4 Park Square, Milton Park, Abingdon, Oxon OX14 4RN

and by Routledge
605 Third Avenue, New York, NY 10158

Routledge is an imprint of the Taylor & Francis Group, an informa business

© 2025 selection and editorial matter, Carla Amorós Negre and Gabriela Prego Vázquez; individual chapters, the contributors

The right of Carla Amorós Negre and Gabriela Prego Vázquez to be identified as the authors of the editorial material, and of the authors for their individual chapters, has been asserted in accordance with sections 77 and 78 of the Copyright, Designs and Patents Act 1988.

All rights reserved. No part of this book may be reprinted or reproduced or utilised in any form or by any electronic, mechanical, or other means, now known or hereafter invented, including photocopying and recording, or in any information storage or retrieval system, without permission in writing from the publishers.

Trademark notice: Product or corporate names may be trademarks or registered trademarks, and are used only for identification and explanation without intent to infringe.

British Library Cataloguing-in-Publication Data
A catalogue record for this book is available from the British Library

ISBN: 9781032687063 (hbk)
ISBN: 9781032687070 (pbk)
ISBN: 9781032687087 (ebk)

DOI: 10.4324/9781032687087

Typeset in Times New Roman
by Newgen Publishing UK

Contents

Notes on Contributors   vii

Introduction: Ethnographic landscapes and language ideologies in the Spanish state   1
CARLA AMORÓS NEGRE AND GABRIELA PREGO VÁZQUEZ

1 Minority language (in)visibility and layered asynchronous dialogue along the Camino del Norte   16
PAUL SEBASTIAN

2 An ethnography of Valencian language policy and planning through the linguistic landscape   40
CARLA AMORÓS NEGRE AND KAROLINA GRZECH

3 Multilingualism in the linguistic landscape of the city of Granada   64
DANIEL M. SÁEZ RIVERA, MARÍA HEREDIA MANTIS, IRANIA MALAVER ARGUINZONES, LUIS PABLO NÚÑEZ AND MARCIN SOSINSKI

4 A feminist discourse in the linguistic landscape of Málaga (2016–2024)   92
DIANA ESTEBA RAMOS

5 Bilingual and monolingual *universcapes*: Language choices and multimodal patterns of communication   123
IZASKUN ELORZA AND VASILICA MOCANU

6 "Iruinkokoa" and the Basque semiotic landscape: Transgressive
  carnival voices taken to the streets 146
  AGURTZANE ELORDUI, JOKIN AIESTARAN AND SAMARA VELTE

7 Ethnographies to localize (in)visibility and complexity: A
  collaborative study in higher education to explore the Bengali
  linguistic landscape in Madrid 166
  ADIL MOUSTAOUI SRHIR AND CARLOS ALIAÑO PÉREZ

8 *Street Languages*: An insight into linguistic landscapes for
  critical language education 194
  LUISA MARTÍN ROJO, CAMILA CÁRDENAS-NEIRA AND CLARA MOLINA

9 Ideologies around "Galicianness" commodification in the
  multilingual linguistic landscapes of marketplaces in Galicia:
  A participatory action research with high school students 217
  GABRIELA PREGO VÁZQUEZ, LUZ ZAS VARELA,
  PABLO MONTAÑA PRIETO AND CELTIA REY BRANDÓN

Index 244

Notes on Contributors

Jokin Aiestaran is a lecturer in the Basque Language and Communication Department at the Faculty of Social and Communication Sciences of the University of the Basque Country (UPV/EHU). He has worked on the fields of multilingualism and education, language attitudes, and linguistic landscape. Aiestaran has participated in the project Gaztesare and is currently a member of the project ESTANDAREV (PID2021-124673NA-I00).

Carlos Aliaño Pérez (Complutense University, Madrid) is a graduate student of Modern Languages and their Literatures. He is working as a certified Spanish teacher while he keeps doing research on Linguistic Landscapes (LL) since he presented his thesis on "Virtua exploration of the Linguistic Landscape of Lavapiés and its signs: The case of Arabic and Bengali." He is interested in Sociolinguistics, Linguistic Landscape, and the application of modern technology in sociolinguistic researches.

Carla Amorós Negre is a PhD in Linguistics and Associate Professor at the University of Salamanca in the General Linguistics Area (Spanish Linguistics Department). Her main areas of scholarly interest include Sociolinguistics, Language Policy and Planning, Multilingualism, Anthropological Linguistics, and Applied Linguistics. She is currently leading ESTANDAREV research project "Language Standardization Revisited: Mediatization, Vernacularization and Language Ideologies in Contemporary Spain."

Camila Cárdenas-Neira is an Assistant Professor at the Institute of Social Communication of the Universidad Austral de Chile and Juan de la Cierva Postdoctoral Fellow at the Center for Multilingualism, Discourse and Communication (MIRCo) of the Universidad Autónoma de Madrid (Spain). Her areas of teaching and research involve Critical Discourse Studies and Social Semiotics, and she has specialized in the analysis of multimodal discourses and linguistic landscapes of social movements.

Agurtzane Elordui is a professor at the University of the Basque Country. Her current research interests include language ideologies, minority languages, multilingual practices in social media, stylization in audio-visual discourse, and sociolinguistic and ideological change among Basque youth. She has been the main researcher of the Project *Gaztesare*, Multilingualism and glocal identities among Basque youth in the social networks (2018–2022). She is currently a member of the project ESTANDAREV (PID2021-124673NA-I00).

Izaskun Elorza leads LINDES Research Group at the University of Salamanca (Spain), where she is an Associate Professor in English Linguistics. Her research focuses on multimodal discourse analysis from the perspective of Halliday's systemic-functional linguistics, Kress and Van Leeuwen's visual semiotics, and corpus linguistics. Currently, she leads the research project AMULIT (Ref. PID2021-124786OB-100), which examines the applicability of multimodal texts about migration to multilingual and multicultural contexts.

Diana Esteba Ramos is an Associate Professor at the Department of Spanish Philology of the University of Málaga. Apart from her work on linguistic landscapes, she is a member of the HUM 558 group and collaborates with the CHER at the University of Strasbourg and on the project "Limes: Limits and Margins in the History of Spanish."

Karolina Grzech is a researcher working on evidentiality and epistemicity, with particular emphasis on how epistemic markers are used in natural discourse. Her research interests include semantics, pragmatics, language endangerment, and methodology of linguistic fieldwork, with special reference to the indigenous languages of South America and the Quechuan language family. She is also interested in the socioeconomic issues which affect speaker communities using minority and endangered languages.

María Heredia Mantis is Assistant Professor at University of Granada, PhD in Language and Culture for the University of Huelva. Her research is focused on Historical Linguistics (History of Spanish Language in the Spanish Golden Age) but also more recently Linguistic Landscape. She is a core member of PLANEO, Andalusian Linguistic Landscape, https://paisajelinguistico.es/.

Irania Malaver Arguinzones is a professor and researcher, currently at University of Granada. She is an anthropologist with a Master's in Linguistics from Universidad Central de Venezuela and a PhD in Applied Linguistics from the University of Alcalá. Her research areas are sociolinguistics and dialectology.

Luisa Martín Rojo is a Full Professor of Linguistics at Universidad Autónoma de Madrid, Spain, and head of the Interdisciplinary Research Centre on Multilingualism, Discourse and Communication (MIRCo). She has conducted research in the fields of discourse analysis, sociolinguistics, and communication, mainly focused on immigration and racism. She served as President of the Iberian Association for Studies on Discourse and Society (EDiSo) and is leading the EquiLing research project.

Vasilica Mocanu is Associate Professor at the University of Salamanca (Spain). Her research employs mixed methodologies in order to explore the relationship between language and identity in mobility contexts triggered by globalization. Vasilica is a member of *LINDES* (Linguistic Descriptions of English) Research Group since 2019 and has been a visiting researcher at Simon Fraser University (Vancouver, Canada), and at the Institute of Multilingualism (University of Fribourg, Switzerland).

Clara Molina is an Associate Professor of English Language and Linguistics at Universidad Autónoma de Madrid (Spain). Her teaching and research interests involve the overlapping fields of language variation and change, multilingualism and identity, language ideologies, linguistic landscapes, semantics and pragmatics, and communication consultancy. She is a member of the EquiLing research project.

Pablo Montaña Prieto is currently working as a teacher of Spanish Language and Literature in a secondary education center in Galicia. His academic publications focus on the Galician linguistic landscape and language teaching. He belongs to the MetalingüisTICa research group at the Universidade de Santiago de Compostela.

Adil Moustaoui Srhir (Complutense University, Madrid) is an Associate professor in the Department of Linguistics and Oriental Studies. He is interested in issues in multilingualism and language policy within transnational Moroccan families and linguistic repertoires, practices, and identity construction in student youth of Moroccan origin in Spain. He has published articles on multilingualism, Moroccan heritage languages, and translanguaging.

Luis Pablo Núñez, PhD, is currently teaching at University of Granada. Pablo Núñez's main research focus involves the fields of lexicography, linguistic historiography, publishing history, and digital humanities. He is currently researching on unpublished manuscript vocabularies from the late eighteenth, nineteenth, and early twentieth centuries for the ExploLEX project: http://wpd.ugr.es/~luispablo/.

Gabriela Prego Vázquez is Associate Professor of General Linguistics at the Universidade de Santiago de Compostela. She belongs to the MetalingüisTICa research group at the Universidade de Santiago de Compostela. Her fields of study are critical sociolinguistics, ethnography, and language education. She is a member of the EDiSo Association in which she has held the positions of vice president, member of the Discourse and Social Justice Commission and coordinator of the Discourse Observatory.

Celtia Rey Brandón currently works as a Galician Language and Literature teacher in Tomiño, Galicia, where she conducts research on linguistic landscape and linguistic biographies with her students. She belongs to the MetalingüisTICa research group at the Universidade de Santiago de Compostela.

Daniel M. Sáez Rivera is currently Associate Professor at University of Granada, with a BA in Spanish and Romance Philology and a PhD in Spanish Linguistics, in both cases from Complutense University of Madrid. His research interests are broad: History of Spanish Language, Historiography of Linguistics, and Applied Linguistics and Sociolinguistics, especially Linguistic Landscape and Migration Linguistics. He is a side member of PLANEO, *Andalusian Linguistic Landscape* https://paisajelinguistico.es/.

Paul Sebastian is Assistant Professor in Spanish and TESL/Applied Linguistics at Appalachian State University (United States). His research is rooted in the relationship between language and the constructed environment, whether that be physical, virtual, or hybrid. Within this central focus, his specific interests lie in the areas of learning space design, place semiotics, and technology-enhanced language learning and teaching.

Marcin Sosinski is Associate Professor at the Spanish Language Department in the University of Granada. His research activity is focused on Spanish as a Foreign Language, Sociolinguistics, and Phraseology. He has co-ordinated European projects regarding educational training for teachers of migrant adults and has published several materials for teaching literacy.

Samara Velte is a researcher at the Faculty of Social and Communication Sciences of the University of the Basque Country (UPV/EHU) and member of the research group NOR (IT881-16). Her research focuses on the discursive construction of identities of youths and adolescents within social conflicts and the construction of collective memory from a symbolic and sociocognitive perspective.

Luz Zas Varela is *Profesora Contratada Doctora* of General Linguistics at the University of Santiago de Compostela and belongs to the MetalingüisTICa research group. Her publications focus on the analysis of linguistic ideologies in educational contexts, communicative practices of superdiversity, and critical linguistic education. She was vice president of the International Association EDILIC (Education for Linguistic and Cultural Diversity, 2014–2016) and co-coordinator of the EDiSo Discourse Observatory.

Introduction

Ethnographic landscapes and language ideologies in the Spanish state

Carla Amorós Negre and Gabriela Prego Vázquez

Introduction: Rationale of the volume

As is very well known, linguistic landscape studies have become the focus of international scholarly attention in the last decades, confirmed by the increasing number of academic publications, projects, and conferences all over the world.[1] In fact, the interest in the linguistic landscape reflects the spatial turn in Sociolinguistics, Applied Linguistics and Linguistic Anthropology that foregrounds the interrelationship between languages, discourses, identities, and places. Already in 1968 the French sociologist Lefèbvre emphasized the importance of space in the projection of social hierarchies and the significance of analyzing it to observe how it is appropriated and transformed by different groups of people and speakers in very different and complex settings.

Nevertheless, it was not until the end of the twentieth century when linguistic landscape (LL) research was defined explicitly in one of the classic works as "visibility and salience of languages on public and commercial signs in a given territory or region" (Landry and Bourhis 1997, 23) and since then it has been used by different disciplines as a proxy to explain how languages and communicative resources are distributed and represented in the public space, through different linguistic traces such as billboards, store signs, graffiti posters, etc. LL studies have shown the symbolic and/or informative functions that different languages perform in a given territory; how the monolingual or bi-multilingual signs combinations can index different linguistic profiles of social groups who inhabit or transit particular settings; how speakers mobilize distinct ideologies (authenticity, anonymity, internationalism, etc.) in different local, national, or global spheres with the production of signs in different languages and varieties, etc. Thus, linguistic landscapes provide a kind of "social cartography" and have become strategic resources for observing processes of linguistic commodification (Heller 2010; Heller, Pujolar and Duchêne 2014) and gentrification. Similarly, linguistic landscapes highlight the fluidity of different linguistic repertoires and the role of language in both perpetuating inequalities and discrimination, as well as advocating for visibility, asserting identity, or resisting linguistically (Blackwood, Lanza and Woldemarian 2016).

Within this context, this volume focuses on the Spanish state, a geopolitical area with diverse sociohistorical, political-economic, and linguistic realities.

DOI: 10.4324/9781032687087-1

2 Ethnographic Landscapes and Language Ideologies in the Spanish State

Spanish, as the hegemonic language, competes for space with other major and hypercentral languages like English, while coexisting with others that vary in degree of minorization: languages tied to historical communities of the territory, both co-official (Catalan, Galician, Basque, Aranese) and non-official (Leonese, Asturian, Aragonese, Fala, Barranqueño, Dariya, Amazigh), as well as non-territorial and migrant languages. Our aim is to move beyond the territorialization of identities within Spain as a nation-state and view it as a geopolitical framework comprising multiple and *superdiverse* spaces where various agents contribute to its symbolic construction. The reference to "superdiverse spaces" relates, thus, to the concept of "superdiversity" coined by Vertovec (2007) in his critique of the naturalization of nation-states as culturally and linguistically homogeneous national communities. With *superdiverse spaces*, we aim to emphasize the adoption of non-essentialist epistemologies that reject the static view of languages as discrete and autonomous entities to properly manage ethnic and linguistic plurality. Following this critical sociolinguistic approach (cfr. Blommaert and Rampton 2011), the focus is on the dynamism of linguistic usage, the heteroglossia of speakers, whose communicative practices are always socially, politically, historically situated and connected to complex social identities that are constantly under construction.

Indeed, one of the means of identity construction and negotiation is precisely the linguistic landscape, through which speakers can challenge bottom-up the monoglossic and monocultural ideologies of the nation-state, its principles of territoriality and stability. Therefore, we are interested in observing how different spaces in officially monolingual and bilingual Spanish regions contribute to the embedding of power in language and how language in the public sphere is employed by speakers to affirm, resist, or challenge language hierarchies in different scenarios (Spolsky 2009). Landscapes are discursive spaces where linguistic imaginaries and ideologies are constructed and deconstructed. These are understood as systems of ideas and beliefs that articulate notions of language and the languages of speakers with the social, political, and economic order (Woolard 1998) of local, regional, national, or global scopes.

In this context, the initial studies on linguistic landscape in the Spanish territory paid special attention to the vitality of minority co-official languages and constituted interesting tools for checking the success of the processes of language planning, by making it possible to verify the visibility and symbolic values of these languages in the public space. The work developed in the Basque Country by Jasone Cenoz and Durk Gorter (2006, 2008) can be considered pioneer in this regard (cfr. Aiestaran, Cenoz and Gorter 2013; Gorter and Cenoz 2015a, 2015b; Fernández Juncal 2020a, 2020b, etc). In the Galician context, different studies addressed later on how bilingualism and the Galician/Spanish conflict materialized in the public space (cf. López Docampo 2011; Dunlevy 2012; Regueira, López Docampo and Wellings 2013; Rodríguez Barcia and Ramallo 2015; Lago Caamaño, Hervella and Gómez Martínez 2020). Likewise, the visibility of Catalan in Mallorca (Bruyel and Garau 2015), Barcelona (Camajoan 2013), or the linguistic conflict in Valencia (Lado 2011) have also been explored (cf. Sáez Rivera and Castillo Lluch 2013), without overlooking the attention to the invisibilization of other more minoritized and unofficial languages of the Spanish state, such as Asturian, in the work of Sebastian (2019).

Initial studies adopted a predominantly quantitative approach by counting the written signs of the linguistic landscape to observe the real impact of language normalization policies in bilingual regions of the state. Following the classic distinction in the subdiscipline of language planning (Calvet 2007), a differentiation was made between *in vitro* signs, produced top-down by national, regional, or local organizations, administrations, and governments (public road signs, railway stations, seaports, toponyms, as well as governmental services) and *in vivo* signs, produced by all kinds of speakers in non-regulated or unofficial domains (signage in commercial and advertising spaces, graffiti, etc.). Over time, linguistic landscape studies have prioritized qualitative and ethnographic research (Blommaert 2013; Blommaert and Maly 2014; Moriarty 2014; Shohamy 2015) or mixed quantitative-qualitative approaches in the analysis of signs (cf. Blackwood et al. 2016) to shed light on the ethnolinguistic vitality of language(s), the degree of multilingualism and contact among languages within a territory, the commercialization of languages on the product labels of popular and stereotyped products (Leeman and Modan 2010), samples of migrants' interlanguages and this is also the case with studies concerning languages of Spain (cf. Calvi 2018; De la Torre García and Molina-Díaz 2022; Gubitosi and Ramos 2021)

In this respect, the imprint of linguistic diversity connected to migration and globalization has been the focus of important linguistic landscape research in the Spanish territory. Pioneering has been the project "Lenguas pa'la citi," coordinated by Luisa Martín Rojo, Clara Molina, and Carmelo Díaz de Frutos in 2012 in Madrid, which has paid attention to the polycentric distribution and hierarchization of the new emerging multilingual ecologies (cf. Martín Rojo and Díaz de Frutos 2014). Madrid's multilingualism has also been addressed in the work of Muñoz Carrobles (2010), Castillo and Sáez (2011), Saiz de Lobado (2021) or in the research of Moustaoui Srhir (2013), focused on the presence of Arabic in contact with other languages in this city. The impact of migration and multilingualism has also been covered in research conducted in different Andalusian cities: Pons Rodríguez (2012) in Seville; Esteba Ramos (2018) in Málaga or Franco Rodríguez (2013) in Almería. In the Valencian Autonomous Community, it is worth noting the works of Yujing (2017), Gómez-Pavón and Quilis (2021), and Mocanu and Amorós (2023) in reference to the interplay between Spanish, Catalan, and Romanian in the Mediterranean coast. These multilingual ecologies connected to migration are also the focus of attention in Prego (2020, 2023); Zas and Prego (2016, 2018), Prego and Zas (2018) in the Galician context, where the authors study how Galician and Spanish varieties intersect with the linguistic repertoires of migrants. The educational applications of the linguistic landscape in language teaching have also garnered the attention of researchers in Spain, as seen in publications such as Prego and Zas (2018); Zas and Prego (2018); Alonso and Martín Rojo (2023); Martín Rojo, Cárdenas and Molina (2023); or Galloso Camacho, Cabello Pino, and Heredia Mantis (2023).

Similarly, in the last few decades the emphasis has been directed towards temporary, virtual, and multimodal signs (graffiti, advertisements, leaflets in-transit, visual, oral, kinesthetic elements (Malinowsk and Tufi 2020; Scollon and Scollon 2003, 1–2; Shohamy and Waksman 2009; Malinowsk and Tufi 2020), reflecting the very diversity of discourse and the performative character of signs, many of which cross traditional linguistic boundaries with hybrid linguistic displays. No wonder, then, that Jaworski and Thurlow (2010, 2) prefer to speak in terms of semiotic landscapes, understood as "any public space with visible inscription made through deliberate human intervention and meaning making." In this respect, particularly novel and interesting to explore are the vindictive and rebellious linguistic landscape (Martín Rojo 2023), to which Martín Rojo and Díaz de Frutos (2012) have paid particular attention in relation to the 15M movement in Madrid; the work of Morant and Martín (2017) on political proclamations in Valencia or the effects of the Law of Historical Memory in Granada, discussed in Guilat and Espinosa (2016).

Nevertheless, there is still a need for many landscape studies that, from a mainly ethnographic and qualitative perspective, analyze the semiotic meaning of the different languages and discursive practices in Spain. The sociolinguistics of globalization (Blommaert 2010) has emphasized the need to look towards the dynamicity of linguistic repertoires and practices ("languages in motion," Moriarty 2014) and precisely the ethnographic and semiotic analyses of the landscape allow us to study the tensions and power struggles in the public space (Ben-Rafael et al. 2006; Shohamy, Ben-Rafael and Barni 2010; Van Mensel, Vandenbroucke and Blackwood 2016, 431). As previously noted, landscapes are powerful tools in the analysis of hegemony relationships between speakers of different languages, but "they do not only reflect the status of different languages in society, but also act as a force shaping how languages are being perceived and used by the population" (Gorter 2013, 199). Some repertoires are privileged in top-down institutional environments, while others respond to bottom-up initiatives that envisage complex processes of identity building. Consequently, this volume pays special attention to the agency of speakers and the processes of linguistic hybridization and linguistic-identity claims that are created semiotically. Following both Scollon and Scollon (2003) and Blommaert and Maly (2014), the novelty of the volume lies precisely in the ethnographic and critical perspective adopted in the geo-semiotic analysis of very diverse linguistic landscapes in the Spanish state.

Different contributions deal with the construction whether or not a greater balance between majority and minority languages is achieved in different contexts and spaces nowadays. In this regard, the research carried out by **Sebastian** explores the (in)visibility and hierarchization among the minority languages of the north of the Spanish State, specifically along the Camino del Norte, part of the Camino de Santiago in Spain, which he himself undertook and which crosses the northern regions of the Basque Country, Cantabria, Asturias, and Galicia. Through the taking of photographs along the trail, personal diary entries, pilgrim stamps, and hand-drawn sketches, the author explores the presence and distribution of signs in Basque, Galician, Spanish, and English, connected with specific target groups, as well as the linguistic and cultural intersectionality of those who inhabit these places. Additionally, his work gives a good account of the ideological and sociopolitical tensions regarding the vindication of the official status of the Asturian language.

The fundamental and documented differences between top-down and bottom-up signage observed on the Camino are also very significant in the study conducted by **Amorós and Grzech** in three sociodemographic neighborhoods of Valencia, a touristic city on the Mediterranean coast and the third most populated in Spain. The examination of recent language policies regarding Catalan normalization and urban signage in the territory shows that, although bilingualism in Spanish and Valencian is the norm in official settings, this is not true for semi-public and private signs. In addition to the complexity and different indexical load of monolingual and bilingual signage in the documented and photographed districts, aided by interviews and participant observation, the study demonstrates the potential of private actors in reproducing and reinforcing the existing hierarchy of the two co-official languages of the region, with Spanish remaining the hegemonic language. The lack of consistent language policy and planning measures by successive regional governments is still evident in the Valencian urban landscape and reinforces the tendency of many landscape creators to commodify Catalan/Valencian as a symbol of authenticity (Woolard 1998) and as a language of activism, generally of a leftist orientation.

As we previously emphasized, our aim with the volume was also to include studies that address migrant and international languages in Spain, which is precisely the focus of the chapter authored by **Sáez, Heredia, Malaver, Núñez, and Sosinski**, devoted to multilingualism in the southern city of Granada. This third chapter explores how various population flows – including tourists attracted by the city's Muslim past, migrants, and students from Spain and abroad – contribute to Granada's multilingual character (primarily Spanish, English, and Arabic, but also Chinese, Japanese, Italian, French, etc.). Drawing from Blommaert (2013) and Blommaert and Maly (2014), the authors offer an ethnographic linguistic landscape analysis (ELLA) of three different areas: the city center, the Albayzín neighborhood, and the Beiro district, which has a significant migrant population, to explain the different patterns of social interaction in Granada.

Also focusing on Andalusia, specifically the coastal city of Málaga, **Esteba** examines landscape signs related to feminist slogans in the public sphere during the Women's Day demonstrations held in the city in 2023 and 2024. The author conducts a thorough analysis of these signs in and around the demonstrations, tracking feminist messages throughout the city in 2023 and interviewing various creators of feminist linguistic landscapes. Additionally, the signs are compared with a large collection of photographs taken in Málaga during two different periods (2016 and 2022–2024). Esteba highlights the tension between globalization and the assertion of local identity in the new globalized world order, noting the use of English alongside specific linguistic features of spoken Andalusian Spanish.

As noted earlier, landscape creators use various semiotic resources – not only verbal but also visual (such as design and layout, images, etc.) – to construct meanings in relation to their interests, communicative purposes, and target audiences. Therefore, linguistic landscape analysis should also take into consideration the multimodal aspects of communication today. This is the proposal of **Elorza and Mocanu** in the fifth chapter of the volume, dedicated to the study of the *universcape*, the university semiotic landscape, as a special case of 'schoolscape' (Gorter 2018), in two Spanish universities: Universitat de Lleida (Catalonia) and Universidad de Salamanca (Castile and Leon). Drawing from Kress and Van Leeuwen's (2006) visual social semiotics perspective, and Ravelli and McMurtrie's (2016) spatial discourse studies, the authors compare the institutional voice with the majority students' voice (language choice; typography and other visual and verbal strategies in regulated and unregulated public space) in these two different educational scenarios. Regardless of the officially bilingual (Lleida) or monolingual (Salamanca) contexts, both universities choose to use a single dominant language (Catalan and Spanish, respectively). It is also interesting to note that, despite the significant presence of international students at both universities, English is not used for signage in either of the *universcapes*. This contrasts with previous studies on universities that have adopted internationalization policies.

Particularly novel is the contribution by **Elordui, Aiestaran, and Velte**, dedicated to studying the carnivalesque parody and satire surrounding the 'Iruinkokoa' performances in Pamplona (Navarra). This event is especially meaningful semiotically for exploring power and political conflicts involving the Basque language in this region, taking into account "verbal texts, images, objects, placement in time and space as well as human beings" (Shohamy and Waksman 2009, 314). Creativity enables the group of Basque young people who participate in this Carnival to rework semiotic resources in order to transcend existing social and material constraints, with the intention of reconfiguring social meanings, relations, and structures.

The remaining three chapters in this volume, authored by **Moustaoui and Aliaño; Martín Rojo, Cárdenas, and Molina; Prego, Zas, Montaña, and Rey**, respectively, are noteworthy for their innovative methodological approaches to the study of the linguistic landscape. These chapters exemplify the latest developments in this field, including the implementation of participatory research, the utilization of mobile applications for data collection, tagging and geolocation of linguistic features, and the integration of critical pedagogical approaches within educational contexts. As Purschke (2023, 87) observes: "The field is currently witnessing processes of methodological consolidation, structural institutionalization, and thematic diversification. These processes foster the emergence of new trends in the field, such as participatory research, mobile crowdsourcing, and engagement in educational settings."

Consequently, the field of linguistic landscape has experienced a continuous evolution in its methodology since its inception, becoming an area conducive to innovation. In recent years, one of the most significant developments has been the introduction of participatory research methods for data collection and analysis. This emerging approach aims to actively engage local communities in the research process, with the objective of placing their knowledge at the center of the study. Participatory research, which is aligned with the principles of citizen science (Levy 2004; Rymes and Leone 2014), enables the collection of data that is more diverse and enriching by integrating the views of a wide range of social actors. Furthermore, its implementation in educational contexts not only empowers students as co-researchers, but also strengthens social cohesion within their communities, thereby broadening the understanding of linguistic diversity. For further insight, one might consider projects such as LoCALL (www.ew.uni-hamburg.de/en/internationales/projekte/locall.html) and EquiLing (www.equiling.eu/gl/sobre-equiling/) which place an emphasis on the educational context.

The research conducted in Spain represents a pioneering effort to integrate participatory research methodologies into the analysis of linguistic landscapes. A pioneering example is the aforementioned project, "Lenguas pa'la citi," which was coordinated by Luisa Martín Rojo, Clara Molina, and Carmelo Díaz de Frutos in 2012 and was previously referenced. This project employed participatory research and citizen science methodologies to examine the linguistic landscape of Madrid and was developed within the framework of the subject "Multilingualism and Languages in Contact" of the degree in "Modern Languages, Culture and Communication" at the University Autónoma of Madrid. Its objective was two-fold: first, to enable students to analyze the linguistic landscape of their environment; second, to facilitate a transformation in their perception of it. As the project coordinators emphasized, members of the public were frequently unaware of the linguistic diversity that surrounds them, as their perception was shaped by monolingual ideologies. The findings of the project, which underscore the multilingual character of Madrid's linguistic landscape, were presented in an exhibition and a documentary (Martín Rojo, Molina and Díaz de Frutos 2012), accessible on YouTube.

In 2014, as a result of a collaboration between the EDiSo Association (www.edisoportal.org/) and the researchers of MIRCO (www.mircouam.com/), the EDiSo/MIRCO Discourse Observatory was established. The objective of the observatory, in the period from 2014 to 2019, was to conduct action-oriented participatory research through the open and collective collection of discursive materials from the linguistic landscape. In the context of citizen science, the project concentrated on the examination of linguistic diversity within the urban landscape, with a particular focus on the analysis of the signs present in public space. This approach aimed to elucidate the mechanisms through which power is exercised, the nature of intercultural relations between citizens, and the ideologies and policies that underpin these interactions. Between 2014 and 2019, the *Discourse Observatory* placed special emphasis on studying through the linguistic landscape: micromachisms and microrracisms, the management of urban diversity and relations between different social groups (assimilation, segregation, marginalization, or social integration), and how the appropriation of space and resistance is manifested through the linguistic landscape.

Four of the authors of the last three chapters of this volume (Luisa Martín Rojo, Clara Molina, Gabriela Prego, and Luz Zas) played a dual role in the project, serving as founders of the observatory and as coordinators at various stages of the initiative. Moreover, the Discourse Observatory enlisted the assistance of university students as co-researchers, predicated on the assumption that all perspectives are worthy of consideration and that all social actors offer a valuable contribution to the understanding of the world. From 2014 to 2019, students from the following universities participated in various projects of this observatory: University Autónoma of Madrid, University of Santiago de Compostela, Pompeu Fabra University, University of Navarra, University of Fribourg, University of Entre Ríos, and University of New York.

The *Discourse Observatory* employed a methodology that is consistent with the principles of citizen science, which encourages collective participation in data collection on a scale that would not be feasible with more conventional observation and data gathering techniques. The observatory also resulted in the creation of the online tool Urbanvoices.net (www.urbanvoices.net/), a collaborative platform that allows for the organization and sharing of photographs for analysis from a critical discourse perspective, taking into account the geospatial implications of different discourses. This citizen science tool facilitates the collection of data for diverse research on social processes in different locations. The photographs on Urbanvoices.net (www.urbanvoices.net/) are categorized into two principal areas: "Language Diversity" and "Discursive Violence and Resistance," with detailed subcategories such as linguistic variety and message type.

In recent years, a number of citizen science projects have been initiated with a crowdsourcing approach for the purpose of conducting research on linguistic landscapes. These projects make use of free mobile applications for the collection and analysis of linguistic data. For example, *Lingscape* (https://lingscape.uni.lu/), *Linguasnapp* (www.linguasnapp.manchester.ac.uk/), or the citizen science platform *Voces territorio*, which is currently in its final stages of development within the framework of MIRCO (www.mircouam.com/). Additionally, other tools for geolocation and labeling of the linguistic landscape, specifically adapted to educational environments, have been developed: *LocaLLApp* (https://portalrecerca.uab.cat/en/projects/locall-local-linguistic-landscapes-for-global-language-education--2) and *MAVEL* (http://mavel.avel.cesga.es/).

Such resources permit direct citizen participation in the research process, thereby opening new ways for public involvement in both scientific research and scientific communication. These mobile applications facilitate the collection of a substantial number of geolocated photographs across entire communities and even countries. A significant benefit of this approach is that, as Purschke (2017, 184) notes: "the data we collect represents not our expert view on the landscape but combines thousands of individual perspectivities of visible multilingualism in public space. This basically means that our data collection does not only reflect our particular research interest and perspective on the linguistic landscape, but the many different ways in which our users perceive the linguistic landscape in everyday life."

In line with this, the last three chapters of this volume (**Moustaoui and Aliaño; Martín Rojo, Cárdenas, and Molina; Prego, Zas, Montaña, and Rey**) introduce the concept of participatory linguistic landscape research in an educational context. The chapters in question exhibit several shared characteristics, both in terms of their theoretical approaches, methodologies and study objectives. This concurrence is not fortuitous, as the three studies are situated within the EquiLing project (www. equiling.eu/gl/), which has integrated participatory ethnographies to examine how language mediates the management of social inequalities in contemporary multilingual contexts. Specifically, the chapters by **Moustaoui and Aliaño; Martín Rojo, Cárdenas, and Molina** are part of the EquilingMadrid subproject (www.equiling. eu/gl/madrid/), while the chapter by **Prego, Zas, Montaña, and Rey** is part of the EquilingGalicia subproject (www.equiling.eu/gl/galicia/). In all three cases, the objective of participatory linguistic landscape research is twofold: first, to prompt students to reflect on the inequalities associated with languages through the lens of the linguistic landscape, and second, to cultivate critical linguistic awareness and encourage students to adopt a heteroglossic perspective towards the linguistic landscapes that surround them.

In all three chapters, the use of linguistic landscapes as a fundamental tool for exploring and understanding sociolinguistic dynamics in public spaces is evident, with examples including multicultural neighborhoods, markets, and urban areas. These works promote critical linguistic education, wherein participants are encouraged to develop an awareness of language use and the social inequalities that can be reflected and perpetuated through such use. They explore how different languages and symbols are used to construct and negotiate identities in specific local contexts. Additionally, the chapters examine the tensions between global and local influences on linguistic landscapes, investigating how phenomena such as globalization, localization, and glocalization have a significant impact on the visibility and status of different languages in public spaces. This phenomenon reflects and, at times, reinforces existing social hierarchies and inequalities. Collectively, these studies advocate for a more inclusive and equitable approach to linguistic citizenship that respects and values linguistic and cultural diversity.

While the three chapters share several points in common, they are also distinguished by their specific approaches, study contexts, and the particular objectives they address. For instance, **Moustaoui and Aliaño** present the findings of a collaborative action-research at the University Complutense of Madrid as part of the EquiLingMadrid initiative. This study examines the process of (in) visibility of the Bengali community by analyzing their linguistic practices within the linguistic landscape of Lavapiés, an urban neighborhood distinguished by its linguistic and cultural diversity. By mapping and observing the linguistic landscape (LLS) and the practices of the Bengali community in Lavapiés, the analysis reveals that the signs used are adapted to both the spatio-temporal demands and the sociopolitical, cultural, and economic conditions of the neighborhood. The authors emphasize that, throughout the participatory research, the students develop their critical linguistic awareness, deepening their understanding of multilingualism and the sociopolitical factors that influence the use of languages in public spaces.

The chapter by **Martín Rojo, Cárdenas, and Molina**, which is also part of the EquiLingMadrid project, presents an educational initiative that was developed through participatory research with students from the University Autónoma of

Madrid. This initiative, situated within the context of open science for popular education, focuses on the interactions between linguistic, sociocultural, and urban processes. Its objective is to explore how the spatial approach in the study of linguistic landscapes can reveal their co-construction. The proposal employs examples from the linguistic landscape of Madrid to identify and illustrate the inequalities present in the city's diverse neighborhoods. The chapter presents the theoretical framework of the proposal and describes its implementation in university classrooms. Moreover, the authors have prepared a free-access guide that includes testimonials from students who have followed the proposed guidelines. The objective of this initiative is to empower speakers to advocate for more equitable societies from a sociolinguistic perspective. In this regard, the educational proposal draws inspiration from Paulo Freire's conscientization method (Freire 1970, 1975), which fosters collective awareness and action.

Finally, **Prego, Zas, Montaña** and **Rey** present the findings of a participatory action research project involving secondary school students from two Galician localities: a high school in Tomiño, a semi-urban municipality situated on the border between Galicia and Portugal, and a high school in the center of Vigo, a major Galician city. The analysis is centered on the linguistic landscapes of traditional markets in these regions. The research adheres to a Critical Linguistic Awareness approach, with data analysis situated within the framework of Critical Sociolinguistic Ethnography (Blommaert 2010). The results of this analysis demonstrate how the discursive commodification of the linguistic landscape occurs through the metadiscursive processes of linguistic and semiotic enregisterment (Agha 2007) of global resources and "Galicianness" resources. The study illustrates how "Galicianness" is commodified to construct an identity of utopian authenticity, associated with values of a natural and sustainable environment, in conjunction with the sea, the land, and traditions, within a glocal context. Furthermore, it addresses the symbolic values and ideologies on which these identities (global, glocal, and local) are based, as well as how these are (mis)recognized, reproduced, or contested by the young students in sociodiscursive processes that renegotiate and reimagine market spaces where the position of the Galician language is situated in a tension between pride and benefit in the multilingual landscape.

Note

1 This book has been produced within the framework of the following projects I+D+I projects Espacios de transformación sociolingüística en el contexto educativo gallego: agencia de los hablantes, repertorios multilingües y prácticas (meta) comunicativas (Plan nacional I+D+I FEDER/Ministerio de Ciencia, Innovación y Universidades – Agencia Estatal de Investigación PID2019-105676RB-C44/AEI/10.13039/501100011033.), Universidade de Santiago de Compostela) and "La estandarización lingüística revisitada. Mediatización, vernacularización e ideologías lingüísticas en la España contemporánea" (Grant PID2021-124673NA-I00 funded by MICIU/AEI/10.13039/501100011033 and by "ERDF A way of making Europe.")

References

Agha, A. 2007. *Language and Social Relations*. Cambridge: Cambridge University Press.

Aiestaran, Jokin, Cenoz, Jasone, and Gorter, Durk. 2013. "Perspectivas del País Vasco: el paisaje lingüístico en Donostia-San Sebastián." *Revista Internacional de Lingüística Iberoamericana* 21, no. 1: 23–38.

Alonso, Lara, and Martín Rojo, Luisa. 2023. "Madrid/Nueva York: La transformación de dos ciudades a través del paisaje lingüístico: una herramienta de acción educativa." In *Superdiversidad lingüística en los nuevos contextos multilingües. Una mirada etnográfica y multidisciplinar*, edited by Gabriela Prego Vázquez y Luz Zas Varela, 157–181. Madrid: Iberoamericana Vervuert.

Amorós-Negre, Carla, and Vasilica Mocanu. 2023. "Las invisibles lenguas de la migración: la identidad lingüística rumana en el paisaje lingüístico del levante español." In *Migración, pluricentrismo y acomodación. Nuevas perspectivas desde la lengua*, edited by Rolf Kailuweit, Sandra Schlumpf-Thurnherr, and Eva Staudinger, 59–87. Berlin: Nomos.

Ben-Rafael, Eliezer, Shohamy, Elana, Amara, Muhammad Hasan and Nira Trumper-Hecht. 2006. "Linguistic Landscape as Symbolic Construction of the Public Space: The Case of Israel." *International Journal of Multilingualism* 3, no. 1: 7–31. https://doi.org/10.1080/14790710608668383

Blackwood, Robert, Lanza, Elizabeth, and Hirut Woldemariam. 2016. *Negotiating and Contesting Identities in Linguistic Landscapes*. London/New York: Bloomsbury.

Blommaert, Jan. 2010. *The Sociolinguistics of Globalization*. Cambridge: Cambridge University Press.

Blommaert, Jan, and Ben Rampton. 2011. "Language and Superdiversity." *Diversities*, 13, no. 2: 1–23. www.unesco.org/shs/diversities/vol13issue2/art1

Blommaert, Jan. 2013. *Ethnography, Superdiversity and Linguistic Landscapes Chronicles of Complexity*. Bristol: Multilingual Matters

Blommaert, Jan, and Ico Maly. 2014. "Ethnographic Linguistic Landscape Analysis and Social Change: A Case Study." *Tilburg Papers in Culture Studies* 100. https://research.tilburguniversity.edu/en/publications/ethnographic-linguistic-landscape-analysis-and-social-change-a-ca-4

Bruyèl Olmedo, Antonio, and María Juan Garau. 2015. "Minority Languages in the Linguistic Landscape of Tourism: The Case of Catalan in Mallorca." *Journal of Multilingual and Multicultural Development* 36, no. 6: 598–619. https://doi.org/10.1080/01434632.2014.979832

Calvet, Louis Jean. 2007. *As Políticas Linguísticas*. Florianópolis: IPOL/Parábola.

Calvi, Maria Vittoria. 2018. "Paisajes lingüísticos hispánicos: Panorama de estudios y nuevas perspectivas." *Lynx: Panorámica de estudios lingüísticos* 17: 3–58.

Castillo Lluch, Mónica, and Daniel Sáez Rivera. 2011. "Introducción al paisaje lingüístico de Madrid." *Lengua y migración* 3, no. 1: 73–88.

Castillo Lluch, Mónica, and Daniel Sáez Rivera (eds.). 2013. "Paisajes lingüísticos en el mundo hispánico." *Revista Internacional de Lingüística Iberoamericana* 21: 9–22.

Cenoz, Jasone, and Durk Gorter. 2006. "Linguistic Landscape and Minority Languages." *The International Journal of Multilingualism* 3: 67–80. https://doi.org/10.1080/14790710608668386

Cenoz, Jasone, and Durk Gorter. 2008. "The Linguistic Landscape As An Additional Source of Input in Second Language Acquisition." *IRAL* 46, no. 3, 267–287. https://doi.org/10.1515/IRAL.2008.012

Comajoan, Luis. 2013. "El paisaje lingüístico en Cataluña: caracterización y percepciones del paisaje visual y auditivo en una avenida comercial de Barcelona." *Revista Internacional de Lingüística Iberoamericana* 21, no. 1: 63–88.

De la Torre García, Mercedes, and Francisco Molina-Díaz (eds.). 2022. *Paisaje lingüístico: cambio, intercambio y método*. Berlin: Peter Lang.

Dunlevy, Deirdre. 2012. "Linguistic Policy and Linguistic Choice: A Study of the Galician Linguistic Landscape." In *Linguistic Landscapes, Multilingualism, and Social Change*, edited by Christine Hélot, Monica Barni, Rudi Jannsens, and Carla Bagna, 53–68. Frankfurt: Peter Lang.

Esteba Ramos, Diana. 2018. "Paisaje lingüístico turístico y residencial en el Mediterráneo español: patrones y usos lingüísticos en Nerja." In *El paisaje: Percepciones interdisciplinares desde las Humanidades*, edited by Emilio Ortega Arjonilla, 193–202. Albolote: Editorial Comares.

Fernández Juncal, Carmen. 2020a. "La estratificación social del paisaje lingüístico de Bilbao." *Revista Internacional de Lingüística Iberoamericana* 35: 117–141.

Fernández Juncal, Carmen. 2020b. "Funcionalidad y convivencia del español y el vasco en el paisaje lingüístico de Bilbao." *Íkala, Revista de Lenguaje y Cultura* 25, no. 3: 713–729. https://doi.org/10.17533/udea.ikala.v25n03a04

Franco-Rodríguez, José Manuel. 2013. "An Alternative Reading of the Linguistic Landscape: The Case of Almería." *Revista Internacional de Lingüística Iberoamericana* 21: 109–134.

Freire, Paulo. 1970. *Pedagogía del oprimido*. Montevideo: Tierra Nueva.

Freire, Paulo. 1975. *Acción Cultural para la Libertad*. Buenos Aires: Tierra Nueva.

Galloso Camacho, María Victoria, Cabello Pino, Manuel, and María Heredia Mantis (eds.). 2023. *Funciones y aplicación didáctica del paisaje lingüístico andaluz*. Madrid: Iberoamericana Vervuert.

Gómez-Pavón Durán, Ana, and Mercedes Quilis Merín. 2021. "El paisaje lingüístico de la migración en el barrio de Ruzafa en Valencia: una mirada a través del tiempo." *Cultura, Lenguaje y Representación* 25: 135–154. https://doi.org/10.6035/CLR.2021.25.8

Gorter, Durk. 2013. "Linguistic Landscapes in a Multilingual World." *Annual Review of Applied Linguistics* 33, 190–212.

Gorter, Durk. 2018. "Methods and Techniques for Linguistic Landscape Research: About Definitions, Core Issues and Technological Innovations." In *Expanding the Linguistic Landscape: Linguistic Diversity, Multimodality and the Use of Space as a Semiotic Resource*, edited by Martin Pütz and Neele Mundt, 38-57. Bristol, Blue Ridge Summit: Multilingual Matters. https://doi.org/10.21832/9781788922166-005

Gorter, Durk, and Jasone Cenoz. 2015a. "Translanguaging and Linguistic Landscapes." *Linguistic Landscape: An International Journal* 1, no. 1–2: 54–74.

Gorter, Durk, and Jasone Cenoz. 2015b. "The Linguistic Landscapes Inside Multilingual Schools." In *Challenges for Language Education and Policy: Making Space for People*, edited by Bernard Spolsky, Ofra Inbar-Lourie, and Michal Tannenbaum, 151–169. New York: Routledge.

Guilat, Yael, and Antonio B. Espinosa-Ramírez. 2016. "The Historical Memory Law and Its Role in Redesigning Semiotic Cityscapes in Spain: A Case Study from Granada." *Linguistic Landscape: An International Journal* 2, no. 3: 247–274. https://doi.org/10.1075/ll.2.3.03gui

Gubitosi Patricia, and Michelle F. Ramos Pellicia (eds.). 2021. *Linguistic Landscape in the Spanish-speaking World*. Amsterdam: John Benjamins.

Heller, Monica. 2010. "The Commodification of Language." *Annual Review of Anthropology* 29: 101–114. https://doi.org/10.1146/annurev.anthro.012809.104951

Heller, Monica, Pujolar, Joan, and Duchêne, Alexandre. 2014. "Linguistic Commodification in Tourism." *Journal of Sociolinguistics* 18, no. 4: 539–566. https://doi.org/10.1111/josl.12082

Jaworski, Adam, and Crispin Thurlow. 2010. "Introducing Semiotic Landscapes." In .*Semiotic Landscapes. Language Image, Space,* edited by Adam Jaworski and Crispin Thurlow, 1–41. London: Continuum

Kress, Gunther, and Theo Van Leeuwen. 2006. *Reading Images: The Grammar of Visual Design* (2nd ed.). London: Routledge.

Lado, Beatriz. 2011. "Linguistic Landscape as a Reflection of the Linguistic and Ideological Conflict in the Valencian Community." *International Journal of Multilingualism* 8, no. 2: 135–150. https://doi.org/10.1080/14790718.2010.550296

Lago Caamaño, Clara, Hervella, Silvia, and Lidia Gómez Martínez. 2020. "An analysis of the Compostelian Linguistic Landscape. The Centrality of the Cathedral of Santiago de Compostela." *RiCOGNIZIONI. Rivista Di Lingue E Letterature Straniere E Culture Moderne* 7, no. 13: 93–104. https://doi.org/10.13135/2384-8987/4383

Landry, Rodrigue, and Richard Bourhis. 1997. "Linguistic Landscape and Ethnolinguistic Vitality: An Empirical Study." *Journal of Language and Social Psychology* 16: 23–49. https://doi.org/10.1177/0261927X970161002

Leeman, Jennifer, and Gabriella Modan. 2010. "Selling the City: Language, Ethnicity and Commodified Space." In *Linguistic Landscape in the City*, edited by Elana Shohamy, Eliezer Ben-Rafael and Monica Barni, 182–197. Clevedon: Multilingual Matters.

Lefebvre, Henri. 1968. *Le droit à la ville*. Paris: Editions Anthropos

Lévy, Pierre. 2004. Inteligencia Colectiva: por una antropología del ciberespacio. Panamericana de la Salud. http://inteligenciacolectiva.bvsalud.org/

LoCALL Project. 2019-2022. LoCALL: Lo-cal Linguistic Landscapes for Global Language Education in the School Context. https://locallproject.eu/

López Docampo, Miguel. 2011. "A paisaxe lingüística: unha análise dun espazo público galego." *Cadernos de Lingua* 33: 5–35.

Ma, Yujing. 2017. "El paisaje lingüístico chino-español de la ciudad de Valencia: una aproximación a su estudio." *Lengua y migración* 9, no. 1: 63–84.

Malinowski, David, and Stefania Tufi. 2020. *Reterritorializing Linguistic Landscapes: Questioning Boundaries and Opening Spaces*. London: Bloomsbury.

Martín Rojo, Luisa, and Carmelo Díaz de Frutos. 2014. "#En Sol, revolución: paisajes lingüísticos para tomar las plazas." *Journal of Spanish Cultural Studies* 15, no. 1–2: 1–24. https://doi.org/10.1080/14636204.2014.982889

Martín Rojo, Luisa, Molina, Clara, and Carmelo Díaz de Frutos. 2012. "Madrid multilingüe: Lenguas pa'la citi." www.youtube.com/watch?v=jBFxhXFVi50

Martín Rojo, Luisa, Cárdenas, Camila, and Clara Molina. 2023. *Lenguas callejeras: paisajes colectivos de las lenguas que nos rodean. Guía para fomentar la conciencia sociolingüística crítica*. Barcelona: Octaedro.

Martín Rojo, Luisa. 2023. "Paisajes lingüísticos de los movimientos protesta." In *The Routledge Handbook of Spanish Language Discourse Studies*, edited by Carmen López Ferrero, Isolda E. Carranza and Teun Van Dijk, 270–286. New York: Routledge.

Morant Marco, Ricardo, and Arantxa Martín López. 2017. *Tatuajes urbanos. Los susurros, murmullos y gritos de la ciudad*. València: Tirant Humanidades.

Moriarty, Máiréad. 2014. "Languages in Motion: Multilingualism and Mobility in the Linguistic Landscape." *International Journal of Bilingualism* 18, no. 5: 457–463. https://doi.org/10.1177/1367006913484208

Moustaoui Srhir, Adil. 2013. "Nueva economía y dinámicas de cambio sociolingüístico en el paisaje lingüístico de Madrid: el caso del árabe." *Revista Internacional de Lingüística Iberoamericana* 21, no. 1: 89–108.

Muñoz Carrobles, David. 2010. "Breve itinerario por el paisaje lingüístico de Madrid." *Revista de estudios sobre la ciudad como espacio plural* 2, no. 2: 103–109. http://www.ucm.es/info/angulo/volumen/Volumen02-2/varia04.htm

Pons Rodríguez, Lola. 2012. *El paisaje lingüístico de Sevilla: Lenguas y variedades en el escenario urbano hispalense.* Sevilla: Diputación de Sevilla.

Prego Vázquez, Gabriela. 2020. "Escalas sociolingüísticas." In *Claves para entender el multilingüismo contemporáneo*, edited by Luisa Martín Rojo and Joan Pujolar, 91–129. Barcelona: Editorial UOC.

Prego Vázquez, Gabriela. 2023. "(Des)reconocimiento sociolingüístico y escalaridad en los nuevos repetorios lingüísticos glocales de los jóvenes en Galicia." In *Superdiversidad linguistic en los nuevos contextos multilingües: una mirada etnográfica y multidisciplinary,* edited by Gabriela Prego and Luz Zas, 85–118. Madrid: Iberoamericana Vervuert.

Prego Vázquez, Gabriela, and Luz Zas Varela. 2018. "Paisaje lingüístico. Un recurso TIC, TAC, TEP para el aula." *Lingue e Linguaggi* 25: 277–295. https://doi.org/10.1285/I2239 0359V25P277

Purschke, Christoph. 2023. "Exploring the Linguistic Landscape of Cities Through Crowdsourced Data." In *Language, Society and the State in a Changing World*, edited by Stanley D. Brunn y Roland Kehrein, 57–74. Cham: Springer. https://doi.org/10.1007/978-3-031-18146-7_3

Purschke, Christoph. 2017. "Crowdsourcing the Linguistic Landscape of a Multilingual Country. Introducing Lingscape in Luxembourg." *Linguistik Online* 85, no. 6: 181–202.

Ravelli, Louise J., and Robert J. McMurtrie. 2016. *Multimodality in the Built Environment.* New York: Routledge.

Regueira Fernández, Xosé Luís; López Docampo, Miguel, and Matthew Wellings. 2013. "El paisaje lingüístico en Galicia." *Revista Internacional de Lingüística Iberoamericana* 21, no. 1: 39–62.

Rymes, Betsy, and Leone Andrea R. 2014. "Citizen Sociolinguistics: A New Media Methodology for Understanding Language and Social Life." *Working Papers in Educational Linguistics* 29, no. 2: 25–44 www.gse.upenn.edu/wpel/sites/gse.upenn.edu.wpel/files/29.2RymesandLeone.pdf

Rodríguez Barcia, Susana, and Fernando Ramallo. 2015. "Graffiti y conflicto lingüístico: el paisaje urbano como espacio ideológico." *Revista Internacional de Lingüística Iberoamericana* 25, no. 1: 131–153.

Saiz de Lobado, Ester. 2021. "Construcción identitaria de la inmigración en el paisaje madrileño: Lavapiés y San Diego." *Migraciones Internacionales* 12. https://doi.org/10.33679/rmi.v1i1.2358

Scollon, Ron, and Scollon, Suzie Wong. 2003. *Discourses in Place. Languages in the Material World.* London: Routledge.

Sebastian, Paul. 2019. "Signs of Resistance in the Asturian Linguistic Landscape." *Linguistic Landscape* 5, no. 3: 302–329. https://doi.org/10.1075/ll.18015.seb

Shohamy, Elana. 2015. "LL research as expanding language and language policy *Linguistic Landscape* 5, no. 1–2: 152–171. https://doi.org/10.1075/ll.1.1-2.09sho

Shohamy, Elana, Ben-Rafael, Eliezer, and Monica Barni (eds.). 2010. *Linguistic Landscape in the City*. Bristol: Multilingual Matters.

Shohamy, Elana, and Shoshi Waksman. 2009. "Linguistic Landscape As An Ecological Arena: Modalities, Meanings, Negotiations, Education." In *Linguistic Landscape: Expanding the Scenery*, edited by Elana Shohamy, and Durk Gorter, 313–331. New York: Routledge.

Spolsky, Bernard. 2009. "Prolegomena to a Sociolinguistic Theory of Public Signage." In *Linguistic Landscape: Expanding the Scenery*, edited by Elana Shohamy, and Durk Gorter, 25–39. New York: Routledge.

Van Mensel, Luk, Vandenbroucke, Mieke, and Robert Blackwood. 2016. "Linguistic Landscapes." In *The Oxford Handbook of Language and Society*, edited by Ofelia Garcia, Massimiliano Spotti, and Nelson Flores, 423–450. Oxford: Oxford University Press.

Vertovec, Steven. 2007. "Super-Diversity and Its Implications." *Ethnic and Racial Studies* 30, no. 6: 1026–1056. https://doi.org/10.1080/01419870701599465

Woolard, Kathryn A. 1998. "Introduction: Language Ideology as a Field of Inquiry." In *Language Ideologies: Practice and Theory*, edited by Bambi B. Schieffelin, Kathryn A. Woolard, and Paul V. Kroskrity, 3–47. Oxford: OUP.

Zas Varela, Luz, and Gabriela Prego Vázquez. 2016. "Las Escalas del Paisaje Lingüístico en los Márgenes de la Superdiversidad." *Cescontexto Debates* 15: 6–25.

Zas Varela, Luz, and Gabriela Prego Vázquez. 2018. "A View of Linguistic Landscapes for an Ethical and Critical." In *Galician Migrations: A Case of Emerging Super-Diversity*, edited by Renée De Palma, and Antía Pérez-Caramés, 249–264. London: Springer.

1 Minority language (in)visibility and layered asynchronous dialogue along the Camino del Norte

Paul Sebastian

Introduction

Along the Camino del Norte, between two small coastal towns in the region of Asturias, there is a colorful mural that invites all who pass to pause and reflect on the shared experience of those who walk what is erroneously referred to in the singular as the Camino de Santiago (Way of St James). Figure 1.1 shows the mural located prominently along the main El Norte route. The United Nations Educational, Scientific and Cultural Organization (UNESCO) describe the Camino de Santiago as "an extensive interconnected network of pilgrimage routes in Spain whose ultimate destination is the tomb of the Apostle James the Greater in Santiago de Compostela" (UNESCO World Heritage Convention 2024).

According to the Oficina de Acogida al Peregrino (Pilgrim's Reception Office), which meticulously tracks a variety of statistics pertaining to pilgrims and their pilgrimages to Santiago de Compostela, a total of sixteen distinct Camino routes were officially completed in the year 2022 (Oficina de Acogida al Peregrino 2024). The office's annual statistical report shows that just over half of the 438,307 pilgrims who completed a pilgrimage in 2022 chose the Camino Francés which begins on the French side of the Pyrenees Mountains and winds through the fabled Spanish cities of Pamplona, Burgos, and Leon until it ends where all Caminos de Santiago end, in Saint James' Field of Stars (Santiago de Compostela) where the Christian Apostle Saint James' remains are said to be held in the city's cathedral. In fact, one of the most recognizable symbols of the Camino de Santiago, the scallop shell, is a metaphor that visually attests to the mural's phrase that *"todos los caminos son el camino"* (all the paths are the path). Figure 1.2 shows the shell's fanning ridges and grooves which represent the many Caminos one might take to ultimately arrive at the same destination of Santiago de Compostela, represented by the shell's base.

Regardless of the Camino route one takes, official trail markers usually consist of the yellow arrow, the scallop shell, or a combination of those two symbols. After a month of being led by these signs, finding and following them are done almost without effort. However, during the first few days of walking, wayfinding can be challenging as not all trail markers are prominently displayed. Thus, missing a subtle yellow arrow on the narrow post of a stop sign often results in a few extra kilometers added to the overall length of one's journey. Further complicating

DOI: 10.4324/9781032687087-2

Minority language (in)visibility along the Camino del Norte 17

Figure 1.1 Mural in Spanish reading, "*todos los caminos son el camino*" along the Camino del Norte in Asturias, Spain.

the matter, clever businesses will sometimes add their own yellow arrows which, instead of indicating a more direct route for a given day, will include a detour that just happens to lead right to a pilgrim-catering pub or souvenir shop.

In 2022, just under 5% of pilgrims reported having completed the Camino del Norte which runs along Spain's northern coast from Irún in the Basque Country to Santiago de Compostela in Galicia. Around another 5% of pilgrims indicated they completed the Camino Primitivo which picks up on the Norte in Oviedo but turns inland following mountainous terrain through the Asturian and Galician countryside. From end to end, the Camino del Norte runs through all four of Spain's northern autonomous regions beginning in the Basque Country and then moving west through Cantabria, Asturias, and then finally into Galicia. These linguistically and culturally diverse settings have resulted in a myriad of semiotic analyses including studies in linguistic landscapes (Cenoz and Gorter 2006; Järlehed 2020; Sebastian 2019), and others connected to broader sociopolitical issues (Llera Ramo 2017; Wells 2019). Research conducted in these regions has included the documentation of minority language contestation in physical spaces, identifying barriers to language officiality, and general exploration of the linguistic and cultural intersectionality of those who inhabit these places.

Figure 1.2 Camino marker in Asturias, Spain with typical yellow arrow and scallop shell indicating the route to follow along the Camino.

In addition to data on specific route selection, the Pilgrim's Reception Office also keeps track of pilgrims' nationalities, recorded upon completion of their official journeys to Santiago. In 2022, of the 438,307 pilgrims who completed an official Camino, a total of 239,417 or approximately 55% were from Spain. Following Spain, the next five countries with the largest representation were Italy (6.2%), the United States (5.9%), Germany (5.3%), Portugal (4.6%), and France (2.4%). Sorting the data by specific route reflects similar trends in completion by nationality. For example, when isolating the data set for only the Camino del Norte, Spaniards represented 51% of route completions in 2022 with the next five nationalities in size being identical in order to the sequence when accounting for all routes that year. Filtering the data to show statistics just for the Camino Primitivo, Spanish nationality representation jumps to 61% with the same order of country representation for the next five largest groups as well. Figure 1.3 shows a synthesis of nationality completion rates between 2021, 2022, and 2023 for both the Norte and Primitivo Camino routes.

The current study offers a semiotic analysis of my own Camino journey which began in Irún at the start of the Camino del Norte, branched inland to follow the Primitivo in Oviedo, and ended on a quiet early morning at the Cathedral of

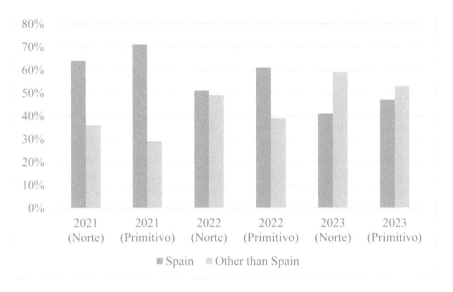

Figure 1.3 Completion of Norte and Primitivo Routes by Nationality 2021–2023.

Source: Oficina de Acogida al Peregrino (2024).

Santiago de Compostela. Prior to completing the Norte, I had previously conducted linguistic landscape research in Asturias, Cantabria, and in the Basque Country where, during the 2019–2020 academic year, I led a study abroad program for US students from the University of North Carolina System. As a follow-up to my previous work in those regions, this study explores the linguistic landscapes of the Camino del Norte and the Camino Primitivo with the following guiding questions in mind:

1. To what extent do pilgrim stamps (*sellos*) gathered along the Camino del Norte and the Camino Primitivo reflect regional languages?
2. To what extent do the Camino del Norte and the Camino Primitivo exist as isolated semiotic spaces within their broader sociolinguistic contexts?

Literature review

Over the last two decades, research on linguistic landscapes has experienced significant growth as exemplified by increases in the frequency and diversity of associated publications (Gorter and Cenoz 2024). From the earlier classic studies of public signage (Backhaus 2006; Cenoz and Gorter 2006) to the thematic semiotic explorations of conflict, resistance, and contestation (Blackwood, Lanza and Woldermariam 2016; Rubdy and Ben Said 2015), linguistic landscape research has provided a powerful multidisciplinary lens for the continued study of social semiotics. This growth in scope has been fueled by calls for expanded analyses of material culture including Aronin and O' Laoire's (2012, 10) invitation to consider how some materialities "are manipulated, moved and staged upfront while others are forgotten or hidden and yet others are not used but kept as memories". The growing body of linguistic landscape literature now includes quantitative and qualitative investigations of a wide array of sociolinguistic matters including issues of underrepresentation of minority language speakers in their respective linguistic landscapes (Hassa and Krajcik 2016; Troyer et al. 2015), language vitality as reflected in the linguistic landscape (Dunlevy 2012; Järlehed 2017; Regueira et al. 2013), and linguistic tokenism, particularly as expressed in areas with high levels of tourism (Pietikäinen et al. 2011; Salo 2012). Yet another vein of linguistic landscape research has emphasized sign semiotics in transitory and momentary contexts including analyses of signs of protest (Hanauer 2013) as well as signs of layered asynchronous dialogue between passing members of the surrounding speech communities (Karam et al. 2023; Sebastian 2019).

This study aims to further expand the work being done in these areas through an analysis of regional language representation as found on pilgrim stamps and the salience of English along two Camino de Santiago routes that span some of Spain's most linguistically diverse regions. Because the Camino attracts pilgrims from around the world, this particular study is also informed by other analyses of English as a global language and as found in areas where it is not commonly spoken by community members just beyond the immediate tourist-centric linguistic landscape. A number of studies have shown English to be a dominant language in a variety of linguistic landscapes with high levels of tourism (Alomoush and Al-Naimat 2018; Zhang and Chan 2017). Such studies show the use of English in these linguistic landscapes as a way for local businesses to cater more effectively to the international tourist audience. However, fewer studies have looked at contexts where English signage in the linguistic landscape is both produced and consumed by the same transient tourist population. Other studies have analyzed the use of regional languages in linguistic landscapes frequented by tourists and have offered potential explanations ranging from supportive local language policies (Bruyèl-Olmedo and Juan-Garau 2015), as in the case of Catalan in Mallorca, to tokenistic motivations (Kelly-Holmes 2014). With these studies as points of departure, the current investigation looks both at the representation of regional languages and the presence of English along the Norte and Primitivo Camino routes. As stamps are granted by local community members living and working along the Camino, these artifacts may be described as signs produced by local community members for what is typically a non-local transient population. In contrast, English signs found along the Camino routes frequently appeared to be authored by and intended for transient pilgrims.

In an effort to answer the exploratory questions, the study applies Scollon and Scollon's (2003) framework of geosemiotics as a theoretical frame and Gorter and Cenoz's (2024) multilingual inequality in public spaces (MIPS) model as an interpretive guide. The former frame helped to focus my attention on strategic juxtapositions of signs and symbols throughout the data collection and data analysis stages of the study. The latter frame was particularly helpful as I then endeavored to make sense of what I observed and experienced within the broader semiotic context of the Camino. The combined application of these theoretical tools contributed to the articulation of my final conclusions which include both a descriptive component (underrepresentation of minority languages in Spain's northern regions) as well as a critical focus (semiotic places of isolation that are not representative of their broader contexts).

Methods

This study employed an emic, mostly qualitative approach and was carried out during my own walking journey along the Norte and Primitivo Camino routes. Although data might have been gathered via intermittent visits to key sections of specific routes, I chose to experience the linguistic landscape precisely as others experience it, walking continuously from one end of Spain to the other. This walking tour methodology (Garvin 2010) has led to important and nuanced analyses of a variety of linguistic landscapes including Kallen's (2010) exploration in Dublin and to my own previous analysis of Asturian in the Asturian linguistic landscape (Sebastian 2019). Acknowledging Blackwood's (2015) support for mixed-methods approaches to linguistic landscape research, the present study situates the qualitative data within the broader quantitative context of Camino route completion rates by nationality as well as simple frequency counts of languages found on pilgrim stamps collected along the way.

Data collection

Data for this study were collected over a span of 35 total days of walking, first along the Camino del Norte from Irún in the Basque Country to Oviedo in Asturias and then on to Santiago de Compostela in Galicia via the Camino Primitivo route option. The first two walking stages were completed as separate day trips in 2019 and 2020, during which time I was leading a study abroad program in Santander in the region of Cantabria. The remaining 33 days were completed without interruption in July of 2022. Data included digital photographs, journal entries, and pilgrim stamps (*sellos*) which were collected in a pilgrim passport (*credencial del peregrino*) often simply referred to as the *credencial*. Stamps were collected at points of interest along the Camino including pilgrim hostels, churches, post offices, tourism offices, as well as at the occasional pub or nearby place of business. Each stamp is a unique combination of image and text upon which the date is written to mark the pilgrim's chronological progression toward Santiago de Compostela. During my trek I collected a total of 56 stamps with an additional and final stamp granted at the Pilgrim Office in Santiago after having my journey officially confirmed. Stamps were collected from all four autonomous regions and along both the Norte and Primitivo routes.

Over 500 photos and videos were taken during my time on the Camino from which I have selected a small sample for inclusion in this chapter. The subset of figures was chosen either to help describe core elements of the Camino experience, as in the case of Figures 1.1 and 1.2, or for their relevance to my central thesis which explores minority language (under)representation as well as the degree to which the Camino itself exists as an isolated semiotic space within a larger context. I used journal entries to document my experience employing both written description and reflection as well as rough sketches of semiotically rich artifacts I encountered along the way. A total of 57 journal entries were recorded between the dates of June 30 and July 31, 2022. Some days included multiple entries and other days no entries were included at all.

Data analysis

Data were analyzed using Scollon and Scollon's (2003) concept of geosemiotics as a general guide. In particular, their notion of place semiotics guided the analysis of two of the three data sources including code preference to analyze pilgrim stamps and emplacement to discuss the use of English in signs photographed along the Camino. Analysis of the third data source, journal entries, follows more general qualitative practices (Maykut and Morehouse 1994) with specific selections being made in order to further contextualize what was being seen and experienced at different intervals along the Camino routes.

As interpretive guide, the present study used Gorter and Cenoz's (2024) multilingual inequality in public spaces model in an attempt to answer the guiding research questions. A final interpretive lens came from my previous study of the Asturian linguistic landscape where I observed public signage being used as a space for asynchronous layered dialogue between unseen actors (Sebastian 2019). These interactions were observed as commodification of existing signage, a behavior that was also observed throughout the Camino linguistic landscapes.

Findings

The Norte in the Basque Country

The Basque Country serves as the point of departure for the Camino del Norte. The Basque language was represented in each of the data categories including pilgrim stamps, research journal entries, and in photographs of public signs. Using a 6-point scale, Gorter and Cenoz (2024) classify Basque as a vibrant level 2 language on the presence and visibility of minority languages in linguistic landscapes with level 1 languages representing majority, highly salient languages and level 6 languages being those with minimal or no presence at all. Basque, as a level 2 language, was found throughout the region including not only in the urban centers of San Sebastián and Bilbao, but also throughout the region's rural areas, including along the quiet walking paths of the Norte route.

At the crest of a particularly challenging climb between the Basque towns of Deba and Markina, I sat down under shade of a tree to sketch a trail marker and to reflect on its semiotic presence along the trail that day. Figure 1.4 shows my

Minority language (in)visibility along the Camino del Norte   23

Figure 1.4 Journal entries recorded in the Basque Country displaying a sketch of a common bilingual trail marker in the region and a sketch of a laundromat in Markina-Xemein with text in both the Basque and Spanish languages.

journal entry which depicts a commonly found trail marker along the Camino in the Basque Country that displays the regionally specific symbol of a rock and pastoral cane in combination with the standard yellow arrow and scallop shell. Under the images, text is displayed first in Basque, *Donejakue Bidea*, and then in Spanish, *Camino de Santiago*. A name of a fellow pilgrim that I had been walking with that day has been blacked out in order to protect their identity.

After a series of small Basque towns, the next prominent stop along the Norte is Guernica. In addition to Picasso's famous immortalization of the city in his artistic critique of violence and war, Guernica is historically important to the Basque people given that its leaders customarily gather under the shade of the Tree of Guernica for important political and cultural ceremonies. This symbolism can be seen in the pilgrim stamp given at the city's tourist office which depicts the Tree of Guernica beautifully embedded within the fanning ridges of the Camino scallop shell. The stamp has the name of the Camino written in Basque prominently displayed above the central imagery and the phrase *Bakearen Hiria* (City of Peace) found at the bottom of the stamp, also written in Basque. Figure 1.5 shows the Guernica tourist office stamp (Stamp 5) along with others from the region that vary in their use of language and imagery. In order to facilitate individual description of some of the

24 Ethnographic Landscapes and Language Ideologies in the Spanish State

Figure 1.5 Pilgrim stamps collected throughout the Basque Country.

stamps seen in Figure 1.5, yellow numbers in black boxes positioned at the upper left corner of individual stamps were added to the original image. In order to focus attention on the stamps from each separate autonomous region, stamps which were collected in other locations or those overlapping on to the same pages have been boxed out during the preparation of the image.

Stamps 2, 5, 10, and 17 include primarily English text. Stamps 8, 9, 11, 14, and 15 display primarily Basque text. Stamps 1, 3, 6, 12, 13, and 16 display a somewhat more balanced display of Spanish and Basque text. Stamps 4, 7, 12, and 18 contain either the name of the location only or image with no text. Together, stamps including either Basque text only or Basque in combination with Spanish text made up 58% of the stamps collected in the Basque Country.

The distribution of stamps as shown in Figure 1.6 is supported by other linguistic landscape analyses in the Basque Country that have demonstrated a healthy and vibrant presence of the Basque language throughout the region (Cenoz and Gorter 2006). After the Basque Country, pilgrims move from a largely multilingual linguistic landscape to one that is primarily dominated by the language of the Spanish state, Cantabria.

The Norte in Cantabria

The challenge of elevation in the Basque Country is replaced by the difficulty of long daily distances in Cantabria. Unlike the other three northern regions in Spain, Cantabria is not associated with a regional language. In a small rural community near the town of Güemes, a good day's walk to the east from the capital city of Santander, pilgrims encounter one of the most prominent hostels along the Norte

Minority language (in)visibility along the Camino del Norte 25

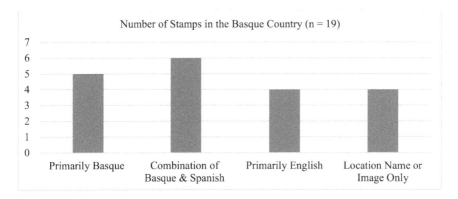

Figure 1.6 Distribution of stamps in the Basque Country based on language representation.

route. Here, rooms are assigned and pilgrims are then invited to gather at the main building of the compound later that evening for a talk about the history and significance of the place. I recall feeling like I had just walked into a village whose sole citizens were transient pilgrims. Having spent the previous night in a peaceful monastery in the town of Laredo, the hostel in Güemes felt detached from its own surroundings. My journal reflection of this place reads,

> Arrived at the hostel in Güemes and it is truly a place of much needed respite. It's sort of a village with little four-person dorms and with other larger communal rooms as well. There's a talk at 7.30p.m. followed by dinner. Everyone seems very much at peace here with lots of open space to reflect and think.

In another entry from that day, I wrote that it "was nice to have so many pilgrims in one place" but that "honestly I loved the simplicity and sincerity of yesterday at the convent more." The very next morning I wrote the following entry in reflection of the experience:

> I darted out of the *albergue* at around 6.15a.m. or so. More snoring that kept me up but this time in close quarters. Probably the first one out the door but watching the sun come up slowly, almost lazily over the cliffs above Somo beach has been worth it.

Ironically, the peaceful seclusion at the hostel near Güemes was something that I was so eager to escape that I woke exceptionally early the next morning and was one of the first pilgrims to leave.

A number of the walking stages in Cantabria take pilgrims right along the jagged coastline, high above the Cantabrian Sea. Weaving back into small coastal towns, signage directed to pilgrims could occasionally be found. One example was an advertisement for a special discount for pilgrims walking between the towns

26   *Ethnographic Landscapes and Language Ideologies in the Spanish State*

Figure 1.7 Pilgrim stamps collected throughout Cantabria.

of Santillana del Mar and Comillas. The sign, which was affixed at the top of a lamppost at the center of a central intersection, was an advertisement for a local bar that read, "10% discount for pilgrims." The sign, although catering to the typically international crowd of pilgrims, was in Spanish only. Furthermore, Figure 1.7 shows that all eight of the pilgrim stamps I collected in Cantabria contained text in Spanish only.

In Figure 1.7, stamp 7 shows the stamp granted at the hostel near Güemes and, like the other stamps collected in this region, displays only Spanish text. After the long walking stages in the predominantly monolingual landscape of Cantabria, pilgrims enter into the region of Asturias where they must decide to either continue along the Norte route passing through the coastal town of Gijón or to take the Primitivo route which turns inward through the mountains beginning in the region's capital city of Oviedo.

The Norte and Primitivo in Asturias

Asturias is a linguistically complex region where the local language, Asturian, struggles to maintain its presence against the ever-increasing dominance of Spanish in the region. Although Gorter and Cenoz (2024) do not include a classification

Minority language (in)visibility along the Camino del Norte 27

for Asturian along their continuum of minority language visibility, I would situate the language at either a level 5 or level 6 based on my own previous investigation of the region's linguistic landscape (Sebastian 2019). In my earlier analysis of Asturian in Asturias, I revealed how resistance was manifested through subtle and asynchronous dialogues between minority and majority language speakers and advocates. Along the Camino route in this region, I encountered a sample of graffiti written both in Asturian and Spanish under an overpass on the outskirts of Oviedo, the region's capital city. The graffiti contained first a line which, written in the Asturian language, was a call for official recognition of the local language, "*L'Asturianu llingua oficial ya!*" The second and third lines were in Spanish and called for protests against population control and poverty. Another sign, found just outside the Asturian town of Villaviciosa, was more purposefully directed to the passing population of pilgrims as the multilingual message board in Figure 1.8 shows.

The message board is affixed to the wall of a small sheltered area where pilgrims can refill water bottles and purchase supplies from vending machines. Messages are written in a variety of languages including Portuguese, English, Hawaiian, German, French, Spanish, as well as others which are written in chalk or left on post-its and tacked to the board itself. Similar to the linguistic makeup of the stamps

Figure 1.8 Multilingual message board for pilgrims to leave messages near Villaviciosa where pilgrims choose to complete the full Norte route or to follow the Primitivo route on to Santiago.

28 *Ethnographic Landscapes and Language Ideologies in the Spanish State*

Figure 1.9 Pilgrim stamps collected throughout Asturias.

collected in the region of Cantabria, Figure 1.9 shows that stamps collected in the region of Asturias depicted primarily Spanish text.

Stamps 6 and 13 could be considered as minor exceptions for their inclusion of the Asturian words "pola" and "texu" in the context of corresponding place names. However, despite the presence of some Asturian signs along and near the Camino routes in the region, the pilgrim stamps were almost entirely void of the regional language. As had been observed at various points along the Camino routes in the Basque Country and Cantabria, the Camino in Asturias also consisted of English-only signs. One such sign was in the form of graffiti near the town of Colunga, just prior to the Norte-Primitivo split. Another was written on a rock found along a particularly challenging stage known as Hospitales. A third sample, which was actually photographed in Galicia, contains text in English with the phrase, "call a taxi" and shows a snake coiled around a branch. The graffiti is clearly directed toward passing pilgrims as a playful temptation to give up and complete the rest of the route via taxi. Figure 1.10 shows each of these signs side-by-side and are grouped together given their semiotic similarities.

Photograph 1 in Figure 1.10 reads in yellow graffiti, "forget the destination" and also contains what appears to be the name "Enzo." The second English-only sign was found on a rock next to the typical yellow arrow trail marker and reads, "Don't stop when the road gets tough. Don't give up when the road ends."

Two journal entries recorded while in Asturias included reflections on the multilingual and multicultural composition of pilgrims. While at a hostel in the town of Berducedo, I wrote the following entry:

Minority language (in)visibility along the Camino del Norte 29

Figure 1.10 English-only signs found along the Norte and Primitivo Camino routes in Asturias and Galicia.

Tonight's *albergue* is nice enough. Right now I'm listening to an ethnically Chinese British guy speak English with an ethnically Vietnamese guy who grew up in the Czech Republic but works in the Netherlands. In other bunks some native Czechs are also talking. Dinner was with two Spaniards, a girl from Brazil, and a girl from Italy.

The following day, I continued to reflect in my journal on the diverse makeup of pilgrims on the Camino. At the hostel in Grandas de Salime, the last stop along the Asturias section of the Primitivo route, I wrote the following:

There are so many storylines here, so many diverse backgrounds. On the Camino, I've met a girl deciding whether or not to dedicate her life to a monastery, people who have just quit their jobs, a filmmaker, medicine, lots of teachers, an author/ motivational speaker, military, a musician/actor, IT workers and lots of others. All on the Camino. All headed in the same direction.

This noted diversity grew even more with entry into the final autonomous region of my journey. The likely reason for this increase is that all Caminos, regardless of their starting points, eventually converge in Galicia. For those coming from the Norte and Primitivo routes, this sudden swell of pilgrims from other Camino routes comes as a bit of a shock given the quiet and solitude of the northern routes.

The Primitivo into Santiago in Galicia

In addition to larger crowds of pilgrims, Galicia marks a return to a region where the local language is both visually and aurally present, earning a level 3

30   *Ethnographic Landscapes and Language Ideologies in the Spanish State*

Figure 1.11   Series of commodified traffic signs in English that have been altered with additional pilgrim-directed messages found throughout Asturias and Galicia along the Camino.

classification along the 6-point continuum of the presence and visibility of minority languages in linguistic landscapes (Gorter and Cenoz 2024). And yet, the linguistically and culturally isolated context of the Camino persisted, even into this last region. Figure 1.11 shows some examples of this persistence in a series of altered traffic signs that first appeared in Asturias and then continued to appear throughout Galicia.

Each of the samples in Figure 1.11 contain altered versions of stop signs which, in its widely used form, includes the English word "stop" in white lettering within a red octagon frame. Modifications varied but all were written in English and appeared to be directed toward pilgrims given their location along the Camino walking routes. Table 1.1 includes the contents of each of the signs along with noticeable attributes and the original text bolded.

The collection of stop signs stands in contrast to the surrounding linguistic landscape consisting of a mix of Spanish or Galician signs and symbols. Galician was observed on official trail signs displaying *O Camiño de Santiago* either as replacement for or in combination with the Spanish *Camino de Santiago*. The difference between the two being denoted by the inclusion of the Galician article "*o*" as well as the tilde mark above the "n" in the Spanish *camino*. Furthermore, Figure 1.12 shows that the pilgrim stamps collected in this region were more reflective of the local language.

Minority language (in)visibility along the Camino del Norte 31

Table 1.1 Descriptions and attributes of stop signs in Figure 1.11

Sign Number	Location	Text	Attributes of Additional Text
1	Along the Camino Primitivo near San Marcelo, Asturias	NEVER **STOP** READING	White, block style letting, similar in design to original sign text.
2	Along the Camino Primitivo near Grandas de Salime, Asturias	DON'T **STOP** BELIEVING	Yellow lettering with some letters having faded or somehow removed. Faint lines can still be seen which allow the altered text to be read.
3	Along the Camino Primitivo near Tineo, Asturias	DON'T **STOP** WALKING	Black lettering, bottom text is added over a removed sticker creating a layering effect.
4	Along the Camino Primitivo near Castroverde, Galicia	Don't **STOP** Walking OR stop and rest and observe if that's what calls you… IT'S YOUR CAMINO <3	Combination of white and black lettering. A smaller additional message is added in the lower left quadrant of the sign.
5	Along the Camino Primitivo near Lugo, Galicia	**STOP** Don't walking!	White lettering added under original sign text creating a grammatically awkward message. **additional arrow is editor marking showing proper syntax of expression** Additional text is separated by a downward facing white arrow.
6	Along the Camino between Santiago and Finisterre, Galicia	**STOP** THiNKiNG	Black lettering added under the original sign text.

Stamps 1, 3, 12, 13 in Figure 1.12 include primarily Galician text. Stamp 10 includes a combination of Galician and English and stamp 6 shows a combination of Spanish and English. Because words like *oasis, catedral, albergue,* and *peregrino* are the same in Spanish and Galician, it is difficult to categorize stamps 2, 4, 5, 7, 8, 9, 11, and 14 as either primarily Spanish or primarily Galician text. If we include this latter set as being representative of Galician, then the Galician language could be said to be included on thirteen of the fourteen stamps collected in the region. If interpreted as Spanish language, then Galician text would only make up five of the fourteen total stamps. Whichever the interpretation, the stamps collected throughout Galicia, similar to those collected throughout the Basque Country, reflect a more vibrant presence of the regional language.

Figure 1.12 Pilgrim stamps collected throughout Galicia.

Discussion

Discussion of the data has been organized using Gorter and Cenoz (2024) Multilingual Inequality in Public Spaces model. Using this framework, the initial guiding research questions of the study were revisited with an attempt to provide additional insight into representation of regional languages on pilgrim stamps and the extent to which the Camino del Norte and the Camino Primitivo exist as isolated semiotic spaces within their broader linguistic landscape contexts. The following conclusions are offered based on the previously mentioned pilgrim stamps, journal entries, and photographs collected during my own trek along the Norte and Primitivo Camino routes.

Language policy processes

Linguistic landscape research on Basque in the Basque Country and Galician in Galicia suggests strong levels of linguistic vitality, reinforcing Gorter and Cenoz's (2024) decision to classify the languages as strong levels two and three respectively on their 6-point continuum of the presence and visibility of minority languages in linguistic landscapes. In justification of their scores, the authors point to a healthy and diverse set of language policies including in the areas of education, commerce, and official public signage mandates. Representation of these languages as found on the pilgrim stamps in these regions supports these claims. In particular, the Basque/Spanish bilingual trail markers in the Basque Country and the switch from the Spanish "El Camino" to the Galician "O Camiño" in Galicia served as frequent moments of contact with the local languages. Asturian, on the other hand, is not officially recognized by the Spanish state and thus has continued to struggle to assert itself within its own linguistic landscape (Sebastian 2019). As Cantabria claims no regional language, the most visible language was Spanish, with additional representation of English observed most often on and near the Camino route. As for language policies specific to the Camino de Santiago in general, UNESCO's (2024) description provides helpful clarification stating that,

> In exercise of their competences, the Autonomous Communities through which the routes pass have each defined the protection of this serial property in their respective territories. The routes are Crown property, and the built components are under a mixture of private, institutional, and public sector ownership, as are the buffer zones.

General oversight is carried out by the Spanish Government's Ministry of Culture with the Jacobean Council (*Consejo Jacobeo*) indicated as the organization in charge of managing the Camino as an official world heritage site. The Jacobean Council works with regional offices of culture, tourism, and linguistic politics to carry out related work including maintenance, outreach, trail marking, and other pertinent tasks (Consejo Jacobeo 2024). Given that the Camino routes pass through a wide variety of private and public spaces, it is difficult to point to any single uniform language policy that shapes the linguistic landscapes encountered along the trail.

Sign-making processes

In its charge to protect and maintain the Camino, the Jacobean Council has provided clear guidelines for official trail markers which outline, in detail, such aspects as arrow directionality, color, size, placement, and even includes details regarding bilingual signage (Consejo Jacobeo 2024). In section 5.3 of their posted guidelines for Camino de Santiago signage, the Council recommends that in those autonomous communities where another official language exists, Camino signage along highways, for reasons involving pedestrian safety, include text duplicated in both content and design. For official signage away from highways, the Council says that the size of text should be reduced proportionally so that text in both languages is included within the prescribed format and dimensions of signs. They do not specify the order of languages but the visual example included in this section for a bilingual Camino sign shows Spanish text above, and then Galician text repeated below in both content and design (Consejo Jacobeo 2024).

As Backhaus (2006) has noted, fundamental differences often exist between top-down and bottom-up signage. Although the Jacobean Council has outlined guidelines for official Camino signage, unofficial signage is not bound by any particular policy. These unofficial signs can be found all along the Camino routes, including, as was noted in Figure 1.11, layered on top of existing top-down signage. A curious case to point out are the pilgrim stamps. My base assumption was that these stamps, given that they make up such an important and visually salient part of the experience, would be governed by some sort of central policy regarding text and style, not unlike the guidelines provided for official trail makers and signs. However, in my investigation I could not find any such guidelines. Furthermore, although stamps are reviewed by the Pilgrim Office in Santiago upon official completion, the office appeared to only corroborate that a sufficient number of stamps had been obtained, with little or no attention to the validity of individual stamps. Again, this is not entirely surprising given that the Camino cuts through a wide variety of public and private sectors. In my own collection of stamps, some appeared to be more top-down, as in those collected at official tourist offices or parishes along the way. Others, however, particularly those offered by hotels, contained no reference to Camino symbols at all. This lack of mandate strengthens the conclusion that the presence of Basque and Galician on stamps in their respective regions were organic signs of vitality, not forced bilingualism as dictated by policy governing text and design of the stamp.

Apart from official Camino signage and pilgrim stamps, the other collection of signs included those produced by, and apparently intended for, pilgrims. This subset of signs contained mostly English as seen in Figures 1.10 and 1.11. In some cases, a mixture of languages was also observed as was seen in Figure 1.8. These pilgrim-authored signs, similar to those I observed in the Asturian linguistic landscape (Sebastian 2019), were sometimes used as an asynchronous forum between pilgrims. Such messages were often inspirational as in the commodified signs in Figure 1.11 but many served as brief philosophical musings as in the message to "forget the destination" as found in Figure 1.10. The use of English in these self-directed signs is interesting and is likely connected with what I observed to be the use of English as a default language among pilgrims, especially when no other common language was found.

Unequal languages on signage in public spaces

English was frequently used in signage along the Camino and as an initial default language among pilgrims. However, the completion rates by nationality, as summarized in Figure 1.3, indicate that only a small minority of pilgrims were from English-speaking countries. In 2021 and 2022, pilgrims indicating Spain as their nationality represented the large majority of all pilgrims on the Norte and Primitivo routes. Spanish nationality representation decreased somewhat in 2023 but the majority still held. Furthermore, in 2022, the year during which this investigation took place, only one of the top six nationalities listed was an English-speaking country. And yet, the signs which appeared to be written by and intended for pilgrims were largely in English. Exceptions containing either Spanish, a regional language, or a mixture of both were mostly noted on official Camino signage which, as I've already noted, is carefully governed by the Jacobean Council. Pilgrim stamps in the

Basque Country and Galician regions also stand as exceptions to the dominance of English signage along the Camino routes. Representation of local languages on the stamps, especially given the lack of any centralized mandated policy regarding content and design, is a strong example of linguistic vitality for both the Basque and Galician languages. The absence of Asturian in Asturias, however, supports the scarcity of visual representation of that language in its own surrounding linguistic landscape.

What people see and read

As for what pilgrims see and read along the Camino, this behavior can change quite significantly over time. In my own experience, and based on similar experiences from pilgrims I walked with, the first few days are spent developing a bit of rhythm for where to find trail markers. Although official signage is often well placed, it takes a while to train the eye to find unofficial yellow arrows and other indicators that mark the way forward. Consequently, due to this settling-in phase, pilgrims are hyper engaged in the linguistic landscape during their first few days on the Camino. After some time has passed, wayfinding becomes a more passive exercise as the skill of following trail markers, both official and unofficial, is better developed. All of this, no doubt, affects what pilgrims see and read along their Camino journeys. The use of signs as forums for asynchronous dialogue was observed in a variety of ways along the Camino routes, Figures 1.8 and 1.11 being just a few examples of the broader collection. Although sometimes written for what appeared to be the general pilgrim reader audience, other signs contained specific messages such as the text seen in the bottom right quadrant of Figure 1.8 which reads "Did you meet Michael? I hope you did." Messages like these were identified elsewhere and were likely a result of pilgrims who, after meeting during an earlier walking stage on the Camino, got separated at some point along the way. This was not uncommon given that pilgrims often progressed at different speeds, synching up occasionally with new pilgrims for a few days of walking and then eventually losing contact with those groups due to differences in pace or general itinerary. Pilgrims who might not have thought to exchange contact information may have been using signage to communicate with one another along the route.

What people think and do

Three walking days out from Santiago I wrote a list of lessons learned during my trek along the Norte and Primitivo Camino routes. Included in the list was the phrase I encountered weeks earlier on a wall in Asturias, "*Todos los Caminos son el Camino*," followed by "All the paths are the path. Exercise understanding when others don't walk the way I walk or take the route I take … all have value." This small piece of the vast linguistic landscape of the Norte and Primitivo routes had stuck with me to the very end. As for what others think and do along the Camino, this investigation is limited to the stamps, pictures, and journal entries collected along the way. Future studies involving participant interviews to understand pilgrims' thoughts and actions as they make their way through the various linguistic landscapes would likely yield insightful results. From this particular data set, I offer a few interpretations regarding thinking and doing along the Camino.

The Camino cuts through a wide variety of rural towns, open countryside, and only a few large cities in Northern Spain. Unlike the major metropolitan areas in Spain, English is not as commonly spoken in these areas. Thus, given the frequency of English signs along the Camino, many pilgrims were surprised at the lack of English spoken in restaurants and other nearby establishments. Another potential interpretation for the frequency of English signs along the Camino routes, is that pilgrims might have assumed that the majority of pilgrims come from English-speaking countries. This would be a fair assumption based on the linguistic landscape but, given the actual completion statistics by nationality, would be an inaccurate conclusion. And finally, the content and design of stamps collected by pilgrims along the way supports the interpretation that in some regions, the Basque Country and Galicia, the regional language is alive and well. On the other hand, given the lack of Asturian on stamps from that region, many pilgrims I spoke with were simply unaware that Asturias was also home to a regional language.

As for what pilgrims do, the commodification of signs revealed that the linguistic landscape was sometimes used as an asynchronous forum for communicating with other pilgrims. English was the language that appeared to be most salient on these pilgrim-authored signs, reinforcing my own observation that it was typically used as a default language between pilgrims, at least until another common language could be identified. Apart from this practice of sign commodification, there were also moments along the Camino where pilgrims could leave their marks in a variety of other ways. Perhaps one of the better-known practices was to bring something from the pilgrim's place of origin to leave at a certain place along the Camino as a symbolic unloading of a burden. My own token was a small shell from Hawaii which I left in a rather unceremonious fashion on a stone pillar marking the official border of the municipality of Santiago.

Conclusion

The linguistic landscapes I observed along the Camino del Norte and Camino Primitivo routes were varied and rich with semiotic complexity. Despite this variation, the data from this investigation helped to reveal two general observations that I offer as partial answers to my original guiding research questions. The first is that the content and design of the pilgrim stamps collected throughout all four northern regions were, in fact, fair representations of the broader linguistic landscapes in those areas. As for the second question, the high prevalence of English signage along the way, particularly given the contrasting nature of linguistic landscapes immediately beyond the buffer zones of the Camino, suggest that the Norte and Primitivo routes did, in fact, exist as isolated semiotic spaces which differed markedly from the surrounding contexts.

Acknowledgments

I would like to extend a special thanks to Jeff Guerrero for granting permission to use his stop sign photos included in this chapter and to my fellow pilgrims along the Camino for their friendship and kindness along the way.

References

Alomoush, Omar Ibrahim Salameh, and Ghazi Khaleel Al-Naimat. 2018. "English as the Lingua Franca in Visual Touristic Jordan: The Case of Petra." *International Journal of Applied Linguistics and English Literature* 7, no. 4: 1–13. https://doi.org/10.7575/aiac.ijalel.v.7n.4p.1

Aronin, Larissa, and Muiris O´Laoire. 2012. "The Material Culture of Multilingualism: Moving Beyond the Linguistic Landscape." *International Journal of Multilingualism* 10, no. 3: 225–235. https://doi.org/10.1080/14790718.2012.679734

Backhaus, Peter. 2006. "Multilingualism in Tokyo: A Look into the Linguistic Landscape." *International Journal of Multilingualism* 3, no. 1: 52–66. https://doi.org/10.1080/14790710608668385

Blackwood, Robert. 2015. "LL Explorations and Methodological Challenges." *Linguistic Landscape* 1, no. 1–2: 38–53. https://doi.org/10.1075%2Fll.1.1-2.03bla

Blackwood, Robert, Elizabeth Lanza, and Hirut Woldemariam. 2016. *Negotiating and Contesting Identities in Linguistic Landscapes.* London: Bloomsbury.

Bruyèl-Olmedo, Antonio, and Maria Juan-Garau. 2015. "Minority Languages in the Linguistic Landscape of Tourism: The Case of Catalan in Mallorca." *Journal of Multilingual and Multicultural Development* 36, no. 6: 598–619. https://doi.org/10.1080/01434632.2014.979832

Cenoz, Jasone, and Durk Gorter. 2006. "Linguistic Landscape and Minority Languages." *The International Journal of Multilingualism* 3, no. 1: 67–80.

Cenoz, Jasone, and Durk Gorter. 2024. *A Panorama of Linguistic Landscape Studies.* Bristol: Multilingual Matters.

Consejo Jacobeo. 2024. "Consejo Jacobeo Directrices para la Señalización del Camino de Santiago." www.cultura.gob.es/consejo-jacobeo/dam/jcr:3baa012b-b976-4887-84e6-43b2ded1a568/directrices%20se%C3%B1alizacion.pdf

Dunlevy, Deirdre A. 2012. "Linguistic Policy and Linguistic Choice: A Study of the Galician Linguistic Landscape." In *Linguistic Landscape, Multilingualism and Social Change*, edited by Christine Hélot, Monica Barni, Rudi Janssens, and Carla Bagna, 53–68. Frankfurt: Peter Lang.

Garvin, Rebecca T. 2010. "Responses to the Linguistic Landscape in Memphis, Tennessee: An Urban Space in Transition." In *Linguistic Landscape: Expanding the Scenery*, edited by Elana Shohamy and Durk Gorter, 107–125. New York: Routledge.

Hanauer, David I. 2013. "Transitory Linguistic Landscapes as Political Discourses: Signage at Three Political Demonstrations in Pittsburgh, USA." In *Linguistic Landscape, Multilingualism and Social Change*, edited by Christine Hélot, Monica Barni, Rudi Janssens, and Carla Bagna, 129–154. Frankfurt: Peter Lang.

Hassa, Samira, and Chelsea Krajcik. 2016. "'Un peso, mami' Linguistic Landscape and Transnationalism Discourses in Washington Heights, New York City." *Linguistic Landscape* 2, no. 2: 157–181. https://doi.org/10.1075/ll.2.2.03has

Järlehed, Johan. 2017. "Genre and Metacultural Displays: The Case of Street-Name Signs." *Linguistic Landscape* 3, no. 3: 286–305. https://doi.org/10.1075/ll.17020.jar

Järlehed, Johan. 2020. "Pride and Profit: Naming and Branding Galicianness and Basqueness in Public Space." In *Namn i skrift. Names in Writing*, edited by Maria Löfdahl, Michelle Waldispühl and Lena Wenner, 147–175. Goteburg: Meijerbergs Institut.

Kallen, Jeffrey L. 2010. "Changing Landscapes: Language, Space and Policy in the Dublin Linguistic Landscape." In *Semiotic Landscapes: Language, Image, Space*, edited by Adam Jaworski and Crispin Thurlow, 41–58. London: Continuum.

Karam, Fares J., Amanda K. Kibler, Amber N. Warren, and Zinnia Shweiry. 2023. "'Beirut You Will Rise Again' A Critical Discourse Historiographical Analysis of the Beiruti Linguistic Landscape." *Linguistic Landscape* 9, no. 2: 133–157. https://doi.org/10.1075/ll.21040.kar

Kelly-Holmes, Helen. 2014. "Linguistic Fetish: The Sociolinguistics of Visual Multilingualism." In *Visual Communication*, edited by David Machin, 135–151. Berlin: De Gruyter Mouton.

Llera Ramo, Francisco J. 2017. *III Encuesta Sociolingüística de Asturias*. Oviedo: Academia de la Llingua Asturiana.

Maykut, Pamela, and Richard Morehouse. 1994. *Beginning Qualitative Research: A Philosophic and Practical Guide*. London: The Falmer Press.

Oficina de Acogida al Peregrino. 2023. "Información Estadística Oficina Peregrino para 2022 hasta diciembre." https://oficinadelperegrino.com/en/statistics-2/

Pietikäinen, Sari, Pia Lane, Hanni Salo, and Sirkka Laihiala-Kankainen. 2011. "Frozen Actions in the Arctic Linguistic Landscape: A Nexus Analysis of Language Processes in Visual Space." *International Journal of Multilingualism* 8, no. 4: 277–298. https://doi.org/10.1080/14790718.2011.555553

Regueira, Xosé Luís, Miguel López Docampo, and Matthew Wellings. 2013. "El Paisaje Lingüístico en Galicia." *Revista Internacional de Lingüística Iberoamericana* 11, no. 1: 39–62.

Rubdy, Rani, and Selim Ben Said. 2015. *Conflict, Exclusion and Dissent in the Linguistic Landscape*. Basingstoke: Palgrave Macmillan. https://doi.org/10.1057/9781137426284

Salo, Hanni. 2012. "Using Linguistic Landscape to Examine the Visibility of Sámi Languages in the North Calotte." In *Minority Languages in the Linguistic Landscape*, edited by Durk Gorter, Heiko F. Marten, and Luk Mensel, 243–259. Basingstoke: Palgrave Macmillan. https://doi.org/10.1057/9780230360235_14.

Scollon, Ron, and Suzie W. Scollon. 2003. *Discourses in Place: Language in the Material World*. New York: Routledge. https://doi.org/10.4324/9780203422724.

Sebastian, Paul. 2019. "Signs of Resistance in the Asturian Linguistic Landscape." *Linguistic Landscape* 5, no. 3: 302–329. https://doi.org/10.1075/ll.18015.seb.

The United Nations Educational, Scientific and Cultural Organization (UNESCO) World Heritage Convention. 2024. "Routes of Santiago de Compostela: Camino Francés and Routes of Northern Spain." https://whc.unesco.org/en/list/669.

Troyer, Robert A., Carmen Cáceda, and Patricia Giménez Eguíbar. 2015. "Unseen Spanish in Small-Town America: A Minority Language in the Linguistic Landscape." In *Conflict, Exclusion and Dissent in the Linguistic Landscape*, edited by Rani Rubdy and Selim Ben Said, 52–76. Basingstoke: Palgrave Macmillan.

Wells, Naomi. 2019. "State Recognition for 'Contested Languages': A Comparative Study of Sardinian and Asturian, 1992–2010." *Language Policy*, 18: 243–267. https://doi.org/10.1007/s10993-018-9482-6.

Zhang, Hong, and Brian Hok-Shing Chan. 2017. "The Shaping of a Multilingual Landscape by Shop Names: Tradition Versus Modernity." *Language and Intercultural Communication* 17, no. 1: 26–44. https://doi.org/10.1080/14708477.2017.1261674

2 An ethnography of Valencian language policy and planning through the linguistic landscape

Carla Amorós Negre and Karolina Grzech
University of Salamanca, Spain
Pompeu Fabra University, Spain

Introduction: Indexicality and the spatial turn in sociolinguistics

In recent years, sociolinguistic research has shown a growing interest in the conscious, intentional variation of linguistic practices, observing that it both stems from and co-creates the social structure of communities. Contemporary sociolinguistic enquiry also attends to the indexicality of signs, i.e., "the semiotic property of pointing to other things" (Kallen 2009, 273). Indexicality is especially interesting in linguistic landscape studies, because signage indirectly aligns with different social meanings, and indexicality allows us to connect the micro-social phenomena to the macro-social frames of analysis (Silverstein 2003, 193). This is the line of research we pursue in this chapter.

We apply the concept of indexicality to an ethnographic study of linguistic landscape (LL) of Valencia, Spain. We show how LL can be used to appeal to a particular ethnolinguistic identity and how signs are rooted in language-related power issues.

Our focus on an urban area also has a theoretical motivation. Cities have become privileged spaces for social exploration (Dunlevy 2020) and Valencia is the third most populous city in Spain, and a popular tourist destination on the Mediterranean coast. It has ca. 800,000 inhabitants in the inner city (Generalitat Valenciana 2010), and ca. 2 million in the urban area. In recent years, Valencia has experienced an increase in multilingualism. However, its native languages – Spanish (the dominant and hegemonic language) and Valencian[1] (the regional and minoritized one) – have also been affected, and so has the dynamics between them. The Valencian case is especially interesting due to the existence of the so-called Valencian linguistic conflict (Ninyoles 1992), i.e. the conflictive dynamics of Spanish-Valencian contact (see "Valencian language policy and planning: Language ideologies in conflict"). This chapter presents an in-depth analysis of the social meaning of the monolingual and bilingual linguistic signs in Spanish and/or Valencian. Our study has two main goals. First, we focus on the regimentation of bilingualism through space: we aim to explain the social value attached to Spanish and Valencian in the construction of Valencia's urban dynamics, and the indexical value associated with the use of both languages. Second, we analyze how the measures of language policy and planning are reflected in the cityscape. In particular, we examine whether the recent

DOI: 10.4324/9781032687087-3

administrative incentives encouraging the use of Valencian brought about their professed aim: promoting symmetrical bilingualism.

Key notions and theoretical background

Since the emergence of the notion of linguistic landscape (henceforth LL), there has been an increasing awareness that the presence of certain languages on public and private signs is neither fortuitous nor arbitrary. Studying LLs allows us to look into the socio-political aspects of language use, and has thus become a fundamental research tool in the analysis of language policy and planning.

Regional language planning measures, e.g. the lettering in official spaces, often reflect decisions made on the national level (Backhaus 2012, 226), However, the true success of language planning measures should be examined on the micro-level. Language policies can only be considered effective if speakers become the main agents using and promoting the language, e.g. through signage of their local businesses. At the same time, the presence of certain languages on unofficial signs does not depend only on language policies. It is intertwined with a range of sociodemographic, political, economic, and ethnic factors. The use of majority and global languages is often related to the desire to project an international and cosmopolitan image. The use of local or minority languages, on the other hand, usually appeals to the ideology of authenticity (Woolard 1998). By the same token, the absence of certain varieties from the linguistic landscape can also be socio-politically and ideologically motivated (Castillo and Sáez 2011, 83).

Early analyses of LL focused mainly on counting and describing permanent linguistic signs. More recent studies have increasingly used qualitative and mixed methodologies (see Blackwood et al. 2016). The latest developments in the discipline feature emic ethnographies, observation, personal interviews, and written questionnaires, whereby both the academics and the inhabitants participate in the fieldwork and the exploration of the data (Malinowski and Tufi 2020; Martínez Ibarra 2021; Szabó and Troyer 2017). This chapter presents a qualitative, discourse-grounded study of the geosemiotics of Valencia. In such an ethnographic analysis linguistic signs are conceptualized as socially situated practices, and the public space is seen as both reflecting and creating the power dynamics within the society (Blommaert and Maly 2014). In line with these assumptions, we conducted an in-depth analysis of LL in three neighborhoods, photographing written-language signs, and taking their historical embeddedness and social agency into account.[2]

In the modern, transnational world, governments no longer have the monopoly over language policy and planning decisions on the macro- or meso-level (Coupland 2011, 79). Today, the possibility of creating top-down linguistic landscape is shared by various actors, including international corporations (see Blommaert 2013; Coupland 2011; Kailuweit 2019; Kallen 2009). For this reason, our study assumes that the distinction between top-down and bottom-up measures is not a dichotomy, but a continuum. We also assume that communication channels can be both vertical and horizontal (Kallen 2011, 43), an example of horizontal communication being e.g. a local shop-owner who puts up a sign and thus communicates with their neighbours and customers.

Valencian language policy and planning: Language ideologies in conflict

Valencia is the capital of the *País Valencià*,[3] one of the 17 autonomous regions of Spain, with over 2.5 million speakers of Valencian. Culturally and linguistically, the Valencian region has strong ties to Cataluña, which borders with it in the north. However, it has also had historically strong ties to Madrid, due to the Castilianization of the region (Aracil 1982; Beltrán 2002), which contributed to the minorization of the Valencian language.

In certain areas of the region, Valencian still has strong status as first language. At the same time, the inhabitants of those regions are strongly stereotyped as having low cultural and socioeconomic capital (Pradilla 2004; Climent Ferrando 2005; Membrado 2012). This contrasts with the situation in Catalonia, where the socioeconomic and cultural elites have been using the local language consistently, especially since the nineteenth-century linguistic and cultural revival (Strubell 1994). The Spanish Constitution, approved in 1978 (Article 3), allowed for making other languages co-official in their respective territories alongside Spanish, the only official language of the whole country. The current Statute of Autonomy (2006) establishes Valencian as the region's *lengua propia* ("own language") but at the same time refers to the region as Comunitat Valenciana ("Valencian Community") rather than *País Valenciá* ("Valencian Country"), which indexes the existence of a clear socio-political identity conflict that takes us back to the draft of the 1982 Statute of Autonomy. Right-wing parties and media in the 1980s and the 1990s came out victorious in the negotiations surrounding the democratic Transition insisting that a (supposedly) genuine Valencian cultural and linguistic identity was to be defended against a Catalan version. It followed that being a "good Valencian" meant to resist the union of Catalan-speaking communities and therefore to be as opposed to Catalonia as possible (Strubell 1994, 244–246).

At present, this ethnolinguistic conflict is still evident, and the use of Valencian has a clear sociolinguistic distribution, influenced by variables such as age, place of birth and residence, and the level of education (cf. Argenter 1995; Boix-Fuster and Vila 1998, 187; Ninyoles 1969, 1992). More than forty years after the implementation of the law regulating the use and teaching of Valencian (*Llei d'ús i ensenyament del valencià,* LUEV 1983), diglossia still persists. Although symmetrical bilingualism is the objective of the *normalization* policy[4] the relationship between the two official languages remains unequal (see Bastardas and Soler 1988; Pardines and Torres 2011; Strubell and Boix-Fuster 2011; Pradilla 2015). In 2021, only 50.6% population of the Valencian region could speak Valencian (Generalitat Valenciana, 2023), which represents a decline of over twenty percentage points for both passive and active language competence in the last fifteen years. In this context, it is not surprising that the regional and country-wide language planning measures have been referred to by some as *counter-planning* (*contraplanificació*, Pradilla 2004, 69; cf. Villaverde 2007; Bodoque 2008).

When the inhabitants of the region were asked to self-evaluate their Valencian skills in terms of speaking, hearing, reading, and writing, the results for the city of

Table 2.1 Which language do you usually use at home? Valencia inner-city and urban area

Always Valencian	10.3%
Generally Valencian	0.9%
More Valencian than Spanish	1.3%
Indistinctly	6.4%
More Spanish than Valencian	4.7%
Generally Spanish	2.8%
Always Spanish	**69.2%**
Other languages	3.5%
Don't know(s)/don't replies	0.9%
Total	100% / (n = 7171) interviews

Source: Adapted from *Generalitat Valenciana* GVA (2023, 23).

Valencia, where the ethnographic study was done, were far from optimistic: 40.7% of the respondents could not write in Valencian; 30.9% reported not being able to read it; and 28% could not speak it at all (Generalitat Valenciana 2023, 7).

In the same survey, the respondents were asked which language they "usually speak at home." Their answers, summarized in Table 2.1, show that nearly 70% of the city's population reports not using Valencian at all. These numbers stand in stark contrast with the professed bilingualism, which exists *de jure*, but not *de facto*.

We cannot lose sight of the fact that between 2015 and 2023, Valencia was governed by a left-wing coalition known as the *Acord del Botànic* ("The Botanical Garden Agreement"). The coalition expressed a strong commitment to advancing the normalization of Valencian (Generalitat Valenciana 2017; Pastor 2017). The government used Valencian as the default language of political advertising, social campaigns, and social media. It was a conscious strategy, particularly evident since 2018, when the regional government created a number of official bodies and institutions to support and promote the use of Valencian (for more details, see Badenes Goterris 2021).

One particularly relevant campaign for the linguistic landscape was *Sempre Teua, la Teua Llengua* ("Always yours, your Language," Generalitat Valenciana 2017; Periódico del Mediterráneo 2018), an initiative in which the municipal government underlined its duty to protect Valencian, increase the speaker numbers, and create social affiliation with the language, also among passive bilinguals. Therefore, since 2017, to foster multilingualism in the city, businesses can incur fiscal benefits if they use Valencian or English in their signage (program *Sello de Calidad Lingüística* "Label of Linguistic Quality.")[5] In the same vein, the authorities also implemented the strategic campaign *El teu comerç parla en valencià, perquè el valencià és marca de qualitat* ("Your business speaks Valencian, because Valencian is a quality brand"). In order to boost signage in Valencian, templates of Valencian-medium opening hours information, bathroom signs, etc., as well as posters with catchphrases encouraging the use of Valencian were designed and distributed in the cityscape. There were also funds included for professionals to enroll in Valencian courses. Another initiative that directly impacted the landscape of the city was the law 69/2017, prioritizing the traditional Valencian toponyms in the Valencian-speaking areas and Spanish in Spanish-speaking regions of the Valencian Community.

It is not insignificant that, for the first time, the *Generalitat Valenciana* survey on knowledge and use of Valencian introduces questions on the evaluation of governmental initiatives to promote the use of this language in the region, particularly the above-mentioned institutional campaign *Sempre teua. La teua llengua*; the passing of the law on multilingualism in the Valencian education system; broadcasts offered by the Valencian public service radio and television station *À Punt*; the creation of the *Oficina de Drets Lingüístics* (Office for Language Rights) and the exams set by the *Junta Qualificadora de Coneixements de Valencià* (JQCV, The Qualification Board for the Knowledge of Valencian) to assess Valencian language proficiency (GVA 2023, 36). These actions were deemed (highly) satisfactory by 37.7% of the population. Although 27% of the respondents were indifferent to such initiatives, it is striking that almost 12% of the population is against these options for the promotion of the minority language and considers the measures taken to be excessive.

An ethnographic analysis of the linguistic landscape of Valencia

Since the 1990s, language policies fostering regional and minority languages became clearly reflected in the linguistic landscapes of many major cities in Europe and North America, with an increase in bilingualism and multilingualism in public spaces (e.g. Wenzel 1996; Ben Rafael et al. 2006; Gorter et al. 2012; Tufi 2016; Van Mensel and Darquennes 2012). The present analysis builds on these studies. It follows Blommaert and Maly (2014) in focusing on the indexical loads of salient monolingual or bilingual signs. Linguistic landscape serves as a proxy for observing the presence and status of the two languages under study in the everyday life of the city and its inhabitants, as well as the effectiveness of the recent language policy and planning measures.

This section describes our methods of data collection and analysis and discusses the sociolinguistic profiles and linguistic landscapes of the analyzed neighborhoods.

Methodology of the current study

This study uses the methodology of semiotic analysis (Scollon and Scollon 2003; Kallen 2011; Blommaert 2013; Blommaert and Maly 2014). The following criteria are relevant to our analysis of linguistic signs:

- Authorship. We consider three categories: public, semi-public and private signs, reflecting the top-down/bottom-up continuum of language policy and planning (see Section "Key notions and theoretical background"). Public signs are those produced by authorities on different levels: municipal, regional, national, and global. Private signs are produced by individual members of society in their private and professional capacity. The in-between category of semi-public signs includes: signs produced by institutions such as churches, which are not private,

but also not state-run; commercial signs produced by actors whose scope goes beyond local shops, such as international corporations and banks; signs created by individuals within their capacity as public servants, e.g. hand-made signs with official information concerning the functioning of public offices.
- Intended audience.
- Function and emplacement. The positioning of signs can influence their legitimacy, and index specific social voices. Regarding functions, we distinguish, after Blommaert (2013, 53–54): (1) landmark function (street, traffic and instruction signs, signage of official institutions and historical sites); (2) recruitment function (signs for shops and services, events-related posters, etc.); (3) public statement function (signs with more elusive authorship, usually of vindictive/ideological character e.g. graffiti, stencils).
- Distribution and role of languages: whether signs are monolingual, bilingual (expressing the same content in Spanish and Valencian), or mixed (different information given in Spanish and Valencian).
- Durability: whether signs are permanent or non-permanent (e.g. event-related).

We analyze three districts, representative of different socioeconomic groups of the population of Valencia, assuming that LL is revealing of a community profiling (Martínez Ibarra 2021, 308). We documented the LL of each neighborhood by photographing public, semi-public, and private signs. The data was collected between February 2019 and August 2023. If a combination of signs could be read by a passer-by at the same time, they were considered a unit. If they could not – like the plaques with street names on two different corners, or a banner with the restaurant's name and a menu in small print – they were considered different units. The photographing of the signs was accompanied by participant observation, as well as by interviews with different linguistic landscape creators in order to learn what motivated their linguistic choices for private signs.

The neighborhoods under study

The city of Valencia is divided into 87 neighborhoods (see Map 2.1). One of our goals was also to establish whether a certain sociodemographic, economic, and historical structure of a neighborhood can both influence and be reflected in the features of its LL. Table 2.2 provides key data obtained from the last 2023 census for each of the neighborhoods under study.

L'Eixample

L'Eixample is one of the richest districts of Valencia and its most important commercial area with high-end shops and restaurants and points of touristic interest. The area is popular for shopping and eating out, but it also has a residential character.

We selected 77 signs in this area, almost 78% (n=60) of which were private signs. What stands out in the LL of L'Eixample is that Valencian is used to index authenticity and localness, rather than to convey information. This is illustrated

46 *Ethnographic Landscapes and Language Ideologies in the Spanish State*

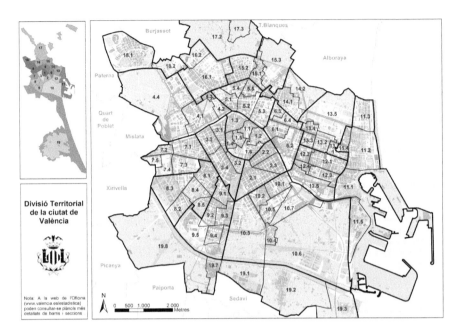

Map 2.1 Neighborhoods of Valencia.

Sources: Adapted from Ajuntament de València (2024a). www.valencia.es/documents/20142/2154295/Valencia_barrios.pdf/6f069b04-8103-05ec-955c-eb159589cd77

Table 2.2 Sociodemographic data for districts under study

District name	L'Eixample (District 2)	Patraix (District 8)	Benimaclet (District 14)
Total population	43565	58833	28317
Population from non-Catalan-speaking regions of Spain	4651	9458	5238
Foreign population	6017	6669	3777
Neighborhoods where data was collected (see Map 2.1)	2.2, 2.3	8.4, 8.1	14.1

Source: Adapted from Ajuntament de València (2024b).

with Figure 2.1, showing a sign for a *casal faller*, i.e. the premises of a *falla*, a neighborhood-based group that participates in the yearly *Fallas* festival.[6]

Since *fallas* are informal associations, the authorship of this sign is private. It is aimed at the local audience – not tourists – and has a landmark function. It does not aim to recruit new members, but rather functions as a public statement, aided both by the monolingual use of Valencian, and by visual elements associated with Valencian identity – the gold and red striped flag with blue rim, evoking the flag of

Figure 2.1 Casal faller. Photograph by the authors.

the region and the bat – the symbol of the city. The sign is permanent, and the combination of the use of the local symbols and language is clearly aimed at sending a message of authenticity.

Authenticity indexed through the use of local language is exploited to a different end by the signs in Figure 2.2. These permanent, private signs belong to a workshop offering renovation and plumbing services, and have a recruitment function. The logo of the shop is a vintage faucet, and the shop's name – *l'aixeta* – means "the faucet" in Valencian, but it is also the only Valencian word on the sign; the practical information about the services are given in Spanish. Therefore, the sign can be classified as mixed rather than bilingual – the vintage illustration and the basic use of Valencian are meant to evoke a certain image, attractive for the local Spanish-speaking clients.

This use of the connotative function of language to evoke authenticity is in line with the results of the sociolinguistic surveys (GVA 2023). Only 27.1% of the respondents stated they generally speak Valencian in their neighborhoods and local stores. Through their design, the signs in Figure 2.2 reference artisan methods, in line with the stereotype of Valencian as the "traditional" language. In this way, they both fit into and reinforce the ideology of authenticity associated with the use of Valencian.

The private signs discussed so far, even if they featured Valencian, contained little to no practical information in the language. The situation is different in the public sign in Figure 2.3, produced by the regional authorities. It has a place-making, landmark function and signals an activity space for seniors, destined for the local residents. It is monolingual in Valencian and also contains visual elements related to the local identity – the logo of the *Generalitat*.

48 *Ethnographic Landscapes and Language Ideologies in the Spanish State*

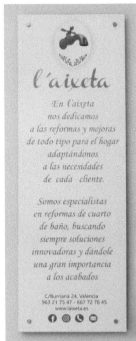

Figure 2.2 L'aixeta, 'renovation company'. Photograph by the authors.

The monolingual use of Valencian in this sign is in line with the policies of the *Generalitat*, implemented since 2015: to raise the profile of Valencian and make it the vehicular language of public administration.[7] However, as Figure 2.4 illustrates, such policies often remain very limited in their application. It is to be expected that they will become even less effective in the coming years, judging by the announcements on language policy that the current government wishes to implement regarding, for example, the modification of the Law on Plurilingualism (starting in September 2024). After these modifications are implemented, Valencian will no longer be the compulsory language of public instruction in subjects other than the linguistic ones in areas where the language is predominantly Castilian (see, e.g. https://valenciaplaza.com/educacion-informa-cambio-ley-plurilingui smo-centros-castellanohablantes).

Figure 2.4 showcases a temporary, public sign, monolingual in Spanish, aimed at the local public and tourists, informing them that parking is not possible for the duration of the *Fallas* festival. The sign has a regulative function and operates within the civic frame of the authorities-general public communication.

In sum, the dominance of Spanish is undisputable in the LL of L'Eixample. Spanish occurred – alone or with other languages – on more than 75% of the signs

Figure 2.3 Aules de tercera edat 'classrooms for the elderly'. Photograph by the authors.

(n=59). The analogous figure for Valencian is 21.7% (n=19). While Valencian only co-occurred on the signs with Spanish, Spanish co-occurred both with Valencian and with other languages such as English, Greek, Japanese, Italian, and German. This provides further support for the observation about the mainly connotative function of Valencian in the LL of the area. In case of private signs, the local language is used particularly in the names of the businesses or in some token words without informative value, which points to its commodification, indexing authenticity and localness, as the interviewees reinforced. The function of Spanish, on the other hand, is more informative and utilitarian, pointing to its default use as language of broader communication.

Patraix

Patraix was a separate town until its annexation to Valencia in 1870, and still conserves some of its town-like architecture and character. It expanded in the Franco era, during which immigrants from other parts of Spain arrived in the rapidly industrializing Valencia. According to the latest census (see Table 2.2), 27% of the population of Patraix comes either from abroad, or from non-Catalan speaking regions of Spain.[8] It is a middle-class district with many shops and restaurants.

50 *Ethnographic Landscapes and Language Ideologies in the Spanish State*

Figure 2.4 Prohibido estancionar 'No parking'. Photograph by the authors.

In Patraix, we chose 83 instances of LL. Just like in L'Eixample, private signs were dominant. However, what we also found noteworthy were the semi-public temporary signs (see Figures 2.5 and 2.6) – created by public servants in their professional capacity, but not officially regulated.

Figure 2.5 shows two pieces of paper, which we consider as one sign. The intended audience are the local residents, and the function of the sign is informative within the civic frame. The first sheet informs about the procedure of getting subsidized tickets for public transport. Only the name of the voucher (*Bono Amb Tu* "Voucher With You") is in Valencian, and the informative content is provided in Spanish. The second sheet details the procedure of making appointments with the city council. It is bilingual, with Valencian preceding Spanish, and featured more prominently. The difference in the use of Spanish and Valencian clearly shows that, despite the presence of official language policies, the final shape of the signs is determined by the individual agency/ repertoires of the civil servants. Other similar signs in our dataset confirm this observation.

In Figure 2.6, showing the entrance to a public school, Valencian is used alongside English, but Spanish is absent. This supports the point made above: official

An ethnography of Valencian LPP the linguistic landscape 51

Figure 2.5 Semi-public sign informing about administrative matters. Photograph by the authors.

Figure 2.6 Local school in Patraix. Photograph by the authors.

Figure 2.7 A greengrocer. Photograph by the authors.

language policy is but an indication, and whether and how it is realized depends on the actors who create the signs.

In the linguistic landscape of Patraix, Valencian is used in the informative function more often than in L'Eixample. Due to the character of this neighborhood, the commercial establishments cater to locals rather than tourists. It is possible that the greater use of Valencian in the landscape mirrors a similar pattern of linguistic behavior among the neighbors.

This can be appreciated on the private signs in the district and in the interviews with the linguistic landscape creators. The storefront shown in Figure 2.7 is a greengrocer shop, aimed at the local public, and fulfilling the recruitment function. It is a bilingual sign, and the use of Spanish and Valencian is almost symmetrical – the only difference being that Spanish is present on the permanent signage, and Valencian – on the graffiti on the blind, which can only be seen when the shop is closed. When asked about his choice of signage, the shop owner observed that symmetrical bilingual signage was not deliberate, but a product of chance. The sign in Spanish reflected the official name of the business, and the writing on the blind was the choice of the artist who painted it. Our interlocutor also said that he was not aware of the city government's financial incentives promoting signage in Valencian.

The informative function of Valencian in Patraix can be appreciated in Figure 2.8, showing a permanent private sign. It is a storefront of a shop selling traditional accessories worn during *Fallas*. The sign has a recruitment function and is directed at a very specific local public, actively participating in *Fallas*. Despite its association with a traditional craft and sector, the sign is monolingual

Figure 2.8 Accessories for *Fallas*. Photograph by the authors.

in Spanish – apart from the word *complements* ("accessories"), but it seems that the use of this word, rather than Spanish *complementos*, is due either to a typo or to lack of space. The owner's choice of Spanish signage was due to the fact that he uses Spanish in his everyday life. The sign is much older than the city government's campaign promoting Valencian signage, and the owner observed that the campaign would not have been a sufficient incentive to change the sign, especially since most of the words that appear on it are near-identical in Spanish and in Valencian. If we compare this sign with the *Casal faller* in L'Eixample (Figure 2.1), we can appreciate that this shop also appeals to the local tradition and identity, but here, there is no use of Valencian to evoke it. In the LL of L'Eixample, the view of Valencian is much more tokenistic and 'essentialist' – associating the language with a traditional identity, whereas in the LL of Patraix Valencian appears to be authentic, and likely being used for everyday interactions. This is confirmed by the LL of the informative plaques created by the local neighbors' association, describing local's sights of interests. Some of them are monolingual in Spanish, and other – in Valencian. This points to a relatively stable bilingualism of the intended audience, able to read both languages. Consequently, we can conclude that the situation in the LL of Patraix is more bilingual, compared to a more diglossic one in L'Eixample.

All in all, Spanish is also dominant in the LL of Patraix. It occurred – alone or with other languages – on 68.2% (n=58) of the signs. Valencian – alone or with other languages – appeared on 48.2% (n=41) of the documented signs. However, qualitative analysis and in-depth participant observation suggest that the advantage of Spanish over Valencian is less pronounced than in L'Eixample.

Benimaclet

Benimaclet was incorporated into the city limits of Valencia as recently as 1972, and a substantial part of the district still conserves a small-town character. It has a vibrant and affordable nightlife, and is home to many grassroots (and often left-wing) political, social, and cultural associations. In Benimaclet, we documented 104 linguistic signs. In contrast with what we found in Patraix,[9] the cultural and neighborhood associations tend to use monolingual signs in Valencian.

Figure 2.9 also shows the informative use of Valencian in private, permanent recruitment signs: a dog groomer and animal shop, called *AmicGos*. On this sign, Valencian and Spanish are mixed to create a wordplay. In Valencian, *amic* means "friend" and *gos* means "dog," but *amigos* is "friends" in Spanish. At the same time, functional information related to opening hours and other announcements is displayed in Spanish. The owner, who is not Valencian, and has passive knowledge of the language, wanted for the name of the business to acknowledge the place where it was located. She admitted that financial assistance for signage in Valencian was initially a motivating factor as well, but that she ended up never actually applying for the aid.

For its part, Figure 2.10 features a greengrocer, where the informative signs are predominantly monolingual in Valencian. The signs are directed towards the local public with a clear recruitment function. The permanent signage with the business name *El camp, la nostra vida* ("The countryside, our life") is accompanied by temporary signs, monolingual in Valencian. The only sign in Spanish

Figure 2.9 AmicGos, a hairdresser for dogs and animal shop. Photograph by the authors.

An ethnography of Valencian LPP the linguistic landscape 55

Figure 2.10 El Camp. La nostra vida, a greengrocer. Photograph by the authors.

is the regulative one about not touching the products. The photograph above was taken in 2019. When we visited the site again in 2024, shortly before submitting this chapter to print, the permanent signage of the shop remained the same, but the temporary signs were now mostly bilingual, with some signs only featuring Spanish.

Based on our analysis, we can affirm that Benimaclet is dominated by the private LL, represented by shops, services, pubs, and restaurants, to a greater extent than the other two studied areas. A plethora of different private associations also influence the cityscape: anti-fascist and feminist non-permanent and event-related signs are especially noticeable, as well as vindictive graffiti (see Figure 2.11), monolingual in Valencian.

The ethnographic analysis of its LL confirms that Benimaclet lives up to its reputation of a vibrant and politically active, pro-Valencian neighborhood. The presence of Spanish – alone or with other languages – amounted to 57% of the documented signs (n=65), which is the lowest figure for all the analyzed neighborhoods.

Discussion and conclusions: From diglossia to social bilingualism?

The qualitative and semiotic analysis allowed us to appreciate that – in this particular case – it is not possible to generalize about the LL of the city as a whole. Our study shows that the situation varies between diglossia and bilingualism depending on the district. The data also reveal differences in linguistic practices of different

Figure 2.11 La seua riquesa, la nostra miseria 'Their wealth, our misery'. Photograph by the authors.

types of actors who produce the signs. In his analysis of the LL of Valencia, Vallès i Sanchis (2003) observed that, even though bilingual signs in Spanish and Valencian are a norm in public signage, this is not true for semi-public and private signs. Twenty years later, our findings confirm that.

What also emerges from our ethnographic analysis is the different indexical load of the monolingual and bilingual signage in the documented districts and the place-making potential of private actors as co-creators of LL. Private actors turn out to be the most active creators of LL, responsible for over three-quarters of the documented signs (75.2%, n=200/266).

This observation is crucial for the discussion of Valencia's sociolinguistic situation and the outcomes of top-down and bottom-up language policy and planning in the city. Our data show that public institutions opt for Valencian-Spanish bilingualism (street names) and display information only in Valencian (names of public institutions). However, it is the private actors who ultimately shape the LL of the streets and make use of their different linguistic resources to negotiate complex processes of language identity construction when addressing particular audiences.

At the same time, the interviews we conducted with private creators of LL suggest that decisions regarding the language of signs are not necessarily related to particular language attitudes. They are also not a part of consistent micro-level language policies associated with the use of Valencian beyond the signage. In that sense, the shopkeepers are reactive rather than pro-active, adapting to the linguistic choices made by their clients.

Qualitative analysis confirms the results of previous studies (cf. Vallés i Sanchís 2003): overall, private LL of Valencia is dominated by Spanish. In 2003, Vallés i Sanchís analyzed 10 streets, observing that only 15% of the commercial and private labels were in Valencian. More recently, Lado (2011) reported that 65% of private signs in Valencia were monolingual Spanish, and 14% were bilingual in Spanish and Valencian. In our data, the presence of monolingual Spanish signs is much lower (38.5%), while the percentage of bilingual signs is in line with Lado's findings: 14.5% of private signs were in Valencian and Spanish, and further 2% also included another language.

Our study shows that shops, restaurants etc. are not, at least as far as signage is concerned, actively promoting the use of Valencian. Rather, commercial actors both reproduce and reinforce the existing hierarchy of linguistic repertoires, whereby Spanish is still the dominant language (see Bruyèl Olmedo i Garau 2015). Given that the different political actors each have their own language policies, and that the legal acts concerning the language of public signs (see Section "Valencian language policy and planning: Language ideologies in conflict") are relatively recent, their effect of the policies we mentioned throughout the chapter is still hard to assess. However, although *de jure* language policy made Valencian more visible on official public signs between 2015 and 2023, it seems to have had little bearing on semi-public and private signs, which are an artifact of their creators' linguistic ideologies and practices.

The scarcity of private signs in Valencian points to the language ideologies whereby Valencian is seen in the city as the *la llengua del poble* ("language of the people"), not used in written communication as much as Spanish, and associated with a traditional, rural identity. The authors of linguistic signs are conscious of their utilitarian function, and presumably choose Spanish or Valencian depending on the type of audience they want to reach (cf. Martínez Ibarra 2021). This ideological embedding has to do not so much with language skills, since the two languages are to a great extent mutually intelligible, but with the assumed sociolinguistic profile of the speakers, or the character of the business, and whether it can be stereotypically associated with the Valencian language.

Another factor bearing on language use in LL is the ideological orientation of language users. Apart from being perceived as the "language of the people," Valencian is also perceived as a language of activism, generally of the leftist orientation

As shown in Table 2.3, those who identify as politically left-wing also show higher level of competence in Valencian across the four language skills. This correlation can also be appreciated in the LL. There is no significant difference between the signs featuring Valencian attested in the middle-class Patraix (42%, n=41) and Benimaclet, perceived and construed as the "alternative," leftist district (45%, n=47). At the same time, as we mentioned above, the presence of Spanish in Benimaclet is less dominant than in the other two neighborhoods under study.

Table 2.3 Valencian population's language skills depending on political orientation

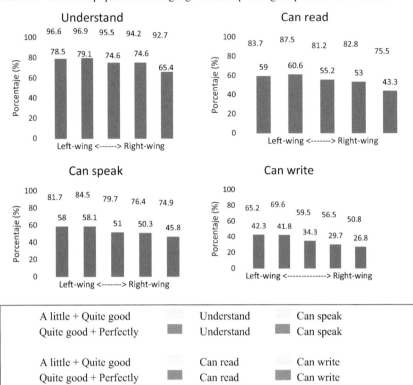

Source: Generalitat Valenciana (2015, 17)

In sum, the assessment of the power relationships between languages and communities in contact is a complex and multi-facetted matter. The multi-layered approach we applied to our data suggests that despite the co-official status with Spanish, Valencian is still perceived as a "marked" choice, representing two types of identities: rural/traditional, or urban left-wing activist.

Almost fifty years have passed since the fall of the Franco regime, which promoted Spanish at the expense of other languages of Spain. Nonetheless, the lack of a consistent language policy and planning on the part of the consecutive regional governments in Valencia is still visible throughout the urban LL.

The analysis of LL, combined with recent language policies, population surveys, participant observations and qualitative interviews all suggest that Valencian still remains a symbol of a particular linguistic identity and local authenticity (Woolard 1998). In this context, the biggest challenge for language policy and planning in Valencia seems to be the ideological component, and the prestige planning associated with it. The 2015–2023 city authorities were indeed attempting to reinforce positive attitudes towards Valencian. The campaigns we discussed throughout the chapter were aimed at promoting everyday use of the language, moving beyond its essentializing association with authenticity. They also promoted allegiance towards Valencian language amongst local residents with passive knowledge of it, drawing on mutual intelligibility with Spanish. While our data show that some elements of these policies were indeed picked up by the public, they also indicate that, for attitudinal change to really take root, a longer time-frame would be needed. Unfortunately, this is not a likely scenario in present-day Valencia. In present day Valencia, given that all the main parties on the regional political scene have their own views on language policy and planning, and aim to legislate in accordance with them as soon as they are voted into power. This is no doubt positive from the perspective of democratic governance, but, at the same time, makes implementing effective and long-lasting language policy and planning measures much more difficult.

Notes

1 Valencian is an occidental variety of Catalan, and the two share the ISO 639-3 code "cat." We use the glottonym "Valencian," as it is preferred by the majority of speakers. Catalan is spoken in Spain (and is the co-official language of Catalonia, Valencian Community, Balearic Islands, and the Eastern strip of Aragon and Carxe region in Murcia), France (the Roussillon plain), Andorra, and Italy (Alghero, Sardinia). In Andorra, Catalan is the only official language.
2 In Patraix: the surroundings of the Patraix Central square; in l'Eixample: Cánovas, Gran Vía, Joaquim Costa, l'Almirall Cadarso and Conte d'Altea; In Benimaclet: carrer d'Emili Baró, Juan Giner, Vicent Zaragoza and carrer d'Enric Navarro, finishing in Benimaclet metro station.
3 We opt to choose the toponym *País Valencià* (Valencian Country), used since the eighteenth century rather than the current official name, *Comunitat Valenciana* (Valencian Autonomous Community), in keeping with the established practice in the field of Catalan sociolinguistics (see, for example, Bastardas and Soler 1988; Boix and Vila 1998).
4 The term *normalization* (*normalització* and *normalitat lingüística*, Aracil 1982) refers to language policy and planning measures aimed at promotion a minoritized language, so as to achieve its effective equality with the majority language, encouraging the use in public administration, education and mass media, and thus reversing the language shift.
5 "El Consell prepara ventajas fiscales para las empresas que cuenten con el sello de calidad lingüística" Accessed February 25, 2024. https://comunica.gva.es/es/detalle?id=359904046&site=174859740.
6 *Fallas* are the most famous popular festival in Valencia, celebrated yearly in March, and considered Intangible Cultural Heritage by UNESCO (since 2019).
7 In May 2023, the conservative Popular Party (Partido Popular) regained the majority in the Valencian regional government and the mayor's office of the city of Valencia. Carlos Mazón was elected president of the *Generalitat Valenciana* and María José Català became the mayor.

8 While this figure is high, the analogous figure is even higher for Benimaclet (31.8%) and only five percentage points lower for L'Eixample (22.2%).
9 Only churches, both here and in Patraix, display monolingual Spanish signage.

References

Ajuntament de València. 2024a. *Padró Municipal d'Habitants*. València. https://pegv.gva.es/es/temas/demografiaypoblacion/0padron (accessed 4 January 2024).

Ajuntament de València. 2024b. *Cartografia dels barris i districtes de València*. www.valencia.es/val/estadistica/per-territori (accessed 4 January 2024).

Andrés Durà, Raquel. 2021. "València destina hasta 2.000 euros por comercio para promocionar el uso del valenciano." La Vanguardia. www.lavanguardia.com/local/valencia/20210402/6624066/valencia-2-000-euros-comercio-promocionar-valenciano.html (accessed 4 June 2021).

Aracil, Lluís V. 1982. *Papers de sociolingüística*. Barcelona: La magrana.

Argenter, Joan A. 1995. "Language Shift: An Overview." *Catalan Review* 9 (2): 39–59.

Backhaus, Peter. 2012. "Language Policy at the Municipal Level." In *The Cambridge Handbook of Language Policy*, edited by Bernard Spolsky, 226–242. Cambridge: Cambridge University Press.

Badenes Goterris, Cristòfol. 2021. "La política lingüística dels governs valencians (2015-2019)." Blog Journal of Language and Law. https://eapc-rld.blog.gencat.cat/2021/03/11/la-politica-linguistica-del-govern-valencia-2015-2019-cristofol-badenes-goterris/ (accessed 10 June 2021).

Bastardas, Albert, and Josep Soler, eds. 1988. *Sociolingüística i llengua catalana*. Barcelona: Empúries.

Beltrán, Adolf. 2002. *Els temps moderns. Societat valenciana i cultura de masses al segle XX*. València: Tandem Edicions.

Ben-Rafael, Eliezer, Elana Shohamy, Muhammad Hasan Amara, and Nira Trumper-Hecht. 2006. "Linguistic Landscape as Symbolic Construction of the Public Space: The Case of Israel." *International Journal of Multilingualism* 3 (1): 7–30. http://dx.doi.org/10.1080/.14790710608668383

Blackwood, Robert, Elizabeth Lanza, and Hirut Woldemariam, eds. 2016. *Negotiating and Contesting Identities in Linguistic Landscapes*. London/New York: Bloomsbury.

Blommaert, Jan. 2013. *Ethnography, Superdiversity and Linguistic Landscapes*. Bristol: Multilingual Matters.

Blommaert, Jan, and Ico Maly. 2014. "Ethnographic Linguistic Landscape Analysis and Social Change: A Case Study." *Tilburg Papers in Culture Studies* 100. https://research.tilburguniversity.edu/files/30402167/TPCS_100_Blommaert_Maly.pdf

Bodoque, Anselm. 2008. *La política lingüística dels governs valencians (1983-2008): Un estudi de polítiques públiques*. València: Universitat de València.

Boix-Fuster, Emili, and Francesc X. Vila i Moreno. 1998. *Sociolingüística de la llengua catalana*. Barcelona: Ariel.

Bruyèl-Olmedo, Antonio, and María Juan-Garau. 2015. "Shaping Tourist LL: Language Display and the Sociolinguistic Background of an International Multilingual Readership." *International Journal of Multilingualism* 12 (1): 51–67.

Castillo Lluch, Mónica, and Daniel M. Sáez Rivera. 2011. "Introducción al paisaje lingüístico de Madrid." *Lengua y Migración* 3: 73–88. www.redalyc.org/pdf/5195/519551811004.pdf

Climent-Ferrando, Vicent. 2005. "L'origen i l'evolució argumentativa del secessionisme lingüístic valencià. Una anàlisi des de la transició fins a l'actualitat." *Mercator – Documents de treball -Working Papers de CIEMEN* 18.

Coupland, Nikolas. 2011. "Welsh Linguistic Landscapes From Above and From Below." In *Semiotic Landscapes. Language Image, Space*, edited by Adam Jaworski, and Crispin Thurlow, 77–101. London: Continuum.

Dunlevy, Deirde A. 2000. "Blurred Lines: The Effect of Regional Borders on the LL in Northern Spain." In *Reterritorializing Linguistic Landscapes Questioning Boundaries and Opening Spaces*, edited by David Malinowski, and Stefania Tufi, 236–260. London: Bloomsbury.

Generalitat Valenciana. 2010. *Enquesta de coneixement i ús social del valencià*. València: Generalitat Valenciana.

Generalitat Valenciana. 2015. *Enquesta de coneixement i ús social del valencià*. València: Generalitat Valenciana.

Generalitat Valenciana. 2023. *Enquesta de coneixement i ús social del valencià*. València: Generalitat Valenciana.

Generalitat Valenciana. 2017. Decret 61/2017, de 12 de maig, del Consell, pel qual es regulen les llengües oficials en l'Administració de la Generalitat [2017/4338]. *Diari Oficial de la Generalitat Valenciana*. València: Generalitat Valenciana.

Generalitat Valenciana. 2017. "Sempre Teua, la Teua Lengua." http://sempreteua.gva.es/va/per-que (accessed 16 January 2024).

Gorter, Durk, Jokin Aiestaran, and Jasone Cenoz. 2012. "The Revitalization of Basque and the Linguistic Landscape of Donostia-San Sebastián." In *Minority Languages in the Linguistic Landscape*, edited by Durk Gorter, Luk Van Mensel, and Heiko F. Marten, 148–163. Basingstoke, UK: Palgrave-Macmillan.

Kallen, Jeffrey L. 2009. "Tourism and Representation in the Irish Linguistic Landscape." In *Linguistic Landscape: Expanding the Scenery*, edited by Elana Shohamy, and Durk Gorter, 270–283. London/New York: Routledge.

Kallen, Jeffrey L. 2011. "Changing Landscape: Language, Space and Policy in the Dublin Linguistic Landscape." In *Semiotic Landscapes. Language Image, Space*, edited by Adam Jaworski, and Crispin Thurlow, 41–58. London: Continuum.

Kailuweit, Rolf. 2019. "Linguistic Landscapes and Regional Languages in Southern France – A Neo-Semiotic Approach to Place-Making Conflicts." In *Linguistic Landscape Studies. The French Connection*, edited by Mónica Castillo-Lluch, Rolf Kailuweit, and Claus D. Pusch, 131–161. Freiburg: Rombach Verlag.

Lado, Beatriz. 2011. "Linguistic Landscape as a Reflection of the Linguistic and Ideological Conflict in the Valencian Community." *International Journal of Multilingualism* 8: 135–150.

Malinowski, David, and Stefania Tufi. 2020. *Reterritorializing Linguistic Landscapes: Questioning Boundaries and Opening Spaces*. London: Bloomsbury.

Martínez Ibarra, Francisco. 2021. "An Analysis of How Business Owners Use Valencian and Spanish in the Linguistic Landscape." In *Linguistic Landscape in the Spanish-speaking World*, edited by Patricia Gubitosi, and Michelle Ramos Pellicia, 293–312. Amsterdam\Philadelphia: John Benjamins.

Membrado, Joan C. 2012. "Identity Conflict in the Land of València During the Post-Franco Democratic Period." *Saitabi. Revista de la Facultat de Geografia i Història* 62–63: 187–210. http://dx.doi.org/10.7203/saitabi.62-63.3861

Ninyoles, Rafael L. 1969. *Conflicte lingüístic valencià*. València: Tres i Quatre.

Ninyoles, Rafael L. 1992. "Sociologia de la lengua." In *La sociedad valenciana de los 90*, edited by Manuel García Ferrando, 421–438. València: Alfons el Magnànim.
Pardines, Susanna, and Nathalie Torres 2011. *La política lingüística al País Valencià: Del conflicte a la gestió responsable.* Barcelona: Fundació Nexe.
Pastor, Estefanía. 2017. "Sempre teua. Educació desvela la seua campanya de promoció del valencià." https://valenciaplaza.com/Sempreteua-Educacio-desvela-la-seua-campanya-de-promocio-del-valencia (accessed 2 November 2021).
Periódico del Mediterráneo. 2018. "Sempre teua. La llengua de tots." www.elperiodicomediterraneo.com/noticias/sempreteua/sempre-teua-llengua-tots_1156549.html (accessed 2 November 2021).
Pradilla, Miquel À. 2004. *El laberint valencià. Apunts per a una sociolingüística del conflicte.* Benicarló: Onada.
Pradilla, Miquel À. 2015. *La catalanofonia. Una comunitat del segle XXI a la recerca de la normalitat lingüística.* Barcelona: Institut d'Estudis Catalans.
Scollon, Ron, and Suzie W. Scollon. 2003. *Discourses in Place. Languages in the Material World.* London: Routledge.
Shohamy, Elana. 2006. *Language Policy and Language Planning. Hidden Agendas and New Approaches.* London: Routledge
Silverstein, Michael. 2003. "Indexical Order and the Dialectics of Sociolinguistic Life." *Language & Communication* 23 (3–4): 193–229. http://dx.doi.org/10.1016/S0271-5309(03)00013-2
Strubell, Miquel. 1994. "Catalan in Valencia: The Story of An Attempted Secession." In *Sprachstandardisierung. 12 Kolloquium der Schweizerischen Akademie der Geistes-und Sozialwissenschaften*, edited by Georges Lüdi, 229–254. Freiburg: Universitätsverlag Freiburg.
Strubell, Miquel, Emili Boix-Fuster, eds. 2011. *Democratic Policies for Language Revitalisation: The case of Catalan.* New York: Palgrave Macmillan.
Szabó, Tamás P., and Robert A. Troyer. 2017. "Inclusive Ethnographies. Beyond the Binaries of Observer and Observed in Linguistic Landscape Studies." *Linguistic Landscape* 3 (3): 306–326. http://dx.doi.org/10.1075/ll.17008.sza
Tufi, Stefania. 2016. "Constructing the Self in Contested Spaces. The Case of Slovenian Speaking Minorities in the Area of Trieste." In *Negotiating and Contesting Identities in Linguistic Landscapes,* edited by Robert Blackwood, Elizabeth Lanza, and Hirut Woldemariam, 101–116. London/New York: Bloomsbury.
Valencia Plaza. 2024. "Educación informa de los cambios en la ley de plurilingüismo a centros castellanohablantes". https://valenciaplaza.com/educacion-informa-cambio-ley-plurilinguismo-centros-castellanohablantes (accessed 14 March 2024).
Vallés i Sanchis, Ismael. 2003. "Aproximació a la imatge lingüística de la ciutat de València." Cuadernos de geografía 73–74: 391–400. https://roderic.uv.es/handle/10550/31282 (accessed 20 November 2021).
Van Mensel, Luk, and Jeroen Darquennes. 2012. "All is Quiet on the Eastern Front? Language Contact Along the French-German Language Border in Belgium." In *Minority Languages in the Linguistic Landscape*, edited by Durk Gorter, Luk Van Mensel, and Heiko F. Marten, 164–180. Basingstoke, UK: Palgrave-Macmillan.
Villaverde, Joan A. 2007. "Comportament dels grups lingüístics i representacions sobre la llengua." In *Llengua i societat als territoris de parla catalana a l'inici del segle XXI: L'Alguer, Andorra, Catalunya, Catalunya Nord, la Franja, Illes Balears i Comunitat Valenciana*, edited by Ernst Querol, 143–181. Barcelona: Generalitat de Catalunya.

Wenzel, Veronika. 1996. "Reklame en tweetaligheid in Brussel: Een empirisch onderzoek naar de spreiding van Nederlandstalige en Franstalige affiches." *Brusselse thema's* 3: 45–74. https://journals.aiac.org.au/index.php/IJALEL/article/view/5656

Woolard, Kathryn A. 1998. "Language Ideology as a Field of Inquiry." In *Language Ideologies: Practice and Theory,* edited by Bambi B Schieffelin, Kathryn A. Woolard, and Paul V. Kroskrity, 3–49. New York: Oxford University Press.

3 Multilingualism in the linguistic landscape of the city of Granada

Daniel M. Sáez Rivera, María Heredia Mantis, Irania Malaver Arguinzones, Luis Pablo Núñez and Marcin Sosinski

Introduction: State of the art on linguistic landscape studies of Granada, study objectives, and identity-focused main hypothesis

Until recently, the linguistic landscape of the city of Granada (Andalusia, Spain) had been largely overlooked, a notable exception being the widely cited article by Leeman and Modan (2010) mainly on the commodification of Chinese in Chinatown in Washington, D.C., which includes a brief sampling of the linguistic commodification of Arabic as a symbolic resource in service of tourism in Granada.[1] Arabic is, however, the focus of the seminal study by Monjour (2014), who draws attention to the use of the language as a resource for fostering a pseudo-Andalusian identity. Guilat and Espinosa Ramírez (2016) also reflect on identity and memory construction, albeit in the wake of Spain's 2008 Historical Memory Law, which recognized Franco-era victims and condemned the Francoist regime. Subsequent work by the same authors (Espinosa Ramírez and Guilat 2019) also examines identity construction through memory in Granada, this time with regard to the Muslim past, as in Monjour (2014).

Other recent explorations (Malaver and Sosinski 2022; Pablo Núñez 2022) have detected a complex multilingualism in which global languages like English figure prominently alongside languages spoken by migrants such as Arabic. The case of Arabic is particularly noteworthy, as it is both a commodified language for tourism in the city center (Leeman and Modan 2010), as well as a resource for inward and outward displays of local identity, but also a tool for communication and identity-building among Arab and Muslim migrant populations in suburban Granada.

Another trend both in the LL of Granada and LL studies of the city is graffiti (see Aguilera Carnerero 2020a, 2020b, 2021; Romera Manzanares 2023a, 2023b), usually more in the tagging style or *pintadas* (Reyes Sánchez and Vigara Tauste 1996–1997, *apud* Aguilera Carnerero 2021, 81) than street art (though there are high-quality street art practitioners, like the well-known Raúl Ruiz, a.k.a. Sex or "Niño de las Pinturas," i.e. 'Paintings boy,' see Aguilera Carnerero 2020b, 80). Most graffiti in Granada is in Spanish, although monolingual handwritten messages can also be found in English, Bulgarian, Basque, Arabic, French, Russian, and German according to Romera Manzanares (2023a, 180). Other graffiti is bilingual,

DOI: 10.4324/9781032687087-4

written mostly in English and Spanish (Romera Manzanares 2023a, 181). This graffiti can also serve as a valuable pedagogical tool (Aguilera Carnerero 2020a; Romera Manzanares 2023b).

This chapter explores the ways in which different population flows fueled by tourists drawn to the Muslim past and the Alhambra, by migration, and by the influx of students from Spain and abroad contribute to a multilingual linguistic landscape in Granada. Our analysis draws on data concerning the languages visually displayed in the city as shapers of the urban semiotic space (Leeman and Modan 2010) and as means of local identity expression. Identities, or mechanisms of self-perception among members of a group, tend to arise in situations of contact with other groups and provide a means of distinguishing the we-group from the them-group (Eriksen 1993). Communities develop and manifest these mechanisms of cohesion by performing religious rituals in the public space; by transforming the urban landscape through the creation of community sites such as places of worship, ethnic stores, or leisure spots; and in outward displays of group identity through the use of the language orally and in the LL. Thus, members of different groups make use of their language in public spaces as means of expressing identity or fending off threats of assimilation by the dominant group in diglossic situations such as those characterized by migration.

Following this introduction, population statistics of Granada are presented in "Population statistics of Granada," followed by a summary of the history, politics, and processes of identity-building in the section "History, politics, and local identity in Granada." The study methodology is explained in detail in "Methodology," and results are presented in "Results: insights on data," before "Conclusions and discussions."

Population statistics of Granada

According to 2022 census data, the province of Granada has a population of 926,019, including 233,680 in the city proper (25.23%). As 92% of the population of the city and province are of Spanish nationality, it can be assumed that they are native Spanish speakers. To this statistical data we should add, at minimum, the percentage of Central Americans (0.6%) and South Americans (1.6%) who, with the exception of Brazilians (1.43% of the foreign population of the province), can be considered Spanish native speakers. With roughly 8% of its residents originally from overseas, Granada is below the national average for foreign-born population. Table 3.1 shows the distribution of foreign inhabitants by nationality in the city and the province of Granada.

Most foreigners in the province of Granada are of Moroccan (25.27%), Romanian (11.55%), British (9.67%), Colombian (4.3%), and Senegalese (3.85%) nationality. It is noteworthy that the ratio of foreigners with Moroccan, British, Senegalese, Bolivian and Argentine nationality is bigger than the average in Spain. Nevertheless, the presence of nationals from American countries with indigenous languages such as Bolivians or Colombian (many of whom are also Aymara or Quechua speakers), does not seem to create a display of Native-American languages as it does in Madrid (see Castillo Lluch and Sáez Rivera 2011; Sáez

Table 3.1 Foreign population in Spain and the province and city of Granada in 2022[15]

Nationality	Total Spain	Granada province	Granada city	Relative Frequency Granada city vs. province	Relative Frequency Granada city	Relative Frequency Granada province	Relative Frequency Spain
Total	47,486,727	926,019	233,680	25.23%	100.00%	100.00%	100.00%
Spanish	41,977,681	855,004	214,518	25.09%	91.80%	92.33%	88.40%
European Union member states (EU 27)	1,646,427	18,973	2,998	15.80%	1.28%	2.05%	3.47%
Non-member European countries	581,356	9,252	1,232	13.32%	0.53%	1.00%	1.22%
African	1,194,561	22,084	6,752	30.57%	2.89%	2.38%	2.52%
North American	73,456	1,593	675	42.37%	0.29%	0.17%	0.15%
Central American and Caribbean	365,179	3,197	1,333	41.70%	0.57%	0.35%	0.77%
South American	1,162,017	12,038	4,060	33.73%	1.74%	1.30%	2.45%
Asian	479,054	3,769	2,059	54.63%	0.88%	0.41%	1.01%
Oceanian	3,423	77	38	49.35%	0.02%	0.01%	0.01%
Stateless	3,573	32	15	46.88%	0.01%	0.00%	0.01%
Foreigners	5,509,046	71,015	19,162	26.98%	8.20%	7.67%	11.60%

Multilingualism in the linguistic landscape of Granada 67

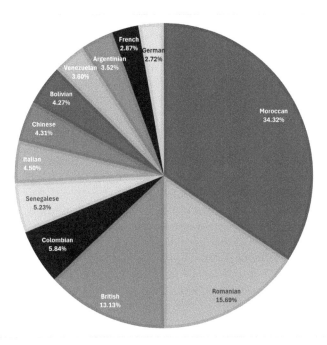

Figure 3.1 Depicts the 12 most common nationalities among the foreign-born residents in the province of Granada in 2022.[17]

Rivera and Castillo Lluch 2012; Sáez Rivera 2014). Among the Arabic population, only Moroccans actually have left their mark on the linguistic landscape, although in a way that appeals to a pan-Arabic/Muslim identity and not linked to any particular nation (see Figure 3.1).

According to 2023 census data provided by the City Council of Granada, the foreign population (12.8% of the whole population) is distributed throughout all the neighborhoods and districts of the city.[2] The neighborhoods of De la Cruz (Beiro district), Cerrillo de Macarena (Chana District), Camino de los Neveros, Castaño-Mirasierra, Cervantes and Lancha del Genil (Genil District), and La Paz (North District) have the lowest ratio of foreign inhabitants, below 8% of the total population. The neighborhoods with the highest prevalence of foreigners, above 20% of the overall population, are Albayzín (Albayzín District) and Campo Verde, Cartuja, and Casería de Montijo (North District). And, in absolute numbers, the neighborhoods with the highest concentration of foreigners, at over 1000 inhabitants per neighborhood, are Albayzín (Albayzín District), Centro-Sagrario and Centro San Matías (Downtown District), Chana-Encina-Angustias (Chana District), Cartuja and Casería de Montijo (North District), Camino de Ronda and Figares (Ronda District), and, far surpassing the others, the Zaidín-Vergeles neighborhood (Zaidín District), with 6,319 inhabitants. The data show that the foreign population is not clearly concentrated in any given neighborhood, with the exception of some neighborhoods where high densities of certain foreign communities relocate after a critical mass of their fellow countrymen have established themselves there, thus attracting future migrants from their country of origin.

Incoming migration has been rising throughout the province of Granada in recent years,[3] increasing by 138.5% from 2012 to 2021. Most new residents are Moroccan (1763 new inhabitants in 2021), Spanish (895), British (583), Colombian (441), Italian (287), US-American (262), Venezuelan (252), Senegalese (223), French (223), German (208), and Romanian (207). As seen in Figure 3.2, between 2012 and 2021 the number of migrants from Ireland, Mali, Norway, Argentina, Venezuela, and Honduras increased, whereas the population originally from Bulgaria, Romania, Lithuania, Moldova, Nigeria, the Dominican Republic, Bangladesh, and Pakistan has diminished.

Whereas Granada receives a remarkable number of migrants, international tourism is less substantial. Moreover, after the sudden dropoff in 2020 and 2021 due to the Covid pandemic, tourism in the city has only recovered to 2015 levels, and the number of individuals visiting the city has increased by a meager 10.5% since 1999.[4] Furthermore, of all the 661,276 incoming foreign tourists, which represent 42% of the total, most were from the European Union (45.8%), and there is a noteworthy proportion of tourists from France (11.9%), Italy (8.6%), Germany (7.9%), the UK (7%), and the USA (15.3%). Based on these figures, one may assume that the tourism-related LL would feature signs in English, French, Italian, or German. In any case, provisional statistics for 2023 reveal a modest 10.5% increase in visitors to the city, from 1,573,189 visitors in 2022 to 1,738,581 visitors in 2023. In addition, the change in the proportion of foreign visitors with respect to the total number of visitors is also meaningful, from 42.03% in 2022 to 50.68% in 2023 (see Table 3.2).

Tourism, a likely source of multilingual LL, is also international in the province of Granada, which received 926,328 foreign visitors in 2022, representing 36% of all visitors to Granada. Tourism outside the city accounts for 3% of the industry for the whole province. Nevertheless, most foreign visitors only visit and stay in the city (71.4%), compared with 28.6% finding accommodations in other towns, including those in the so-called Tropical Coast (Motril, Salobreña, and Almuñécar). Therefore, international tourism in Granada is focused on urban tourism and coastal resorts, with few popular destinations in the countryside.[5]

In addition to a site for leisure travel, Granada is a popular destination among university students. The University of Granada is one of the European universities with the highest number of foreign students. Of the 55,593 foreigners who came to Spain for the 2019–2020 academic year, 2997 studied at the institution, representing 5.4% of all such students nationwide. For the 2021–2022 academic year, a similar number of international students studied in the classrooms of the University of Granada,[6] mostly from Italy (24.4%), France (13.5%), Germany (12.8%), and the United Kingdom (6%), although foreign nationals studying at the institution come from more than 70 different countries. These students stayed in the city between 4 and 9 months, although it appears this was time enough to make an impact on the

Multilingualism in the linguistic landscape of Granada 69

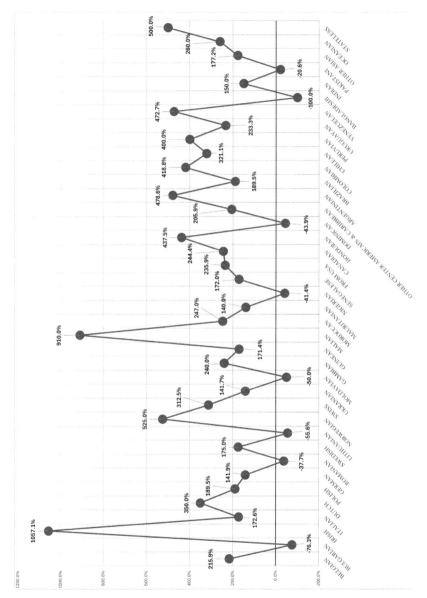

Figure 3.2 Difference in migrant flows from 2021 compared with 2012.

Table 3.2 Number of incoming travelers in the city of Granada[16]

	Number of travelers Granada city 2022	Number of travelers Granada city 2023
Total	1,573,189	1,738,581
Residents in Spain	911,913	857,411
Non-residents in Spain	661,276	881,170
Residents of European member states	302,627	
Germany	52,334	
Belgium	16,452	
France	78,770	
Italy	57,069	
Netherlands	25,266	
Portugal	16,821	
Other Europeean countries	55,915	
United Kingdom	46,308	
Japan	6,992	
China	4,864	
United States	101,576	
Others	198,909	

LL of the city as seen in the number of stickers in different languages found everywhere, particularly in the city center.

We must not overlook the presence of Spanish students from other parts of Spain in the University of Granada. For a semester or two, these individuals bring other Spanish languages to Granada, such as Galician, Catalan, or Basque, as seen in graffiti.[7]

History, politics, and local identity in Granada

Social identity is not uniform, and diverse identities coexist in Granadan society, sometimes overlapping with ethnic, linguistic, cultural, and religious identities. On the one hand, Granada is a socio-historical space with a marked presence of the Muslim culture of Spain, and the Muslim past is one of the hallmarks of the city both domestically and abroad. As Álvarez de Morales Ruiz Matas (2008) states, "Granada is going to be present throughout the history of Muslim Spain. As a province (*Ilbira's cora*) depending on a central power […] as a part of the North African Almoravid and Almohad empires, and as an independent kingdom twice, with the last one, the Nasrid kingdom, closing the historical cycle of the Muslim presence on the Iberian Peninsula."[8] The most widely known Muslim dynasty in Granada is certainly the Nasrids (1232 to 1492), although we must also recognize the Taifa kingdom under the rule of the Berber Zirid dynasty in the eleventh century. This past explains how the city's identity is rooted in the magnificent architectural site of La Alhambra, El Generalife, and the Albayzín quarter, material and cultural embodiment of its Muslim-Arabic history, monuments declared World Heritage by UNESCO from 1984 onwards.

Other dimensions also make up the city's identity, including its transformation into a Christian city, as well as nineteenth-century Orientalism and the twentieth-century urban transformation linked to the Civil War and Franco's dictatorship (Espinosa Ramírez and Guilat 2018, 23). The Nasrid Palace offers thus "a mystical resymbolized Muslim past" which powerfully atracts people from other places (with the ongoing economic success of massified tourism but also its complications) and which permeates the local identity and social imaginary. Espinosa Ramírez and Guilat (2018) state that the linguistic landscape of Granada's street names reflects the historical tensions of local identity: the memory of the Muslim kingdom of Granada (both Zirid, but mainly Nasrid), nineteenth-century Orientalism, Francoism, and the return of democracy. Romanticism reflects an interest in the Middle Ages and exotic places, which were both present simultaneously in the Nasrid past of Granada. At the beginning of the twentieth century, Orientalism was at its peak, an example of which is seen in the trend by which residents photographed themselves in the Alhambra disguised in oriental garments: still today, Alhambra Photo, Ruiz Linares' Photographic Gallery founded in 1886, provides this service using an indoor Alhambrian stage. It is no surprise that the ten most popular monuments in Granada, according to the City Hall Tourism website, features the item, "Travel in time visiting the Alhambra from Granada": a past which is not linked with the present in the collective identity. This is possible because the Alhambra complex, which welcomes more than 2 million visitors each year, can be accessed directly from the highway, thus bypassing the city, and many tourists visit the Nasrid palaces without entering the city itself. A similar parallelism can be drawn with members of the Romani community. They inhabit the neighborhood of Almanjayar in the north of the city and the neighborhood of Sacromonte in the east, on top of the hills. The Romani community of Sacromonte is treated as a folkloric element of the city and has been touristically exposed to increase the number of visits.

The language found in the urban landscape is not always clearly identity-laden. Tourists visiting Granada beyond the Alhambra encounter a multicultural and multiethnic city, with Chinese or Arab businesses and an array of restaurants offering all manner of international food, while signs in the tourist spots are written in Spanish, English, and other languages. The pervasive use of English is no longer exclusively linked to any nation, but is rather the language of globalization. The use of Arabic can be twofold: while Arabic writing in halal butcher shops transmits a sense of belonging to the local cohort of Arab-speaking migrants (but also non-Arabic Muslims or Spanish converts to Islam), the Arabic used for tourists is a commodity, a souvenir of Muslim culture frozen in the past.

Although the Muslim community in Granada has never been homogeneous, its formation can be better understood by taking into account certain important facts. According to Rosón and Tarrés (2013), the community began to take shape in 1945 with the founding of the House of Morocco, a dormitory for Moroccan students studying in the city. A second milestone dates back to the 1960s, when Arab students from Morocco and elsewhere promoted the foundation of the Islamic

Center of Granada and the Student Muslim Center of Granada. The 1970s saw a wave of conversion to Islam among part of the Spanish population, initially linked to cultural movements that had taken root in the previous decade. As the Spanish economy improved toward the end of the 1980s, incoming migration intensified. Granada was one of the most attractive spots for these new citizens, especially those from Morocco, which explains the high percentage of Moroccans in the city. In 2003, after a twenty-year process marked by controversy, protests, and bureacratic problems, the Great Mosque was inaugurated. The first to be built in the city after the conquest by the Catholic Kings in 1492, the mosque has been managed by the Islamic community in Spain since its founding.

The collective identity of Granada is in a constant state of balance between the acknowledgment of this Andalusian past and the rejection of the Muslim other as promoted by the fraught narrative of the Reconquest, which legitimizes the reclaiming by the (Christian) Spaniards of what was taken away from them by the (Muslim) Arabs from 711 on. This view of history inevitably sidelines or purposefully erases the Arab and Islamic heritage of the city and its perceived value. The tensions caused by these two opposing perspectives regarding the presence of Arabic or Islam within the collective imagination of Granada is widely manifested, and sometimes not peacefully. Examples of violence in the name of identity can be seen in the derogatory graffiti written on the sculpture of the head of the Great Captain, the most famous general of the Spanish Empire and a Granadian native, or the frequent controversies and confrontations surrounding the local holiday commemorating the conquest of Granada, held annually on January 2, or the 2017 xenophobic attack of the Great Mosque of Granada.

Methodology

We have selected only some areas of the city for extensive fieldwork, since a comprehensive city-wide study such as the one by Pons Rodríguez (2012) for Seville or Backhaus (2007) for Tokyo would be unwieldy. Rather, our research takes an ethnographic perspective in the vein of Blommaert (2013) and Blommaert and Maly (2014). We performed an "ethnographic linguistic landscape analysis" (ELLA) of the neighborhood – or, in our case, several. This approach creates an optimal source of material and is used as our analytical framework, which we linked to the tentative tracing of urban distribution patterns of the linguistic landscape, checking whether the patterns found for Madrid by Castillo Lluch and Sáez Rivera (2011) are also applicable.

The three areas selected for study, and researched thoroughly, included the city center, which is the main tourist attraction, as well as the Albayzín neighborhood and the Beiro district. Although considerably gentrified, central Granada and the Albayzín neighborhood maintain their traditional allure as seen in the myriad traditional shops that populate these areas. The Beiro district, a suburban neighborhood with a significant migrant population (see "Population statistics of Granada," is also a site of study.

Photos were taken by the entire team of researchers and interns[9] between September 2022 and April 2024. The objective of this effort was to locate examples of languages other than Spanish, but also local Spanish vernacular. Additional spontaneous photos were taken in various other areas of the city. The present analysis is limited to the multilingual signs photographed; the remaining signs will be the subject of a study in the near future. Signs were classified according to the languages used in them and the well-known distinction by Ben-Rafael et al. (2006) between top-down vs bottom-up signs.

All authors are Granada residents and professors of Spanish linguistics at the University of Granada, although none is a native of the city, which brings an outsider ethnographic gaze and a degree of participatory observation of the linguistic landscape of the city and its non-stop state of change.

Some methodological considerations must be made. Similar to ELLA, the interaction of languages in the LL will be examined in a way that is informed by our insider perspective. Temporality, as discussed by Sáez Rivera (2014) and highlighted at the 2nd International Conference on Linguistic Landscape: Reflections from the Past into the Present and the Future (Granada, June 3–5, 2024) is thus a key interpretative tool. Blommaert and Maly (2014) describe three temporal axes: who produced the sign (past axis), the prospective public (future axis), and how it is emplaced (present axis), which can be analyzed in geosemantic terms (Scollon and Wong Scollon 2003).

Signs that make up the linguistic landscape must be analyzed as situated discourse, reflecting the original concept of context of situation of Malinowski (1972 [1923]) which geosemantics promotes. Like oral discourse, linguistic landscape signs build texts collectively and collaboratively. For instance, shop signs are often industrially mediated, and many different signs may populate a shop window. Franco-Rodríguez (2009, 5) distinguished between "text" (the entire array of signs chosen by an actor in a shop) and "sign" (each framed piece of this text), thus aligning with the classical definition of sign by Backhaus (2007, 66–67). Graffiti is often cumulative, containing language in response to other graffiti appearing on walls, while manually written or printed parasite signs (as defined by Castillo Lluch and Sáez Rivera 2012, 2023) are adjacent to each other, resembling the interactive and creative nature of conversation in improvisational arts such as jazz or improv theater (see Sawyer 2001).

The ethnographic method must be precise. In ELLA, participatory observation is always subtle: analysts are passers-by, interpreters, and even users of signs, but not producers in the traditional sense of ethnography. The analysis cannot be strictly ethnographic, but rather holistic, as is customary in linguistic anthropology. Ethnography provides a method, but not the interpretation. We will revisit the distinction between informative and symbolic use appearing in the seminal work by Landry and Bourhis (1997), though in a nuanced way when necessary, as information signs can also have symbolic aspects.

The following section presents the results of the study qualitatively.

Results: Insights on data

Recursive urban patterns? The center and periphery logic

The search for patterns in the use and appearance of signs in public spaces is a central aspect of LL studies, as highlighted by Gorter and Cenoz (2024, 371) in their recent overview of the field. In Madrid, Castillo Lluch and Sáez Rivera (2011) and Sáez and Castillo (2012) found five recurring patterns of urban geographic configuration in the LL of the city that can also be applied to Granada.

1. *Monopoly*: main streets populated by stores, with signs usually appearing in the local language (Spanish in this case) and global languages such as English, with a connotative-symbolic commercial use but also to inform tourists, e.g. Gran Vía in the city center and Calle de Bravo Murillo in the Tetuán district. In Granada, the street known as Gran Vía de Colón, a local equivalent to Gran Vía in Madrid, or Calle de los Reyes Católicos and Calle Recogidas in the city center could be considered main streets for this purpose. In Madrid, the surrounding side streets are characterized by the presence of migrant languages or language variants, as in the following pattern.
2. *Ethnic area*:[10] high density of non-hispanic LL on streets closer to main streets, which act as outer borders, examples from Madrid being Calle de Leganitos next to Gran Vía in Madrid, *Little Caribe*, mainly populated by Dominicans and surrounding Calle de Bravo Murillo on both sides (see Sáez Rivera 2015), Usera's Chinatown (any street except Calle de Marcelo Usera), and so forth. A similar street in Granada is Calle de Elvira, which runs parallel to Gran Vía de Colón and contains many Arab restaurants, pastry stores, and teahouses.
3. *Progressive LL*: streets that progress from a local LL to a migrant LL, like Calle de Monte Igueldo in the traditionally working-class and newly migrant neighborhood of Vallecas in Madrid.
4. *Spotted LL*: migrant LL can be identified all around the city, as in Chinese or Latino grocery stores, restaurants, or shops.
5. *Silenced or Silent LL*: *silenced LL* is exemplified by the use of co-official languages of Spain other than Spanish (i.e. Galician, Basque, Catalan) during the Franco era, when these languages were prohibited from the LL. *Silent LL* occurs when the language of a significant migrant population is barely displayed in the LL, as is often the case with Romanian, partially due to cultural mores of adaptability and discretion.[11]

These patterns suggested a likely correlation with the sociolinguistic integration of migrants: high integration if the migrant language is found in monopoly or spotted LL, or low integration if restricted to an ethnic area or a progressive LL. The patterns in Madrid seem to recur in a way that resembles a fractal, in which each copy assumes the same shape as the whole,[12] at least in a cosmopolitan city such as the capital of Spain (for more on the fractal configuration of cities, see Zarza 1996; regarding the fractality of LL, see Blommaert 2013).

While similar patterns can be found in Granada, a more suitable description of the LL of the city is the center vs periphery dichotomy suggested by Malaver and Sosinski (2022) and Pablo Núñez (2022), by which migrant languages are mainly found in the outskirts as opposed to the city center.

Global languages

Our analysis takes into account English, the global language par excellence, but also other Western languages used in tourism and as a vehicle for information transfer such as French, German, or Italian, although these languages are also used in a connotative and symbolic way.

Unsurprisingly, English is the dominant foreign language in the LL of Granada. In the city center, English is the main (and sometimes only) language for providing information to tourists, like in the Cathedral or the Royal Chapel, where the Catholic Kings and their family are buried. Nevertheless, the information appearing in top-down signs placed by the City Council of Granada is sometimes surprisingly scarce or incomplete: e.g. directional signposts in the city center are exclusively in Spanish, with the exception of signs pointing to the tourist office, and in large upright maps of the city the only information in English is the "You are here" indication. This pattern contrasts with that of signposts on monuments and emblematic buildings of the City Council in the city center and the historic neighborhoods of Albayzín (the Arab old town) and Realejo (the Jewish old town), which have signage both in Spanish and English (Spanish at the top and English below when the sign is closer to a wall, or Spanish on one side and English on the other when there is ample room for both). Figure 3.3, from the Madraza, is particularly illustrative in that it epitomizes the whole history of the city: a former Quranic school (madrasa) later converted into the old City Council, rebuilt in Renaissance and Baroque style, and which today is part of the University of Granada campus.

French is sometimes used as a secondary tourist language alongside English, as seen in signs related to public transportation, such as those for the city bus to the Alhambra in Plaza Nueva, an example of a top-down sign. Bottom-up signs on menus in restaurants catering to tourists may also feature a third language, as in Figure 3.4, taken from the restaurant Rabo de Nube ("Cloud tail," the title of a famous song by Cuban folk singer Silvio Rodríguez), located on the highly touristic Paseo de los Tristes, where you can have an al fresco meal facing the Comares Tower of the Alhambra; the vegetable section on the menu is titled "Verde que te quiero verde" ("Green, I love you green"), the famous verse by local poet Federico García Lorca, a figure also commodified in the city. A minority of bottom-up signs contain languages beyond English and French, including German, Italian, Russian, Japanese, or even Arabic, as in the Nuba Andalusí crafts and souvenir shop on Calle Darro by the river.

From an informational but also symbolic point of view, English is used for its high status, sometimes in bottom-up signs appearing in shops, hairdressers, bars, or restaurants with a mixed local and tourist clientele, as in the many specialty coffee

Figure 3.3 Informational plaque containing a historical explanation of the monument on the Madraza (old Quranic school).

shops that now fill the city center, such as Sur Coffee Corner in Plaza de Romanilla (see Figure 3.5). In the city center, most restaurants use English to describe the cuisine they serve: "Korean food," "ramen bar," and "pasta burger restaurant," among others. Other types of establishment, like hotels or hair salons, use English exclusively in all signage. Invevitably, some restaurant names are in Italian, like La Piccola Carmela Ristorante e Pizzeria (the Italian restaurant of the local chain La Carmela), or in ice-cream parlors, like Fior di Granada, "Heladería Italiana, Gelato Artesanal," a peculiar mixture of Italian ("fior" 'flower' and "Gelato" "ice-cream") and Spanish ("Heladería italiana" "Italian ice-cream shop" and "artisanal" or "craft," actually in Italian "artigianale").

A highly prevalent and noticeable medium that has become more popular of late in Granada and other Spanish and European cities is stickers. Mostly in English

Figure 3.4 Restaurant menu in Spanish, English, and French.

but occasionally featuring text in other languages like German, Italian, French, or even Portuguese, these signs can be seen glued to walls and street furniture such as benches, street lamps, or traffic signs, and contain messages that are most

Figure 3.5 Sur Coffee Shop: "Specialty Coffee" offered.

commonly transgressive, witty, whimsical, or personal. Many express a fondness for tattoo culture or support for European football clubs, or contain political messages. In the LL of Granada, stickers can be found on many traffic and street signs in Plaza Nueva (see Figure 3.6), a highly popular gathering spot. Plaza Nueva is both a tourist hub – it is the starting point for the easiest walking route to the Alhambra Palace, through the Cuesta de Gomérez – and a traditional meeting place, where the old Palace of Royal Justice ("Real Chancillería") is located. According to informal interviews with international students in Granada, the people who place these stickers in the LL are among others European Erasmus students who print their own stickers to mark the places they travel to or where they study, as a way of expressing personal and community identity abroad.[13] These stickers may also be affixed by Spaniards who are fond of urban culture and operate in so-called "crews," spreading the same message on the walls of one or more cities, or who run a small business and need low-cost publicity (Heredia Mantis 2024).

In Granada, stickers of this type can be seen in the same square containing a remarkable Latin epigraph inscribed on the door of the Chancillería. Indeed, the city is full of old script in Arabic (Alhambra and other centuries-old Arab palaces like Dar Al-Horra), but also Latin and Old Spanish on the façades of buildings like churches, monasteries, or university buildings.

Another noteworthy use of English – more symbolic than informative – is found in graffiti of all kinds. While Spanish is the main language used in graffiti in the city (in contrast to English, which is more common in stickers), thereby suggesting that graffiti is usually the work of Spanish locals, the use of English connects the

Figure 3.6 Stickers in Plaza Nueva.

users with the globalized urban culture. But other languages can also be found, like some poems in Italian in the north of the city center, Sagrario ("Sanctuary"), others in French in the San Matías area in the now trendy neighborhood of Realejo, and more in Bulgarian in the Figares neighborhood (on the outer limits of the city center). Written with a ballpoint pen and often in response to other graffiti, this kind of graffiti is a public display of intimacy by people of non-Spanish origin using a non-Spanish language.

Graffiti such as that found in the main tourist attractions like the promenade by the Darro River can be the work of tourists or locals, as in the *horror vacui* tagging on the back wall of the Colegio de Ave María (advertised in the front as an English-Spanish bilingual school) in the Placeta de la Victoria ("Victory Little Square," containing an Eastern peninsular diminutive that is typical of Granada[14]), also a hidden spot from which to view the Alhambra Palace, which explains the beautiful drawing of the Alhambra that we authors call the "Alhambrita" ("Little Alhambra"), surrounded by tagging, and even social network tags (see Figure 3.7). This results in a blend of physical linguistic landscape and the Internet as personal means of youth expression (Sáez Rivera 2023). Graffiti in Latin like "Hic erat KKhuete" ("Peanuts was here") on the Slope of Rolling Stones ("Cuesta de los Chinos") to the Alhambra reveals the high educational level of many who visit or live in the surrounding area.

As in the case of Madrid (Castillo and Sáez 2011), other languages of Spain behave like global languages ("international languages" in the cited reference), that is, they appear in restaurants or banks, like CajaSur KutxaBank (the name of a credit institution with a name in Spanish and a blend of Basque and English) or CaixaBank (a Catalan-English blend) on Gran Vía de Colón, where the locally

Figure 3.7 "Alhambrita" ("Little Alhambra") in Placeta de la Victoria sorrounded by miscellaneous tagging in several languages.

famous ice-cream shop "Los Italianos" is also located. We can also find graffiti in Basque (like the one written in Basque, *Zuriz dagoelako koloreztatzen dugu* ("We color it because it is white" on the touristy Calle del Santísimo, next to the Darro River; see Reguero Ugarte 2024, 25) or much more frequently in Catalan, like "Tropessarem amb la necessitat de sentirnos amb vida" ("We will stumble upon the need to feel alive") on Calle de Elvira 94 (see Figure 3.8), both examples of poetic-philosophical graffiti, according to the taxonomy by Aguilera Carnerero (2020a, 2020b, 2021), applied also by Romera Manzanares (2023b). All graffiti can be problematic to interpret due to its anonymous authorhip. As a result, any interpretation must be built on certain assumptions. For instance, both examples of graffiti in Basque and Catalan are the work of Basque or Catalan residents, not tourists, since the Basque graffiti was erased and then redone, which suggests that it was written by someone living in the neighborhood or at least in Granada, and the graffiti in Catalan is on a side street adjacent to the main street, Gran Vía de Colón, as well as Calle de Elvira, replete with Arab stores and restaurants, but not eminently touristic. We surmise that the Catalan graffiti was also written by a Catalan speaker who resides in the area, possibly a student who speaks Catalan. Other graffiti on Calle de Elvira reads, "Nunca máis" ("Never again"), a Galician political slogan, which is also found in graffiti like in the Beiro district, a migrant but also student neighborhood.

Multilingualism in the linguistic landscape of Granada 81

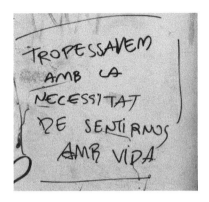

Figure 3.8 Graffiti in Catalan.

Arabic superdiversity: International, historical, and migrational

Since the seminal study by Blommaert (2013) on ELLA, superdiversity has become a trope of sorts within multilingual linguistic landscape studies. Precisely because it is a cliché, and likely an instance of academic branding, the term has drawn criticism from Pavlenko (2019) and Sáez Rivera (2021, 169, n. 51), among others. As originally conceived by Vertovec (2007), however, this notion of different layers, times of arrival, professional status, or degrees of education among migrant populations with the same origin (Arab-speaking in this case) can still be useful.

For instance, the well-known use of Arabic in building the Orientalist identity of Granada explains the appearance of the Arabic qāf letter ق in place of the G in the name of the Granada city tourist train (when it is actually a voiceless velar consonant in Arabic, not a voiced one like in Granada), see Figure 3.9. The informational signpost indicating the location of the train is in Spanish, English, French, and German.

Surprisingly or not, Arabic is one of the languages available for the free audioguide, though only for the city tourist train and the Nasrid Alhambra Palace; in contrast, all linguistic landscape information for tourists in the Alhambra is bilingual in Spanish and English. Real multilingualism is only offered in live and, especially, recorded guides. (The tourist train's audioguide is avalaible in Spanish, English, French, Italian, German, Portuguese, Chinese, Japanese, Russian, Korean, Catalan, and Arabic, and visitors may listen to the free audioguide for the monument in Spanish, Dutch, Portuguese, Japanese, Arabic, Korean, Russian, Chinese, English, Italian, French, and German).

We can also find the *Selling Granada by the Dirham* phenomenon, a play on words inspired by the progressive rock album by Genesis, *Selling England by the Pound*. This includes not only the sale of tiles with Arabic script or offers to have one's name written in Arabic (as noted in Leeman and Modan 2010), but also T-shirts featuring slogans such as "God is the vanquisher," which are pervasive in the

82 *Ethnographic Landscapes and Language Ideologies in the Spanish State*

Figure 3.9 Granada City Tour train information post in Spanish, English, French, and German, offering a multilingual audioguide indicated by country flags.

area surrounding the Alhamba. An example can be seen in Figure 3.10, which shows a T-shirt for sale on a street next to the Cathedral in an Arab-owned business. This phenomenon is possible in large part because of the presence of a permanent Arab-origin population, some of whom make a living selling Orientalist souvenirs like these. Immigrant populations have also put up teahouses, Arab candy stores, and bazaars along the street of Calderería Nueva in the Albaizín. The area is therefore

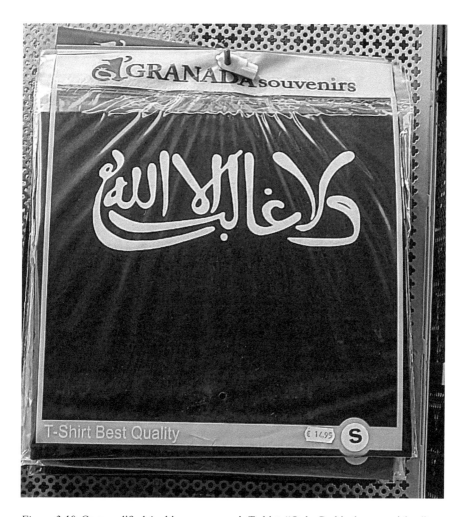

Figure 3.10 Commodified Arabic on a souvenir T-shirt: "Only God is the vanquisher."

a two-sided space: mainly owned by Arab migrants but enjoyed mostly by locals and tourists seeking an Orientalist experience. Calle de Elvira, where Calle de Calderería ends on its way down from the Albayzín hill, is also an interesting transitional space, full of Arab restaurants and bazaars, but also barbershops that serve as local meeting points for the Arab ethnic community (similar to spaces in Madrid for Dominicans, but also Arabs, see Moustaoui Shrir 2013 and Sáez Rivera 2015).

Although a certain monopoly/ethnified pattern can be established in Granada, this frame of analysis is not a perfect fit for the city's LL: on Gran Vía, offices advertise legal translations into Arabic, as in Beiro (alongside other languages, as in a sign near a police station offering Spanish, English, French, Arabic, Italian, Russian, and Portuguese translations; see Figure 3.11). Beiro is part of a peripheral

Figure 3.11 Translations offered in several languages in the Beiro district.

area, following the center vs periphery pattern that adequately explains the distribution of the linguistic landscape in Granada city. In the peripheral neighborhoods, graffiti in Arabic is also on display.

Therefore, apart from the Great Mosque in the Albayzín next to the most touristy lookout point of Saint Nicholas, Arabic is mostly used for informational purposes in suburban contexts, signaling mosques, halal butchers, feasts (see Figure 3.12), and a range of services in Arabic like private lessons for secondary-school students. These informational signs are also an act of resistance, signaling community identity, much like in Madrid (Moustaoui 2013). In addition to religious shrines,

Figure 3.12 Informational (but also symbolic) Arabic: announcement of the Feast of the Lamb and advertisement for a halal butcher shop.

associations and foundations are other means of maintaining an Arab identity, as in the Euro-Arab Foundation, created in October 1995, or the Al-Andalus Foundation for Education, with a site in Albayzín, temporarily closed at the present time but home to the Madrasa publishing company, which sells Spanish translations of classical and contemporary books on Islam.

Other languages

Beyond Spanish, English, and Arabic, the most noteworthy languages in the LL of Granada are linked to other populations residing in the city (see the section on "Demography"). Although to a lesser extent, these groups leave their mark on the linguistic landscape: from Chinese and Japanese, to Slavic languages like Polish, Russian, or Ukrainian, as well as Romance languages like Italian, French, Portuguese, or Romanian. The presence of languages further removed from Spanish in geographical, cultural, or economic terms, such as Baltic languages and certain languages of Asia, is anecdotical or non-existent.

Migrant populations concentrate in suburbs with older apartment buildings and lower rents, although there is no clear concentration of communities (see

"Population statistics of Granada"). However, these population trends follow the aforementioned center vs periphery pattern in the linguistic landscape.

Migrants, migrant language, and displays of this language in the linguistic landscape depend on three main factors:

1. Religion: as in the case of Muslims and Arab speakers, migrants have a main gathering point in places of worship, like the Russian Orthodox Church in Saint Bartholomew Square in the Albayzín neighborhood (the same quartier where the Great Mosque is located). Constructed in 2021, the church holds services for Russians, Ukrainians, Bielorrusians, and Kazakhs. The church has no signs on its exterior in Russian or any other language except for the customary monument signpost explaining the history of the building in Spanish and English. This absence of signage in the languages of the churchgoers is most likely to avoid drawing unwanted attention to the institution stemming from the Russian-Ukrainian War. Inside, Catholic sculptures have been replaced by Orthodox icons, and the signage is in Spanish and mainly in Russian.
2. Ethnic shops: these are usually grocery stores, such as "La Pequeña Europa, Magazin Romanesc" ("Small Europe: Romanian store"), located in an ethnically diverse neighborhood near the bus station on Joaquina Eguaras. However, the complexity and diversity extend beyond this, linked to cultural idiosincrasies. One example is a Chinese parapharmacy next to Camino de Ronda, on the edge of the city center.
3. Associations: usually promoting activities or providing help for a given nationality, these have not taken hold in Granada city, but have in the coastal city of Motril, as in the Acuarum Cultural Association of Friends of Romania (from 2007 onwards) or the Romanian Association for Integration and Development. Another case is the Slava Ukraini Association of Granada, created with the support of the Civil Guard ("Guardia Civil") and providing support for Ukrainian refugees fleeing from the war.

Nevertheless, migrant populations tend to focus more on the virtual linguistic landscape, since intra-group communication is mainly through social networks, websites (e.g. "Ukrainians in Spain," https://ucranianos.com/es), Facebook pages, and Whatsapp.

In some cases, the migrant category does not accurately describe the population in Granada: while most migrants leave their country for economic motives, other foreigners are often considered expatriates drawn to Granada out of curiosity or affinity. This could be the case of the Japanese nationals in Granada studied by Heredia Mantis (2023). The author points out the scarce presence of Japanese in tourist communication and offers a case study of the store known as Detalle ("Detail"), a Japanese-owned business on Calle de San Juan de Dios in the city center. The establishment sells Japanese articles such as porcelain figures, tea sets, anime merchandising, and silver jewelry. The ethnographic component of the study highlights the low Spanish proficiency of the shop owner and several signs in sometimes incorrect Japanese and broken or interlanguage Spanish.

Conclusions and discussions

Our experience, contact, and field work with multilingualism in the linguistic landscape of Granada reveals a complexity of language use. Context of use or situation as displayed in the linguistic landscape seems paramount to the analysis: English is the predominant language of tourist communication and a means of signaling belonging to global culture (e.g. chic graffiti and stickers in English); other Western languages like German or French seem secondary to English; Italian, however, maintains some degree of prestige as a language of gourmands. Most important and nuanced is the case of Arabic: this provider and symbol of the local identity due to its rich past is relegated to a migrant language mostly restricted to suburbs, but at the same time Arab migrants (mostly Moroccan but also Syrians or Lebanese) offer a more commodified version of Arabic. Migrants of all kinds gather around religious shrines, ethnic shops, and associations and influence the linguistic landscape. Another important contribution of multilingualism (including other languages of Spain like Catalan and Basque) comes from students and expatriates attracted by the city's beauty and standard of living, its prestigious university and high-spirited music, as well as the local arts and literature scene.

The city of Granada mirrors global tendencies such as the predominance of English for international communication and as a trait of global pop culture, but with its own idiosyncrasies, like the multifaceted use of Arabic or the importance of the many languages spoken in a university city of the twenty-first century.

More and deeper studies can be conducted on this topic. These may focus on a single language (e.g. English, Arabic) or linguistic landscape format (tourist information, local shops or restaurants, graffiti and newly placed stickers). Furthermore the use of local vernacular Spanish as a source of identity construction remains unexplored, and as pointed out by Sáez Rivera (2024a), the presence of old Spanish merits further study.

Notes

1 This chapter forms part of the research output of the *Linguistic Landscape Observatory of Granada* https://blogs.ugr.es/paisajelinguisticogranada/ and *Paisaje lingüístico andaluz: cartografía del multilingüismo y la heteroglosia en la ciudad de Granada (PLANEO.GR) (Andalusian Linguistic Landscape: cartography of multilingualism and heteroglossia in Granada city)*, a 2023 MediaLab project of the University of Granada coordinated by María Heredia Mantis, of which the rest of the study co-authors are research members. The study data were gathered by the whole team and some student interns, although the chapter has been edited in its entirety by Daniel Sáez, who also wrote the introduction and the methodology section; the second section, on population statistics of Granada is the work of María Heredia; the section entitled "History, politics, and local identity in Granada" was written by Irania Malaver and Marcin Sosinski; finally, results as well as conclusions and discussion were written by the whole team. Part of this chapter was presented as a poster to celebrate the Cultural Year of Spanish in the School of Translation (Heredia et al. 2023). We want to thank Oliver Shaw, PhD, professional translator and fellow linguist, for revising the text for English grammar and style.

2 Notice that these data differ from the City Census in the INE. The data provided by the City Census are from 2022, whereas the City Council of Granada gives 2023 figures.
3 Instituto Nacional de Estadística, "Migration flows coming from abroad by province, year, and nationality, province of Granada, 2012–2021."
4 Ayuntamiento de Granada (City Council of Granada), "Granada Tourism Information," https://turismo.granada.org/es/datos-turisticos-granada-ine.
5 Instituto Nacional de Estadística, "Travelers and overnight stay by Autonomous Communities and Provinces 2022, province of Granada."
6 Universidad de Granada, "Statistical Appendix 6. Internationalisation," in *Memory. College Year 2021/2022*.
7 Sadly, statistics are not available.
8 Our translation for "Granada va a estar presente a lo largo de toda la historia de la España musulmana. Como provincia (*cora de Ilbira*) dependiente de un poder central [...], como parte del imperio de los almorávides y los almohades norteafricanos, o como reino independiente en dos ocasiones, el último de los cuales, el Nazarí, cerró el ciclo histórico de presencia musulmana en la Península."
9 The following interns worked under the supervision of María Heredia and Daniel Sáez: Thalía Compán and Cecilia González, who provided a thorough photograpic account of the city center during the 2022–2023 academic year, and Alba Fernández and Miguel Ángel Díaz, who performed photographic field work in Beiro in the 2023–2024 academic year, as well as Elena Juanmartí, who took photographs of Asturian and other Spanish languages in the city center.
10 In previous versions of the model this was called *ghetto* or *spider web*, a term that has since fallen into disuse because it does not adhere to the real facts (i.e. even if a foreign population is large or predominant in an area, it is not exclusive) and because of its negative connotation.
11 Cultural traits according to our Romanian colleague Doina Repede, personal communication.
12 The Mandelbrot fractal model attributes the following characteristics to a geometrical object with a fractal structure: it is far too irregular to be described in traditional geographical terms and it is self-similar, its form made by recursive copies of the same figure.
13 This is also the case in the Dutch stickers in Málaga analyzed by Sáez Rivera (2024b, 53), though Dutch was not found in our sample.
14 On the use of diminutives in Granada, see Manjón-Cabeza (2012) and Malaver (2021); on the display of diminutives in the linguistic landscape, but in the case of Madrid, see Hu and Sáez Rivera (2022).
15 Source: Instituto Nacional de Estadística (National Statistics Institute), "Resident population according to date, sex, and nationality (by national groups) and birthplace (by national groups), Spain and the province of Granada," as well as "Ongoing Census. Population according to sex and nationality (by big groups) in the municipality of Granada."
16 Instituto Nacional de Estadística, "Survey of hotel occupation in 2022, travelers coming in some touristic spots and by country of residence, Granada" and "Survey of hotel occupation. Travelers and overnight stay by tourist attraction."
17 Instituto Nacional de Estadística, "Foreign Population by communities and provinces, nationality and sex, province of Granada." INE does not provide data in the City Census of nationality of foreign population according towns.

References

Aguilera Carnerero, Carmen. 2020a. "El graffiti como motor del pensamiento crítico en lengua extranjera." *Onomazein Extra* 6: 189–208.

Aguilera Carnerero, Carmen. 2020b. "Urban Wall Monologues: A Critical Discourse Analysis of graffiti in Granada." In *Fuzzy Boundaries in Discourse: Theoretical, Methodological and Lexico-Grammatical Fuziness*, edited by Péter B. Furkó, Ildikó Vaskó, Csilla Ilona Dér and Dorte Madsen, 77–109. Cham (Switzerland): Palgrave MacMillan.

Aguilera Carnerero, Carmen. 2021. "La ciudad como participante comunicativo: Un análisis crítico del discurso del graffiti en Granada." In *Paredes que comunican: Las pintadas como expresión ciudadana*, edited by J. Ignacio 'Iñaki' and G. Chaves, 79–99. Granada: C3FES Comunicación/Ediciones Desde Abajo.

Álvarez de Morales Ruiz Matas, Camilo. 2008. "Granada en la Historia de al-Andalus", Escuela de Estudios Árabes, Consejo Superior de Investigaciones Científicas. Accessed May 14, 2024. www.eea.csic.es/divulgacion/granada-en-la-historia-de-al-andalus/

Backhaus, Peter. 2007. *Linguistic Landscapes: A Comparative Study of Urban Multilingualism in Tokyo*. Clevedon/Buffalo/Toronto: Multilingual Matters.

Ben-Rafael, Eliezer, Elana Shohamy, Muhammad Hasan Amara, and Nira Trumper-Hecht. 2006. "Linguistic Landscape as Symbolic Construction of the Public Space: The Case of Israel." *International Journal of Multilingualism* 3 (1): 7–30.

Blommaert, Jan. 2013. *Ethnography, Superdiversity and Linguistic Landscapes: Chronicles of Complexity*. Bristol/Buffalo/Toronto: Multilingual Matters.

Blommaert, Jan, and Ico Maly. 2014. "Ethnographic Linguistic Landscape Analysis and Social Change: A Case Study". *Tilburg Papers in Culture Studies* 100. Tilburg: Tilburg University. https://research.tilburguniversity.edu/en/publications/ethnographic-linguistic-landscape-analysis-and-social-change-a-ca-4

Castillo Lluch, Mónica, and Daniel M. Sáez Rivera. 2011. "Introducción al paisaje lingüístico de Madrid." *Lengua y Migración* 3: 73–88.

Franco-Rodríguez, José M. 2009. "Interpreting the Linguistic Traits of Linguistic Landscapes as Ethnolinguistic Vitality: Methodological Approach." *Revista Electrónica de Lingüística Aplicada* 8 (1): 1–15.

Gorter, Durk, and Jasone Cenoz. 2024. *A Panorama of Linguistic Landscape Studies*. Bristol: Multilingual Matters.

Eriksen, Thomas Hyland. 1993. *Ethnicity and Nationalism: Anthropological Perspectives*. London/Boulder/Colorado: Pluto Press.

Espinosa Ramírez, Antonio B., and Yael Guilat. 2018. "Memoria e identidad a través del paisaje lingüístico: el caso de Granada." In *Narrativas Urbanas*, edited by Miguel Ángel Chaves Martín, 23–32. Madrid: Universidad Complutense de Madrid.

Heredia Mantis, María. 2023. "'Hola. Bienvenidos. Soy de Japón'. El japonés en el paisaje lingüístico de Granada." *Seminario de Investigación: El paisaje lingüístico de Granada en el contexto andaluz y global,* Workshop paper. Granada, 18-19 de diciembre de 2023.

Heredia Mantis, María. 2024. "Nuevos discursos en el paisaje lingüístico transgresor: Las pegatinas en Granada." *Del Español. Revista de Lengua* 2.

Heredia Mantis, María, Irania Malaver Arguinzones, Luis Pablo Núñez, Marcin Sosinski, and Daniel M. Sáez Rivera. 2023. "Estudios del Paisaje Lingüístico en Granada." *Año cultural de los países que hablan español,* University poster. (Facultad de Traducción, Universidad de Granada).

Leeman, Jennifer, and Gabriella Modan. 2010. "Selling the City: Language, Ethnicity and Commodified Space." In *Linguistic Landscape in the City*, edited by Elana Shohamy, Eliezer Ben-Rafael and Monica Barni, 182–197. Clevedon: Multilingual Matters.

Guilat, Yael, and Antonio B. Espinosa Ramírez. 2016. "The Historical Memory Law and Its Role in Redesigning Semiotic Cityscapes in Spain: A Case Study from Granada." *Linguistic Landscape* 2 (3): 247–274.

Hu, Jingyuan, and Daniel M. Sáez Rivera. 2022. "El diminutivo en el Paisaje Lingüístico de Madrid." *Círculo de Lingüística Aplicada a la Comunicación* 92: 127–138. Accessed May 14, 2024. https://revistas.ucm.es/index.php/CLAC/article/view/76734

Landry, Rodrigue, and Richard Y. Bourhis. 1997. "Linguistic Landscape and Ethnolinguistic Vitality: An Empirical Study." *Journal of Language and Social Psychology* 6: 23–49.

Malaver Arguinzones, Irania. 2021. "Estudio sociopragmático del diminutivo en Granada." In *El español de Granada. Estudio sociolingüístico*, edited by María de las Mercedes Soto Melgar and Anna Zholobova, 246–264. Berna: Peter Lang.

Malaver Arguinzones, Irania, and Marcin Sosinski. 2022. "El árabe en la ciudad de Granada." *I Congreso Internacional sobre Paisaje Lingüístico: el entorno urbano y rural hispánico*. Sevilla: Universidad Pablo de Olavide, 9–11 noviembre 2022).

Malinowski, Bronislaw. 1972 [1923]. "The Problem of Meaning in Primitive Languages." Supplement I In *The Meaning of Meaning*, edited by C.K. Ogden and I.A. Richards, 296–336. 10th ed. London: Routledge and Kegan Paul.

Manjón-Cabeza Cruz, Antonio. 2012. "Los diminutivos en el corpus PRESEEA de Granada." In *Español hablado. Estudios sobre el corpus PRESEEA-Granada*, edited by Edyta Waluch de la Torre, and Juan Antonio Moya Corral, 55–76. Warsaw: Instituto de Estudios Ibéricos e Iberoamericanos de la Universidad de Varsovia.

Monjour, Alf. 2014. "El paisaje lingüístico de la Granada actual y la construcción de una identidad seudo-andalusí." In *Escenarios urbanos: en torno a la ciudad del siglo XXI*, edited by Melanie Würth, 135–158. Genève: Slatkine.

Moustaoui Srhir, Adil. 2013. "Nueva economía y dinámicas de cambio sociolingüístico en el paisaje lingüístico de Madrid: El caso del árabe." *Revista Internacional de Lingüística Iberorrománica* 11 (21): 89–108.

Pablo Núñez, Luis. 2022. "Una primera aproximación al paisaje lingüístico de Granada capital." *I Congreso Internacional sobre Paisaje Lingüístico: el entorno urbano y rural hispánico*. Sevilla: Universidad Pablo de Olavide, 9–11 noviembre 2022.

Pavlenko, Anna. 2019. "Superdiversity and Why It Isn't: Reflections on Terminological Innovation and Academic Branding." In *Sloganization in Language Education Discourse: Conceptual Thinking in the Age of Academic Marketization*, edited by Barbara Schmenk, Stephan Breidbach and Lutz Küster, 142–168. Bristol: Multilingual Matters.

Pons Rodríguez, Lola. 2012. *El paisaje lingüístico de Sevilla: lenguas y variedades en el escenario urbano hispalense*. Sevilla: Diputación de Sevilla: Servicio de Archivo y Publicaciones.

Reguero Ugarte, Urtzi. 2024. "Lenguas cooficiales: El euskera, el gallego y el catalán en las calles de Andalucía." In *Álbum de paisaje lingüístico andaluz: Andalucía, tierra de lenguas, Archiletras*, edited by Lola Pons Rodríguez, 22–25. Madrid: Prensa y Servicios de la Lengua.

Reyes Sánchez, Francisco, and Ana María Vigara Tauste. 1996-1997. "Graffiti y pintadas en Madrid, Arte, Lenguaje y Comunicación." *Espéculo* 4. Accessed May 14, 2024. http://webs.ucm.es/info/especulo/numero4/graffiti.htm

Romera Manzanares, Ana María 2023a. "*Stay rude, stay rebel*: la reivindicación en el paisaje lingüístico de la ciudad de Granada." In *Verba, Anexo 85, Andalucía en su paisaje lingüístico: lenguas, signos y hablantes*, edited by Blanca Garrido Martín, and Lola Pons Rodríguez, 145–184. Santiago de Compostela: Universidad de Santiago de Compostela.

Romera Manzanares, Ana María 2023b. "El paisaje lingüístico como material de innovación docente en las asignaturas de Lengua española." In *Funciones y aplicación didáctica del paisaje lingüístico andaluz*, edited by María Victoria Galloso Camacho, Manuel Cabello Pino, and María Heredia Mantis, 143–163. Madrid/Frankfurt am Main: Iberoamericana/Vervuert.

Rosón Lorente, Francisco Javier, and Sol Tarrés. 2013. "Inmigración, integración y comunidades musulmanas." In *Cuadernos de la Escuela Diplomática 48: El Islam y los musulmanes hoy. Dimensión internacional y relaciones con España*, edited by Olivia Orozco de la Torre, and Gabriel Alonso García, 249–264. Madrid: Ministerio de Asuntos Exteriores.

Scollon, Ron, and Wong Scollon, Suzie. (2003). *Discourses in Place: Language in the Material World* (1st ed.). London: Routledge.

Sáez Rivera, Daniel M. 2014. "El Madrid plurilingüe y pluridialectal: nueva realidad, nuevos enfoques." In *Prácticas y políticas lingüísticas. Nuevas variedades, normal, actitudes y perspectivas*, edited by Klaus Zimmerman, 403–440. Madrid/Frankfurt am Main: Iberoamericana/Vervuert.

Sáez Rivera, Daniel M. 2015. "Viajes lingüísticos de ida y vuelta: el español de los dominicanos en Madrid y su plasmación en el Paisaje Lingüístico." In *La Española – Isla de encuentros, Hispaniola – Island of Encounters*, edited by Jessica Stefanie Barzen, Hanna Lene Geiger and Silke Jansen, 171–195. Tübingen: Narr Verlag.

Sáez Rivera, Daniel M. 2021. "El Paisaje Lingüístico como herramienta pedagógica para la enseñanza de la lingüística: Un estudio de caso en la confección de blogs especializados." *Revista de Recursos para el Aula de Español: investigación y enseñanza* 1 (1): 167–204. Accessed May 14, 2024. https://erevistas.publicaciones.uah.es/ojs/index.php/rr/article/view/1504/846.

Sáez Rivera, Daniel M. 2023. "Notas sobre el paisaje lingüístico ¿fractal? de Granada: la Placeta de la Victoria." *Seminario de Investigación: El paisaje lingüístico de Granada en el contexto andaluz y global.* Granada, 18–19 de diciembre de 2023.

Sáez Rivera, Daniel M. 2024a. "Relaciones posibles entre temporalidad y paisaje lingüístico en español." *Philologia Hispalensis* 38 (1): 171–198.

Sáez Rivera, Daniel M. 2024b. "Neerlandés[:] Una lengua en contacto." In *Álbum de paisaje lingüístico andaluz: Andalucía, tierra de lenguas, Archiletras*, edited by Lola Pons Rodríguez, 50–53. Madrid: Prensa y Servicios de la Lengua.

Sáez Rivera, Daniel M., and Mónica Castillo Lluch. 2012. "The Human and Linguistic Landscape of Madrid (Spain)." In *Linguistic Landscapes, Multilingualism and Social Change: Diversité des Approches*, edited by Christine Hélot, Monica Barni, Rudi Janssens and Carla Bagna, 309–328. Bern: Peter Lang. Accessed May 14, 2024. https://serval.unil.ch/resource/serval:BIB_501E8688DB40.P001/REF.pdf

Sawyer, Keith. 2001. *Creating Conversations: Improvisation in Everyday Discourse.* New York: Hampton Press.

Vertovec, Steven. 2007. "Super-Diversity and Its Implications." *Ethnic and Racial Studies* 30 (6): 10241054.

Zarza, Daniel. 1996. *Una interpretación fractal de la forma de la ciudad.* Madrid: Instituto Juan de Herrera.

4 A feminist discourse in the linguistic landscape of Málaga (2016–2024)

Diana Esteba Ramos

Introduction and hypothesis

Although studies on the linguistic landscape have begun to focus on the crossover between their aim and feminist theories, there are still myriad aspects to be addressed in this field.[1,2] For example, most of these studies deal solely with the slogans used at demonstrations held to celebrate International Women's Day on March 8 (8M), providing a fruitful yet limited corpus of study, which is addressed without considering the language or its varieties used for conveying a feminist message. As these options have not been considered, it is obvious that no attention is being paid to their communicative purpose or the added semiotic value of these signs inasmuch as they are the product of a linguistic choice.

The aim here, therefore, is to refocus the perspective adopted in previous studies through a two-pronged exercise of extension and specification: the extension will be rendered possible by the use of the Ma#PL#aga corpus of study that consists of a large collection of photographs that reflect the micro-diachrony in Malaga's linguistic landscape (2016; 2022–2024) while the specification is prompted by the choice of language or the features of certain varieties of Spanish.

Feminist movements and the use of language: Identity

Personal identity is based on several pillars, of which language is clearly one of the main ones.[3] In a more or less conscious manner, we use language to express ourselves in a hyperconnected society. Within this context, an identity is based on an online/offline construct that conflates the outlines of the self and constantly feeds back off them. This means the link connecting individuals involves the building of translocal and volatile networks (Castells [1997] 2002) in the digital-based *postnational constellation* (Habermas 2001, 5).

The appropriation of territory is an age-old identity practice. This appropriation may be undertaken through linguistic construction and the creation of signs in the public arena, forming the linguistic landscape,[4] as a place that thus becomes a space for expressing relationships of power (Bourdieu 1983; 1993 in Cenoz and Gorter 2024) in which to assert one's own self-identity (in the sense given by Goffman 1963; 1981 in Cenoz and Gorter 2024).[5]

DOI: 10.4324/9781032687087-5

The public arena in a consumer economy is a setting in which a city publicizes itself, yet at the same time it may be considered a disruptive space, as diverse social collectives have the opportunity to speak and enter into a dialogue or confrontation with those that have done so previously in the same place. They do so against a shared background, yet one that at the same time does not fully belong to them because they are subject to the authority of official rules and regulations.[6] Furthermore, these voices, as often as not anonymous, can reach a large audience:[7] the general population that moves about freely in the streets and interacts, in a more or less conscious manner, with the signs surrounding them, in what is undoubtedly an unprecedented density of messages (Gorter and Cenoz 2017, 234). All this without even considering the bombardment of digital messages being received at the same time. This means city dwellers come into contact with slogans that crowd their online/offline environment, as in *continuum*, in endless dialectical interaction (Blommaert 2016, 99).[8]

This interweaving of aspects from online and offline life takes on considerable meaning in studies on the linguistic landscape, insofar as Gorter (2006, 1) contends, the term *landscape* may be understood as the scenario we can see and its representation. We are dealing with a specular reality, as already posited in Esteba Ramos (2024), in which we need to accept both definitions for the following three main reasons: (i) we take photos for our studies and we process these representations in our research; (ii) an online search provides numerous examples of the linguistic landscape that may help to verify our corpus; (iii) the composers of these signs are aware of other similar examples from which they draw their inspiration, and they may even hope that their examples will play the same echoing role. The creative process, therefore, is built upon the collectiveness of the transnational referents that largely condition the examples we are studying. Many of the signs have their origin (and a large part of their functions and meanings) in a "translocal online world" (Blommaert 2016, 113; Blommaert and Maly 2019), which has informed their creation, testing, and discussion, on an even broader audience (MacDowall and de Souza 2018, 3) of a hybrid nature (Campos 2020, 59).

Moreover, when these examples are used in socio-political causes such as feminism, the creation of identity and its collective building become even more important: signs not only claim part of the common space, as they are also part of a given social protest that is clearly rooted in identity, through a critical and alternative discourse (Guerra 2013), which uses this channel of expression because it considers it has no alternative mouthpiece (Gaggero et al. 2002, 109) and it resorts to online information, whereby it establishes a "continuum of involved sociotechnical practices" (Cárdenas 2016, 95). What's more, it is clear that the public space, a setting for discussing matters of common interest according to Habermas, like the society that upholds it, is not fully equal: as a male domain it often excludes women (Fraser 1990) and their demands, although it is now being subverted by the drive of sundry feminist collectives. The linguistic choices that are therefore made in the processing of these examples determine the way in which their authors introduce themselves to the world, in the way they find their place in this ephemeral jungle of signs (cf. Ben-Rafael 2009, 42; Shohamy et al. 2010, xiv–xv). Such messages are most assuredly conditioned by the aforementioned online-offline tension (cf. Fernández-Planells, Figueras-Maz and Feixa 2014), which, especially in protest movements, involves a constant flow and interaction between the internet and the public space (Martín Rojo 2013, 275).

Modern society continues to be pressured by the tensions generated by globalization and movements of place attachment: indeed, globalization itself is the very reason for the flourishing of cultural identities of a local nature in several places throughout the world (Giddens 2001), fostering a kind of glocalization (Robertson 1992).[9] These tensions are reflected in the same way that as individual beings we positions ourselves before these options that are in opposition, yet at the same time interdependent and, to a certain extent, reconcilable. Feminist movements themselves today could be defined en masse by this duality: although the vast diffusion and dissemination of feminist thinking stems from the imperialist world and seems to spread through channels that are closely linked to the dynamics of global communication, which have given rise to the notion of a transnational feminist theory;[10] the particular reception of these ideas may pass through a specific filter that relates it to its closest realities.[11] This gives meaning to the existence of feminism of a markedly local nature, such as the one referred to as *feminismo andaluz* [Andalusian feminism], strongly intertwined with other markers. On the one hand, movements of this kind thrive under the umbrella of the English language slogans from which they draw their inspiration, and which underpin their mission and to a certain extent their specific modes of linguistic expression; nonetheless, on the other hand, they have a manifest vocation for expression through linguistic channels of a markedly local nature.

Variation research appears to confirm that the Spanish spoken in Andalusia has undergone significant changes in recent years, especially on the back of the economic development recorded in the second half of the twentieth century, involving massive migration away from the countryside. This has entailed the forgoing of certain features of the vernacular varieties in the places of origin, prompting a tendency towards convergence with the national standard, reinforced by mandatory schooling and exposure to the media, as noted also in processes elsewhere in other languages. It is important to note also that this process is especially significant in female discourse: women are assumed to choose gentler forms, as the more forceful ones are supposedly reserved for men. This tendency has led to the creation of an intermediate variety in standard and vernacular language (Villena 1996; Villena and Vida 2020), which in turn is seen as natural (especially regarding the syllable coda, and fosters diverse phenomena within this text that are commonplace in the spoken language in Andalusia in general) and prestigious (in upholding the forms of reflecting the national standard in the syllable onset). Following the Le Page model, we might establish a continuum between the vernacular variety, the regional standard, and the national standard (as posited by Villena 2001, 109), correlating with the actual underlying identities in these linguistic systems. The vernacular end of the continuum is occupied particularly by the local varieties of the lower and working classes and is, furthermore, the butt of the discourse among those that decry Andalusians and their culture;[12] hence the reason that when dealing with certain audiences, opting for this markedly Andalusian use may involve highlighting certain values held by its users.

One of the feminist movement's guiding lights in Andalusia,[13] Mar Gallego, stresses the intersectionality of feminism based on the struggle of Andalusian working women subject to a twin process of discrimination: racial-linguistic and misogynist (Rodríguez Iglesias 2022a, 98). In this defence of their identity, it seems logical that the linguistic ideal is located in the area nearest the vernacular end of the continuum. Nevertheless, migratory processes and protracted access to formal education mean that those vernacular traits are being lost, as Gallego herself personally regrets following her time at university and her move from the countryside to the city. In view of this loss, a rebuilding is underway above the level of awareness of the linguistic product, whose repercussions on Andalusia's public messaging space are worth tracing.

There is no doubt that society, and especially its younger members, bases its array of communication options on what Blommaert describes as multilingualism, the partial access to different language units that constitute "truncated repertoires" that "are grounded in people's biographies" (Blommaert 2010, 102). In these repertoires, English occupies a privileged position and the focus towards other languages. Moreover, the building of identity discourses such as the feminist one may in some way operate as an international lingua franca, as occurs in other collectives, providing access to a global community (cf., initially, Nelson 2010, and subsequently Epstein 2023), which nonetheless creates tension with the local input (Bucholtz and Skapoulli 2009).

Therefore, when feminist voices in places such as Andalusia seek to become encapsulated in the form of written signs, they may encounter at least three different kinds of expression: (i) the use of the Spanish language without any special kind of linguistic varieties influence; (ii) the use of English as the globally recognized lingua franca, without any particular cultural attachment and encompassing a broad and non-defined audience, and (iii) the use of Spanish spiced up with certain language patterns associated with the varieties in Andalusia.[14]

The Internet plays a key role in this identity-building: modern reality cannot be separated into independent online/offline ambits, and this impossibility is reaffirmed by social struggles, whose impact will be greater as their audience increases. For example, the 8M demonstrations themselves may be considered "global media events," of considerable interest to scholars of globalization (Sandvoss 2015, 395): these mass events create a virtual community that is based on a common textual output. It is a given, furthermore, that urban art has a powerful impact on socio-political movements (Gonçalves and Milani 2022, 432). This stresses the importance of dealing with social media as a vehicle for disseminating ideologies (Lee and Lim 2014), which merge identity and territorial slogans through ephemeral forms of expression (Gonçalves 2019, 147) that may circulate globally thanks to the Internet (Blommaert 2016).

In short, the choice of one of these means for the voicing of feminist demands in Andalusia reflects a more or less conscious choice of identity. Hence, and in keeping with the positions adopted here, this chapter propounds a descriptive reflection that in no way seeks to be judgemental on how the linguistic landscape in Malaga adopts these modes of expression and places them at the service of the feminist struggle. It will be expedient to reflect upon the semiotic value of the examples, the specific mechanisms themselves of the linguistic (re)construction of the discourse, the media in which these modes of expression appear, and their possible direct sources.

Method

The Ma#PL#aga corpus

Initially, the Ma#PL#aga corpus is the outcome of this author's individual work for an unpublished lecture delivered in 2016, being subsequently completed, tweaked, and extended thanks to the collaboration of members of the project "The linguistic landscape in Malaga; approached and mapped from a gender perspective (*Paisaje lingüístico malagueño: aproximación y cartografiado desde una perspectiva de género*)."[15] It consists of examples of linguistic signs in the public arena that have been collected in two different timeframes: 2016, with more than 150 examples, and the period 2022–2024, which remains open and in constant growth, with over 1000 items. Both sets of examples have several aspects in common: (i) on the one hand, they have been collected in Malaga in Andalusia (Spain), a coastal and cosmopolitan city that is both home to and visited by people from all over the world; (ii) it has also been chosen because of its ties, in the broadest sense, with realities involving women: the use of feminist messages and slogans; the expressions of sentiments linked to the female domain, and the numerous linguistic strategies use to shed light on gender,[16] and finally (iii) its composition reflects a wide variety of types, ranging from placards and banners in demonstrations, stickers, graffiti, and business signs and stencils, among others.

The two timeframes used here are especially significant: when in 2016 I accepted an invitation extended by the University of Malaga's Association of Historical Studies on Women (*Asociación de Estudios Históricos sobre la Mujer*) I did not realize that I had built up a corpus that contained examples from the moment before decisive events for the history of feminism, such as La Manada rape case, the #MeToo movement, and the great purple wave of the feminist strike and demonstration on 8M 2018. This first timeframe provides a comparison with the ongoing subcorpus that is being gathered since 2022, and enables us to analyze how these social milestones have impacted on the messages visible in the public arena. In other words, we have a vantage point that enables us to observe possible changes in the linguistic landscape and therefore in its actual discursive makeup.

In terms of other significant methodological aspects, it should be noted that the language examples we use are labelled and constitute a database that provides us with information on their location, content, medium, and the language or variety used.

Research method

This chapter has used a quantitative and qualitative methodology informed by the processing and analysis of the Ma#PL#aga corpus, in addition to open interviews with sundry creators of examples of a feminist linguistic landscape. The research's ethnographic contribution has been made via a member of the now-defunct feminist collective, La Medusa Colectiva, responsible for artistic displays of a feminist nature that can still be seen on walls in the city center; what's more, I was present at the creation of the placards for the autonomous block for the demonstration on 8M 2024, and I met some leading members of other blocks representing different organizations; finally, I attended the 8M demonstrations in 2023 and 2024 and, insofar as the possibilities that events of this kind provide, I talked to the individuals carrying placards of interest to this research and which I had photographed.[17]

Results

Signs in other languages

Malaga's linguistic landscape has numerous features of multilingualism, as I reported in a prior study (Esteba Ramos 2014). On that occasion, nonetheless, I was not interested in addressing the conflation between the use of language other than Spanish and messages of a feminist nature: but it seemed plausible that some feminist messages, composed in English-speaking ambits, kept to this language as a globalizing aspect that imbued them with an international and identity nature.

Indeed, the walls in Malaga often feature slogans in English: within these examples, some of them also involve messages with a feminist content, although solely in the subcorpus corresponding to the second timeframe (2022–2024). An analysis of the micro-diachrony reveals a greater use of English for these purposes.

The signs in English in the public arena may be painted on or graffiti, especially circumscribed to the city centre. Some of them are simply reaffirmations of identity, labels of female empowerment, such as those that say *pussy power* or its partial translation *chocho power* (Figure 4.1), which has already been studied elsewhere (Esteba Ramos 2024). As we have seen, the search for the hashtag #chochopower on Instagram shows results for wall slogans in other Spanish cities such as Barcelona, Madrid, and Granada. If the search uses #pussypower instead, there are over 350,000 hits, including some in the public space. Not only do we find examples of the linguistic landscape on social media with this hashtag, a Google search finds many on the retail websites for clothes or accessories with superimposed phrases. In addition, there are several songs by international performers that contains this reaffirmation in their title or in their lyrics. We thus encounter an expression coined by the feminist movement in English, where it is strongest, and partially translated into Spanish.

Figure 4.1 Graffiti in English reading, "Pussy Power." Málaga, Spain.

The graffiti that uses these words is sprayed on in black and purple paint, in keeping with the colours associated with feminist movements. In addition, it is usually accompanied by a depiction of a vulva, as a genital portrayal that is becoming increasingly more commonplace in the streets of Malaga together with phallic images, which are still much more frequent. This is undoubtedly a new symbolic appropriation of a space previously restricted to depictions of male genitalia, which accompany and complement the linguistic message.

We have also found stickers with feminist messages in English. Amongst these, there is one that states, "Dump your porn addicted boyfriend,", Figure 4.2., an invitation that also appears in some songs and whose appearance on stickers is available online. The web even has a photo of a sticker that is identical to the one in our corpus, with both taken in Malaga and posted in Wikimedia commons.[18] We cannot say whether or not this was a more or less concerted act with several examples throughout the city, as our corpus only records a couple of cases. Moreover, a Spanish translation of this slogan also appears in the city's streets, although there is no evidence of bilingual texts or the successive appearance of the two messages as a bilingual sign: their presence is clearly separate.

There is a single recorded case of "Trans lives matter," Figure 4.3, on a flyer taped to a lamppost on the El Ejido university campus. This message is linked to "Black trans lives matter," which in turn is associated with "Black lives matter"; in other words, with the prominent BLM movement that arose in 2013 following the death of T. Martin, and unfortunately reinforced following the deaths of other individuals, especially in the USA. Over and above the movement itself, this phrase became a tag for social media and even an identity slogan that is globally recognized today, and which is reflected on numerous consumer items: bags, t-shirts, mugs... There is no record of a Spanish translation in Malaga's linguistic landscape, probably because of the profound impact that the phrase had

A feminist discourse in the linguistic landscape of Málaga   99

Figure 4.2 Sticker in English, reading "Dump your porn addicted boyfriend." Málaga, Spain.

in English and its adoption in other languages, mediated by its digital tag: it often happens that certain slogans involving social demands, forged in specific linguistic contexts and disseminated as catchphrases on social media, remain untranslated on public signs, faithful to the unifying hashtag under which they were created.[19]

Other slogans are sprayed onto walls, such as the one that affirms "Woman is not a feeling," Figure 4.4, which is widely echoed in its Spanish translation on other walls, *"ser mujer no es un sentimiento,"* all in the city center. This slogan, moreover, is associated with a phrase used by the so-called trans-exclusionary radical feminist (TERF) movement, and it can be found on consumer items that can be purchased online.

The banners in the demonstrations in 2023 and 2024 bore texts in English, with a clear increase from one year to the next. Although they are not at all in the majority, the English slogans have a space of their own on individually composed placards carried by young women. None of these slogans is original: they all reflect other texts that have gone viral on the web, whether originating in a specific demand ("support all your sisters, not only your cis-ters," whose translation would have meant forgoing the play on words; "for all womankind,", Figure 4.5., by the illustrator

100 *Ethnographic Landscapes and Language Ideologies in the Spanish State*

Figure 4.3 Paper taped to a post, reading "Trans lives matter." Málaga, Spain.

behind the artistic expression of the #MeToo movement, represented in the poster with a design clearly inspired by it), or reflecting the lyrics of a song, reproduced literally ("Anything you can do, I can do bleeding," Figure 4.6, a 2018 song by Mary More; "Sex is cool, but have you ever fucked the system?," Figure 4.7, from a 2020 song by Pussy Riot; "I am sick of running as fast as I can," Figure 4.8, from a 2018 song by Taylor Swift) or altering them ("Girls just wanna have equality," Figure 4.9, as an alternative to "Girls just wanna have fun," by Cindy Lauper in 1983). In all these cases, the texts have to remain in English to uphold the play on words or direct references to artistic expressions.

A particularly curious example combines Spanish and English in a play on words that works only by interpreting the English part from a Spanish-speaking perspective: "I'm art (*estoy harta*, meaning "I'm sick and tired")," Figure 4.10. The phrase emphasizes the artistic quality of the issuer ('*soy arte*' – "I'm art"), yet at the same time its continuation in the Spanish segment "*estoy harta*" suggests a

A feminist discourse in the linguistic landscape of Málaga 101

Figure 4.4 Graffiti in English reading, "Women is not a feeling." Málaga, Spain.

translation of the English by phonetic similarity between "art" and "*harta*." In this case, the two languages are playing off each other in an apparently new slogan, but one that is still not original, as other examples have been found online and on consumer items.

Using English in other cases is more superfluous, as in the case of the following texts: "To all the men feeling attacked right now. ¡Maybe you should be smiling!" [note the Spanish inverted exclamation mark], Figure 4.12, and "Destroy the patriarchy, not the planet," Figure 4.13, slogans that have been appearing in social media particularly since 2018 and which feature on a range of commercial products, or "I am an object", Figure 4.11 (swapping the "o" for ♀, which would have also been perfectly possible in Spanish), as a slogan that has also been reproduced on t-shirts and other items.

Yet not all texts can be used to support feminist demands. There are also examples of the Spanish linguistic landscape with an anti-feminist slant. Thus, the walls on a school in the working-class district of Cruz de Humilladero, one of the areas of the city with the largest migrant populations, bear the slogan "fuck femismo", Figure 4.14 (sic). It seems that French-, Italian-, and Spanish-speaking youths are making increasing use of *fuck* to denigrate movements they do not agree with, as was also apparent on posters in the 2024 demonstration, with the

102 *Ethnographic Landscapes and Language Ideologies in the Spanish State*

Figure 4.5 Banner of the Women's Day demonstration (2024), reading in English "For all woman kind." Málaga, Spain.

simple phrase "fuck you" framed within female sexual organs in which the fallopian tubes appeared as hands with raised index fingers making an insulting gesture.[20]

In short, none of the feminist-related signs in English is original; in other words, they echo global discourses that have gone viral online and been embraced particularly by young people through processes of copying and intertextuality (Kristeva

Figure 4.6 Banner of the Women's Day demonstration (2024), reading in English "Anything you can do, I can do bleeding." Málaga, Spain.

1967).[21] Many of the slogans that appear in these examples revisit the death of the author (cf. Barthes [1988] 2002 and Foucault 1977), diluted in the digital crowd. These (re)creations resort to humour and other devices to have an impact on the reader, all with a view to gaining recognition and urging their consumers to share them online (Martín Rojo 2013, 281).

With the exception of the examples described above, all the messages are monolingual, thereby assuming their audience's linguistic capability. The individuals interviewed that carried the banners bearing these slogans, the only actual authors identified in this linguistic landscape, are Spanish speakers that have used these forms of expression because of their particular mastery and affective proximity to this language. The phrases belong to a collective and international feminist imaginary that is also expressed in the lyrics of songs and on a range of commercial items, which may serve, when used in the street, as other features of the mobile linguistic landscape. These slogans carry a huge symbolic and emotive charge and have the ability, when photographed and shared online, to perpetuate the echo of these viral messages.[22]

104   *Ethnographic Landscapes and Language Ideologies in the Spanish State*

Figure 4.7 Banner of the Women's Day demonstration (2024), reading in English "Sex is cool but have you ever fucked the system?" Málaga, Spain.

Figure 4.8 Banner of the Women's Day demonstration (2024), reading in English "I am sick of running as fast as I can, wondering if i'd get quicker if I was a man," just next to other Spanish banners. Málaga, Spain.

A feminist discourse in the linguistic landscape of Málaga 105

Figure 4.9 Banner of the Women's Day demonstration (2024), reading in English "Girls juts wanna have equality."

Presence of varieties of Spanish

The emergence of an Andalusian feminism that reflects its linguistic variety in the spoken language, as well as intentionally embracing it in some of its written expressions in favor of an Andalusian spelling, requires us to explore the examples of the linguistic landscape to discover whether they also resort to these devices, and if so, which ones specifically. These linguistic options stand in contrast to the

Figure 4.10 Multilingual banner of the Women's Day demonstration (2024), reading "[English] I'm art,[Spanish] I am fed up" Málaga, Spain.

Figure 4.11 Banner of the Women's Day demonstration (2024), reading in English "I am an object," with the words "am an" crossed out.

A feminist discourse in the linguistic landscape of Málaga 107

Figure 4.12 Banner of the Women's Day demonstration (2024), reading in English "To all the men feeling attacked right now. ¡Maybe you should try smiling!" [note the Spanish inverted exclamation mark]. Málaga, Spain.

use of English, the lingua franca of globalization with no local roots. This therefore generates tension between global and local that is readily apparent in Malaga's linguistic landscape, albeit far from doing so in equal measures. As opposed to the neutral "despatialization" involved in the use of English, this linguistic choice focuses on the user's specific background.

Indeed, some of the graffiti on the walls in Malaga contains words that may be considered as influenced by the Andalusian variety of Spanish, as they have been composed in Andalusia and reflect the existence of the local feminist movement mentioned earlier. This may be the case, although it should be noted that in isolation these messages might be associated with other varieties of Spanish.

Particularly significant are the city's surviving stencils, created by the now defunct group La Medusa Colectiva, Figure 4.15. They feature spellings that reflect the loss of the final -s in the syllable coda of the word simply through the ellipsis of the consonant itself. The same stencil uses the definitive article "er" instead of "el," reflecting the rhotacism that appears in some speech varieties in Andalusia, in a routinized and a little bit vulgar sentence that insists on the fact that women are very fed up.

108 *Ethnographic Landscapes and Language Ideologies in the Spanish State*

Figure 4.13 Banner of the Women's Day demonstration (2024), reading in English "Destroy the patriarchy, not the planet." Málaga, Spain.

This loss or aspiration is represented on wall messages by a purple *h* in the slogan "Andalusah levantaos. 8M," Figure 4.16, which echoes and alters the phrase in Andalusia's anthem that says "Andaluces, levantaos" [Andalusians rise up!]. This example, moreover, reflects a seseo sound in the spelling.

Some of the features we have reported might be considered by their creators as typically Andalusian, although there is actually no reason for this. These are devices

A feminist discourse in the linguistic landscape of Málaga 109

Figure 4.14 Graffiti in English reading, "Fuck femismo [sic]." Málaga, Spain.

that are typical of diaphasic varieties linked to colloquial speech, such as apocope procedures involving *pa*, *to* and *toas*. Some of the slogans, such "*Metralleta pa to el que te someta*" [Machine-gun for everyone who oppresses you], Figure 4.17, with the *pa* and *to* replacing *para* and *todo* originating in hip-hop culture: in this case, from a feminist rap band called IRA, from Madrid. This is, furthermore, a clear choice of the vernacular, as these apocopes are less frequent in the normal speech of the urban middle classes in Andalusia (Villena and Vida 2020, 161), as seen also in Figure 4.18.

Figure 4.15 Stencil reading in Spanish "No tenemo er chichi pa farolillo." Málaga, Spain.

In terms of spelling, a further highlight in wall messages and slogans is the use of dissident forms such as the use of *k* instead of *c*, in Figure 4.19 (which is also a reflection of protest ideologies, Screti 2015, 206) or *x*, which in this case is used for prepalatal voiceless fricative (or affricate, in which case it reflects an Andalusian spelling), in Figure 4.20. These letters are typical of protest discourses, which include the slogans in question here. Nevertheless, they do not involve a dialectal adscription, but a diaphasic one instead.

Apart from these apocopes typical of informal registers, the examples of slogans seeking to reproduce local Andalusian features appear solely in graffiti and stencils, and we have not been able to record any cases in the actual demonstrations.[23] These are aspects, moreover, that are related mainly to the syllable coda, which means they are mostly compatible with the intermediate variety; nevertheless, there are also aspects of syllable onset that are largely recorded in Malaga itself, such as the *seseo*, with the possible intent of vernacular adscription.[24]

Conclusions

In sum, feminism is a movement in which identity takes central stage. Linguistic choices have a more or less conscious role to play in identity-building itself.

A feminist discourse in the linguistic landscape of Málaga 111

Figure 4.16 Graffiti in Spanish reading, "Andalusah levantaoh," Málaga, Spain.

The feminist slogans analyzed in Malaga in these two timeframes inform the following findings: (i) these signs are a further manifestation of the tension between globalization and the recovery of the local, as we have recorded examples of signs that resort to English, the global lingua franca and the language in which the bulk of feminist theories have been expressed, and signs that seek to interweave

112 *Ethnographic Landscapes and Language Ideologies in the Spanish State*

Figure 4.17 Stencil reading in Spanish "Metralleta pa to el que te someta." Málaga, Spain.

A feminist discourse in the linguistic landscape of Málaga 113

Figure 4.18 Banner of the Women's Day demonstration (2024), reading in Spanish "Un besazo para toas las flores que estremecen el cemento." Málaga. Spain.

feminism and the more immediate reality of Andalusian culture, which involves the imitation of certain linguistic features associated with the way Spanish is spoken in this region; (ii) English appears much more often on banners in demonstrations than in graffiti. The reason for this is that many of the slogans in demonstrations are inspired by online social media, whereby they are part of a globalized world, which at the same time is part of daily online/offline reality; (iii) the use of local features appears to be restricted more to certain more militant social groups and their messages on the city's walls; (iv) both tendencies are much more developed in recent examples of the diachrony that we have described in our corpus: that is, they appear to be in full development and we do not know how this tension will be resolved; (v) in both types of examples, as in most of the texts in Spanish that we have discarded for this research, we can hear the echoes of today's interconnected society, which means they are wholly lacking in any form of originality: the slogans are informed by the global culture of music or other cases of online significance, which in turn are stamped on different consumer articles on the market. They often involve international slogans that are reproduced with few changes throughout the world. These examples, furthermore, often become mass consumer items in a process of intersemiotic transposition (Milani 2022), a device linked to a fetish for the word.

114 *Ethnographic Landscapes and Language Ideologies in the Spanish State*

Figure 4.19 Stencil reading in Spanish "Akelarre feminista local." Málaga, Spain.

There is still a lot of work to be done, and this has been simply an overview that paves the way for a reflection on a kind of hybridization that defines this discourse. The following studies are called for: (i) verification of this tension between global and local in other towns and cities in Andalusia and comparison of the features reproduced in their imitation of Andalusian idiosyncrasies; (ii) verification of this tension in other diatopic varieties both in Spanish and in other languages; (iii) more detailed observation of the processes of appropriating lexical terms from English in combination with other languages, for a

A feminist discourse in the linguistic landscape of Málaga 115

Figure 4.20 Graffiti in Spanish reading "Maxo malo abre el no." Málaga, Spain.

more comprehensive description of phenomena of a seemingly international nature, such as the combination of *fuck* with nominal syntagma in the languages in which it is used.

Above all, a study is required of a truly interdisciplinary nature. Studies on the linguistic landscape are aware of this approach, as recently highlighted by Gorter and Cenoz (2024). It may be, nonetheless, that other studies will not have such a broad range of perspectives as those that characterize the research on the linguistic landscape. The English-speaking world, and especially the USA, is showing considerable interest in studying feminist movements, urban cultures, and their rhetorical and linguistic expression, although in many cases through the theoretical framework of cultural studies and not specific approaches that provides the setting for the analyses of the linguistic landscape. These studies are therefore being drafted without our findings and, to a certain extent, ours without theirs, because of mutual unawareness. It should never be forgotten that we are dealing with a study topic that is of interest to myriad specialists and that a diversity of approaches and perspectives will always be enriching.

Notes

1 This chapter is part of the project "The linguistic landscape in Malaga: Approach and mapping from a gender perspective," in Malaga University's 2nd Research, Transference, and Scientific Dissemination Plan for Young Researchers. Lead Researcher Livia C. García Aguiar. This

project has led to the creation of the corpus Ma#PL#aga, whose results will be publicly disclosed in 2025. The author is a member of IGiuma, the University of Málaga Gender Institute.

These institutional acknowledgements would be incomplete without referring to the discussion of ideas the author has held with different colleagues: Ávila Muñoz, Frabotta, García Rivero, Rodríguez Iglesias and Von Essen, all of them from the University of Málaga, along with Maux and Salgado Robles from Strasbourg University and The City University of New York.

2 In the Spanish case, mention should be made of the texts by Marín Romero and Ribas 2021 and Molina Martos 2021. More recently, the author has addressed the topic jointly in Esteba Ramos and García Aguiar (2024) and individually in Esteba Ramos (2024). Furthermore, there are several online Master's presentations available at academia.edu, such as those by Marín Romero et al. (2017) and Dackow (2020).

3 The language-identity relationship has a long research history in (socio)linguistic studies. Since Labov (1963) used this correlation to explain his study findings at Martha's Vineyard, or Lakoff (1973) linked it to women's discourse, the list of studies devoted to its analysis is extensive and has numerous connections with sociology, anthropology, and psychology. An overview of the genealogy of this relationship can be found in Llamas and Watt (2010).

4 A dedicated study of this nature would render redundant the genealogy of the label *linguistic landscape*, whereby we refer to the introduction to this volume. This is undoubtedly the right time to call upon the different studies on public signs to consider the research published in languages other than English, and especially those studies in Spanish, with an abundant and highly significant literature output in recent decades.

5 This interpretative explanation of the public arena has been accepted since the first research into the linguistic landscape (cf., for example, Ben Rafael et al. 2006, 9), as summarized and explained by Cenoz and Gorter (2024).

6 This has been highlighted on several occasions in seminal studies, such as the one by Ben-Rafael et al. (2006, 8), and repeated particularly in studies on graffiti and wall messages, such as the one by Blommaert and Maly (2014, 3).

7 We are considering the extent to which the public at large is aware of the linguistic landscape and is impacted by it. We are concerned solely by the possibility that this is indeed the case. We agree with those that since the earliest research on the linguistic landscape advocate an analysis of the perception and analysis of these signs, even as the field's major challenge (Gorter and Cenoz 2017), which today should be based on eye-tracking technologies. There is no doubt that the ultimate aim of many of the examples analysed is to ensure that the *ethos*, the emitter's identity, both individualized and minority, takes hold in society (cf. Ramalle and Rodríguez Barcia 2015, 133), whereby the online-offline conjunction will be of inestimable assistance.

8 We should not ignore the fact that this plethora of signs is growing in step with the aesthetic value given to words nowadays (cf., Järlehed and Jaworski 2015, based in turn on Jaworski 2015), whereby many people become a kind of *walking advertisement*, responsible for bearing slogans that reveal their own perception of their identity (or, at least, of how they want to present themselves to the world). At the same time, this linguistic landscape constitutes a commitment by those that choose it on the grounds of certain causes (Jaworski and Jia Lou 2021, 131).

9 In linguistic terms, globalization involves the ongoing diffusion of a common vocabulary referring to people, places, and ideas that are shared the world over and which are undergoing constant renewal (Gorter, Cenoz and Van der Worp 2021, 190), either in the original or in its translation into local ones.

A feminist discourse in the linguistic landscape of Málaga 117

10 Transnational feminists have had a major voice between global and local life, establishing a community that overcomes cultural, moral, and ideological barriers, in its struggle against global neoliberalism (Radhakrishnan 2009, 36–39).
11 Based on the three historical forms of identity-building proposed by Castells ([1997] 2002), feminism pivots between *identidad resistencia* [resistance identity], in that to a certain extent it opposes globalization and resorts to local roots in which to create a haven of solidarity, and *identidad proyecto* [project identity], which seeks a new identity in favour of transforming the social structure.
12 From the perspective of a critical sociolinguistics, the belittling of the Andalusian people and their culture has been studied by Rodríguez Iglesias (2022b).
13 For a general view of the movement, cf. Chacón-Chamorro, and Terrón-Caro (2021). This chapter proposes 2016 as the date for the creation of the Andalusian feminist movement, as opposed to hegemonic feminism, as instigated by the work of Mar Gallego. Its precepts include the notion that within this context gender is compounded by other discriminatory variables. The demands made include the recovery of flamenco, carnival festivities, and Andalusian varieties, in line with multicultural and post-colonial theories.
14 A current of thought has emerged in recent years that argues that the linguistic identity of peoples should have an orthographic correlate (cf. Ávila Muñoz 2021, 44, who cites studies on the Afro-American context by Young 2007 and Young et al. 2014). Indications have been forthcoming accordingly in other languages to foster writing guidelines that promote social justice and equity (cf. Inoue 2015). As part of this trend, one might include the spelling proposal (in Spanish) put forward by the EPA (Er Prinçipito Andalûh) group for the Spanish used in Andalusia (https://andaluhepa.files.wordpress.com/2019/10/propuesta-de-ortografc3ada-andaluza-epa-actualizada-2019-docx.pdf, retrieved in March 2024).

It has been inspired by *Er Prinzipito Andalú* by *Huan Porrah* (Juan Porras). Ávila Muñoz (2021, 45) has described it as a complex proposal because it contains heterogeneous and multilayered variations in pronunciation, and Del Rey Quesada and García de Paredes (2022) offer also a critical review of this proposal.

Nevertheless, although certain texts in the feminist linguistic landscape involve the reproduction of a dissident spelling of a particularly Andalusian nature, they do not fully embrace these proposals either because, as we shall see in due course, they above all affect the syllable coda, drawing close to the intermediate Andalusian variety.
15 The consideration made by Milani could not be closer to the truth (2013, 211) regarding his own research: only certain data can be viewed as such at a given moment and when analyzed by a specific person. As an Andalusian woman, I have felt that the data called upon me to analyse them, a call that I have responded to in very good company. After writing this chapter, I am profoundly aware of the meaning of disinterested cooperation and, especially, sisterhood. I should like to express my gratitude to all those people around me that have contributed by submitting examples: not only the students and teaching staff at Malaga University, but also different individuals linked to organizations involved in 8M, together with social media users that have shared their examples and collaborated by providing their geolocation and answering further questions I have asked them (I am referring especially to @mi.cuaderno.rojo).
16 I have used these three lines in three prior contributions, respectively, on my own or in co-authorship with García Aguiar, which has led to the article by Esteba Ramos and García Aguiar (2024). In addition, a sample of the collection used for these

contributions was presented as a photo exhibition at the 2nd IGiuma seminar held in March 2024.
17 Although this research proposal is eminently linguistic in nature, it stands to reason that an approach to the linguistic landscape in this ambit is greatly enriched by an interdisciplinary viewpoint (Cenoz and Gorter 2024, 56), thereby providing the research with a more semiotic nuance (Canakis 2019, 269) and listening to those individuals that are conducting an analysis of modern society and its gender demands. In order to fall in line with the content of the monographic work in which this chapter appears and for reasons of space, I have not given any greater weight to interdisciplinarity. Subsequent studies will include part of the research stream that is being conducted in the English-speaking world and whose results may be used for comparison with Spain.
18 https://commons.wikimedia.org/w/index.php?search=dump+your+porn+addicted+boyfriend&title=Special:MediaSearch&go=Go&type=image. Last accessed March 2024.
19 Expressions of support have been found in Spanish for the Spanish female football player Jenny Hermoso and her infamous kiss under the hashtag #seacabo (enough is enough), which was worn, for example, by the feminists of the ROSA – Socialist Feminist Movement in Ireland in the summer of 2023.
20 Its accompanying nominal syntagma may be written in English, although cases are also beginning to be reported in other languages, such as Spanish, French, Italian, and German.
21 These networks should be considered in the light of those academic studies that address urban cultures such as hip-hop in relation to feminism, which have been scarcely studied and even dismissed within a European academic context (Marín Villarreal 2020).
22 There is only a relevant token presence of other languages. We have only documented one homemade placard by a French woman that has used her mother tongue to salute the figure of the French politician Simone Veil and support France's recently passed constitutional right to abortion.
23 Two cases might help to explain why these marks do not appear in the demonstrations: (i) when the demonstrators mustered at the Café Feminista, run by the autonomous feminist block, they discussed the possibility of writing "*estamos hartas*" with an aspiration sign on the "h"; although this spelling was discarded in the end; (ii) in an interview with a demonstrator from the Medusa Colectiva group, she explained the need to validate the Andalusian way of speaking, to use it for political purposes, and highlight the meaning of the slogans used in the street; nevertheless, as the groups in the demonstrations are more heterogenous, there is a tendency toward harmonization, thereby depriving them of any linguistic vindication. In both cases, the social players' repertoire of options considers the use of spellings linked to the Andalusian way of speaking, yet for reasons that have not been explained or through a willingness for national "harmonization," this idea is dismissed: the simple consideration of the possibility already implies the need felt for linguistic expression.
24 The samples gathered on an anecdotic basis include a *voseante* placard using the *vos* form of address. We did not have the opportunity to interview its author. It uses a slogan that is frequently seen in demonstrations throughout the Spanish-speaking world, and especially so in the movement in the *rioplatense* [River Plate] area. It might simply involve the repetition of a phrase seen in a demonstration in countries such as Argentina or Chile.

References

Ávila Muñoz, Antonio. 2021. "¿Es legítimo (y necesario) escribir las variedades no estándares de las lenguas? El caso del español de Andalucía." In *Langues romanes non stardard*, edited by Ivona Piechnik, and Marta Wicherek, 43–56. Kraków: Uniwersytet Jagielloński, Biblioteka Jagiellońska Kraków.

Barthes, Roland. 2002. *Oeuvres complètes*, I (1942–1961), II (1962–1967), III (1968–1971), IV (1972–1976) and V (1977–1980), edited by Éric Marty. Paris: Seuil.

Ben-Rafael, Elizer. 2009. "A Sociological Approach to the Study of Linguistic Landscapes." In *Linguistic Landscape. Expanding the Scenery*, edited by Elana Shohamy, and Durk Gorter, 40–54. New York: Routledge.

Del Rey Quesada, Santiago, and Elena Méndez García de Paredes. 2022. "Traducción y normalización lingüística o el triunfo de la divergencia a la fuerza: el caso de *Le petit prince* andaluz." *Nueva revista de filología hispánica*, 70, no. 1: 53–94.

Ben-Rafael, Elizer et al. 2006. "Linguistic Landscape as Symbolic Construction of the Public Space: The Case of Israel." In *Linguistic Landscape. A New Approach to Multilingualism*, edited by Durk Gorter, 7–30. Bristol, Buffalo, Toronto: Multilingual Matters.

Blommaert, Jan. 2010. *The Sociolinguistics of Globalization*. Cambridge: Cambridge University Press.

Blommaert, Jan. 2016. "'Meeting of Styles' and the Online Infrastructures of Graffiti." *Applied Linguistics Review*, 7, no. 2: 99–115.

Blommaert, Jan, and Ico Maly. 2014. "Ethnographic Linguistic Landscape Analysis and Social Change: A Case Study." *Tilburg Papers in Culture Studies*, no. 100: 1–27.

Blommaert, Jan, and Ico Maly. 2019. "Invisible Lines in the Online-Offline Linguistic Landscape." *Tilburg Papers in Culture Studies*, no. 223.

Bucholtz, Mary, and Elena Skapoulli. 2009. "Introduction: Youth Language at the Intersection: From Migration to Globalization," *Pragmatics*, 19, no. 1: 1–16.

Campos, Ricardo M. O. 2020. "Youth Street Cultures: Between Online and Offline Circuits." In *Routledge Handbook of Street Culture*, edited by Jeffrey Ian Ross, and Peter K. Manning, 59–70. Routledge.

Canakis, Costas. 2019. "Further Advances in Linguistic Landscape Research: Language and Identitiy-Work in Public Space." *Punctum*, 5, no. 1: 264–270.

Cárdenas Neira, Camila. 2016. "El movimiento estudiantil chileno (2006-2016) y el uso de la web social: nuevos repertorios de acción e interacción comunicativa." *Última década*, 24, no. 45: 93–116.

Castells, Manuel. [1997] 2002. *La era de la información: economía, sociedad y cultura. Vol. II, El poder de la identidad*. Madrid: Alianza Editorial.

Chacón-Chamorro, Victoria, and Teresa Terrón-Caro. 2021. "Feminismo andaluz: acercamiento a una nueva línea de pensamiento feminista." *Athenea digital. Revista de pensamiento e investigación social*, 21, no. 2. https://doi.org/10.5565/rev/athenea.2845

Dackow, Cynthia. 2020. "Paisajes Semióticos Disidentes. La retórica de los feminismos del 8M y 9M." *Master dissertation*. www.academia.edu

Epstein, Brandon W. 2023. "English as 'The Gay Comfort Zone' of Hybrid Youth Identities." In *The Routledge Handbook of Language and Youth Culture*, edited by Bente Svendsen, and Rickart Jonsson. Routledge.

Esteba Ramos, Diana. 2014. "Aproximación al paisaje lingüístico de Málaga: Préstamos y reflejos de una realidad lingüística plural." *Recherches*, 12: 165–187.

Esteba Ramos, Diana. (2024). "El paisaje lingüístico como fuente de análisis para la creatividad léxica: el caso de los usos neológicos de la esfera de los feminismos." en *La creatividad en las humanidades: perspectivas singulares y universales*, edited by Pedro José Chamizo Domínguez, 53–74. Madrid: Renacimiento.

Esteba Ramos, Diana, and Livia C. García Aguiar. (in press). "¿Cómo reflejan nuestras calles los usos inclusivos? El caso del paisaje lingüístico malagueño (2016-2023)." en *Estudios Aplicados sobre el paisaje lingüístico*, edited by Mercedes de la Torre García. Valencia: Tirant Lo Blanch.

Fernández-Planells, Ariadna et al. 2014. "Communication Among Young People in the #spanishrevolution. Uses of Online-Offline Tools to Obtain Information About the #acampadabcn." *New Media & Society*, 16, no. 8: 1287–1308.

Foucault, Michel. 1977. "What is an Author?." In *Language, Counter-Memory, Practice*, edited by Donald F. Bouchard, 113–138. New York: Cornell University Press.

Fraser, Nancy. 1990. "Rethinking the Public Sphere: A Contribution to the Critique of Actually Existing Democracy." *Social Text*, 25–26: 56–80.

Gaggero, Caterina et al. 2002. "Graffiti, espacio social y política." *Comunicación y medios*, 13: 101–110.

Giddens, Anthony. 2001. *Un mundo desbocado. Los efectos de la globalización en nuestras vidas*. Madrid: Santillana.

Gonçalves, Kellie, and Tommaso M. Milani. 2022. "Street Art/Art in the Street – Semiotics, Politics, Economy." *Social Semiotics*, 32, no. 4: 425–443. DOI: 10.1080/10350330.2022.2114724

Gonçalves, Kellie. 2019. "The Semiotic Paradox of Street Art: Gentrification and the Commodification of Bushwick, Brooklyn." In *Making Sense of People, Place and Linguistic Landscapes*, edited by Amiena Peck, Quentin E. Williams and Christopher Stroud, 141–160. London: Bloomsbury.

Gorter, Durk. 2006. "Introduction: The Study of the Linguistic Landscape as a New Approach to Multilingualism." In *Linguistic Landscape. A New Approach to Multilingualism*, edited by Durk Gorter, 1–6. Bristol, Buffalo, Toronto: Multilingual Matters.

Gorter, Durk, and Jasone Cenoz. 2017. "Linguistic Landscape and Multilingualism." In *Language Awareness and Multilingualism. Encyclopedia of Language and Education*, edited by Jasone Cenoz et al., 233–245. Cham: Springer.

Gorter, Durk, and Jasone Cenoz. 2024. *A Panorama of Linguistic Landscape Studies*. Multilingual Matters/Channel View Publications.

Gorter, Durk et al. 2021. "Global and Local Forces in Multilingual Landscapes: A Study of a Local Market." In *Spaces of Multilingualism*, edited by Robert Blackwood, and Unn Røyneland, 188–212. New York: Routledge.

Guerra, Nicola. 2013. "Muri puliti popoli muti: analisi temática e dinamiche linguistiche del fenomeno del graffitismo a Roma." *Forum Italicum: A Journal of Italian Studies*, 47, no. 3, 570–585.

Habermas, Jürgen. 2001. "El valle de lágrimas de la globalización." *Claves de la Razón Práctica*, 109, 4–11.

Järlehed, Johan, and Adam Jaworski. 2015. "Typographic Landscaping: Creativity, Ideology, Movement." *Social Semiotics*, 25, no. 2: 117–125.

Jaworski, Aam, and Jackie Jia Lou. 2021. "#wordswewear: Mobile Texts, Expressive Persons and Conviviality in Urban Spaces." *Social Semiotics*, 31, no. 1: 108–135.

Kristeva, Julia. 1967. "Bakhtine, le mot, le dialogue el le roman." *Critique*, 239: 438–65.

Labov, Wiliam. 1963. "The Social Motivation of a Sound Change." *WORD*, 19, no. 3: 273–309.

Lakoff, Robin. 1973. "Language and Woman's Place." *Language in Society*, 2, no. 1: 45–80.

Lee, Jayeon, and Young Shin Lim. 2014. "Who Says What About Whom: Young Voters' Impression Formation of Political Candidates on Social Networking Sites." *Mass Communication Society*, 17, no. 3: 553–572.

Llamas, Carmen, and Dominic Watt. 2010. *Language and Identities*. Edinburgh University Press.

MacDowall, Lachlan John, and Poppy de Souza. 2018. "'I'd Double Tap That!!': Street Art, Graffiti, and Instagram Research." *Media, Culture & Society*, 40, no. 1: 3–22.

Marín Romero, Alba et al. 2017. "Paisajes lingüísticos de disidencia: reconstrucción de la imagen de la mujer en las calles de Barcelona." *Master dissertation*. www.academia.edu

Marín Romero, Alba, and Montserrat Ribas. 2021. "Paisajes discursivos en movimiento: análisis de la manifestación feminista del 8 de marzo de 2020 en Barcelona." *Discurso & Sociedad*, 15, no. 3: 647–678.

Martín Rojo, Luisa. 2013. "Paisajes lingüísticos de indignación. Prácticas comunicativas para tomar las plazas." *Anuario Del Conflicto Social*, 2: 275–302.

Milani, Tommaso. 2013. "Expanding the Queer Linguistic Scene: Multimodality, Space and Sexuality at a South African University." *Journal of Language and Sexuality* 2, no. 2: 206–234.

Milani, Tommaso M. 2022. 'Banksy's *Walled Off Hotel* and the mediatization of street art', *Social Semiotics* 32, no. 4: 545–562. doi: 10.1080/10350330.2022.2114730.

Molina Martos, Isabel. 2021. "Urban Discourse and Civil Resistance Against Gender-Based Violence in Madrid." In *Linguistic Landscape in the Spanish-speaking World*, edited by Patricia Gubitosi, and Michelle Ramos Pellicia, 135–158. John Benjamins, Ámsterdam: Filadelfia.

Nelson, Cynthia D. 2010. "A Gay Immigrant Student's Perspective: Unspeakable Acts in the Language Class." *TESOL Quarterly*, 44, no. 3: 441–464.

Ramalle, Fernando, and Susana Rodríguez Barcia. 2015. "Graffiti y conflicto lingüístico: el paisaje urbano como espacio ideológico." *Revista Internacional de Lingüística Iberorrománica*, 25, no. 1: 131–153.

Robertson, Roland. 1992. *Globalization: Social Theory and Global Culture*. London: Sage.

Rodríguez Iglesias, Ígor. 2022a. Desespacialización y privilegio en el discurso glotopolítico en la prensa sobre mujeres andaluzas. Implicaciones para la comunicación intercultural y el multilingüismo. *Círculo de lingüística aplicada a la comunicación*, 91, 97–112.

Rodríguez Iglesias, Ígor. 2022b. *La lógica de inferiorización de las variedades lingüísticas no dominantes: etnografía sociolingüística crítica del andaluz*. Berlín: Peter Lang.

Sandvoss, Cornel. 2015. "Popular Culture, Fans, and Globalization." In *The Routledge International Handbook of Globalization Studies*, edited by Bryan S. Turner, and Robert J. Holton, 395–411. London: Routledge International Handbooks, Taylor and Francis Inc.

Screti, Francesco. 2015. "The Ideological Appropriation of the Letter <k> in the Spanish Linguistic Landscape." *Social Semiotics*, 25, no. 2: 200–208.

Shohamy, Elana et al. 2010. (eds.). *Linguistic Landscape in the City*. Bristol, Buffalo, Toronto: Multilingual Matters.

Radhakrishnan, Smitha. 2009. "Limiting Theory: Rethinking Approaches to Cultures of Globalization." In *The Routledge International Handbook of Globalization Studies*, edited by Bryan S. Turner, and Robert J. Holton, 23–41. London: Routledge International Handbooks, Taylor and Francis Inc.

Villena, Juan A. 1996. "Convergence and Divergence in a Standard-Dialect Continuum. Networks and Individuals in Malaga." *Sociolingüística*, 19: 112–137.

Villena, Juan A. 2001 "Identidad y variación lingüística: Sistema y síntoma en el español andaluz." In *Identidades lingüísticas en la España autonómica. Jornadas Hispánicas de la Sociedad Suiza de Estudios Hispánicos*, edited by George Bossong, and Francisco Báez de Aguilar González, 107–150. Francfort: Vervuert.

Villena, Juan A., and Matilde Vida 2020. "Variation, Identity and Indexicality in Southern Spanish. On the Emergence of a New Variety in Urban Andalusia." In *Intermediate Language Varieties: Koinai and Regional Standards in Europe,* edited by Massimo Cerruti, and Stavruola Tsiplakou, 149–162. Amsterdam: John Benjamins.

5 Bilingual and monolingual *universcapes*

Language choices and multimodal patterns of communication

Izaskun Elorza and Vasilica Mocanu

Introduction

Although recently there has been a growing interest in linguistic landscapes in educational settings, or "schoolscapes" (Gorter 2018), university landscapes have been somehow neglected, and the studies carried out so far present a composite picture which makes any generalization elusive.[1] With the aim of exploring the governing bodies' policies for adopting one specific language for institutional communication (e.g. Legge 2015), studies have compared different universities (Yavari 2012), mismatches between language policy and language use in multilingual contexts (Abbas, Samad, Imam and Berowa 2022; Kadenge 2015; Spolsky and Cooper 1991), or language use in relation to gender inclusiveness (Bosworth 2019). However, in addition to cataloging language policies and use, university linguistic landscape studies (henceforth ULLS) can also reveal the tensions and relationships among the different social groups who populate them. In fact, Blommaert and Maly (2015) contend that, in order to explain the connections between the languages attested in an environment and the communities populating it, the relationships among them, or their patterns of social interaction, it is necessary to adopt "a more maturely semiotic approach, in which the signs themselves are given greater attention both individually (signs are multimodal and display important qualitatively typological differences) and in combination with each other (the *landscape*, in other words)" (193).

In the Philippines, a country linguistically and culturally diverse, Abbas, Samad, Imam and Berowa (2022) carried out a qualitative and descriptive study of the linguistic landscape of Mindanao State University, analyzing the number of languages used, the language choice and the types of signs. They found that one of its campuses was characterized by a sociolinguistic paradox: while the reality of the school community was multilingual, its linguistic landscape showed mostly monolingual signs in English. This goes in line with Kadenge (2015), who examined the linguistic landscape of Wits University, in South Africa, pointing to what the author calls largely a reflection of a failed institutional language policy which reproduced a monolingual, English-based language ideology. In Europe, Legge (2015) analyzed the linguistic landscape of Stockholm University in relation to its linguistic policy to promote parallel use of Swedish and English.

DOI: 10.4324/9781032687087-6

Bosworth's (2019) study of gender-inclusive linguistic practices, as evidenced in a representative corpus of signs photographed in interior spaces of six Parisian universities, found that the signage created by students displayed a considerably higher rate of inclusivity than official signage. Yavari (2012) explored the linguistic landscapes of Linköping University (Sweden) and that of ETH Zürich (Switzerland), two universities particularly interesting because both receive many international students, but as Sweden is a monolingual country and Switzerland a multilingual one, the comparison yielded insightful results regarding the public use of different languages in those linguistic settings and their impact on society. And in the United States of America, Im (2023) analyzed how the strategic changes introduced to respond to the pandemic in a midwestern university broadened its identity into a new "spatial identity,", understanding "space" not just as a physical construct but as a social one.

What all these studies seem to suggest is that ULLS are moving, from an emphasis on cataloging language policies and language use in universities, to an interest in the population who interact in those environments as well.

Im's (2023) study raises the question of the implications of studying language from a spatial perspective. According to spatial discourse analysis (Ericsson 2023; Pennycook 2009; Ravelli and McMurtrie 2016), the choices made in spatial design create meanings about what we perceive in built environments, how we experience them, and how we behave and interact with them. Hence, overlapping with linguistic policies and use in them, buildings constitute "spatial texts" that are inherently multimodal and environmentally situated, and that we "read" when moving around them. Consequently, foregrounding their populating users as part of dynamic meaning-making processes through their interactions, not only *in* the designed environment but *with* the environment as well, is seen in this chapter as an essential part of ULLS, and the shift from an emphasis on language policies and language use into that on language users is understood as a need to approach them as university *semiotic* landscapes instead, what we term *universcapes*.

Some researchers (e.g. Pennycook 2009) argue for a focus on the dynamicity of sign production in a landscape which is constantly under production. In doing so, *universcapes* become also polyphonic spaces where different voices manifest, interact and communicate, in addition to the institutional official voice of governing bodies, who are in control of the semiotic space. In this respect, ULLS have often placed the focus on students' voices.

Students' voices often occupy *universcapes* as graffiti, an area which is still under-researched in ULLS (Chen 2023). Among the recent studies that delve into "campus graffiti," Ferris and Banda (2018) adopted a multisemiotic approach to analyze graffiti in men and women's toilets at the University of Cape Town, shedding light into how students appropriate discourse from other contexts and practices. Interestingly, they found that resemiotization was constructed along a dialogic trajectory across context, space, practice, and time, so that students' discourses were informed by and reflected social and political changes and were also woven dialogically by intertwining the voices of different actors who contribute to them. Lapyai (2003) delved into university students' graffiti in Thailand, where graffiti are deemed illegal, as a form of rebellion and resistance, and hence from a perspective on graffiti as transgressive social action (Pennycook 2009). Through a qualitative content analysis framework, Lapyai (2003) examined graffiti in men and women toilets in three universities in Thailand to try to understand and illustrate how, despite the strictly illegal status of graffiti in the country, students still opted for transgressing legal boundaries and kept on using this means of expression and the toilets as spaces for communication. Although these two studies focus on what has been termed "toilet graffiti," *universcapes* cover other types of "campus graffiti."

University dorms in Iran were the *universcape* studied by Moghaddam and Murray (2023), comparing male and female graffiti to scrutinize their communicative functions and gender differences from a systemic functional linguistic perspective. They found that graffiti allow students to express affective states and personal concerns, which eventually determined the authors to claim for a more "sympathetic view" towards a practice traditionally considered illegal and vandalous (Moghaddam and Murray 2023, 738). Similarly, Chen (2023) examined identity construction through graffiti in the campus walls of a university in Beijing (China) and demonstrated how graffiti artists "engage in information dissemination through both one-way output and two-way interaction," employing "written and pictorial symbols to express their identity" and using "metaphors and symbols to create deeper layers of meaning" (Chen 2023, 47). The study concluded that there is a need for graffiti campus management in order to find a balance between the freedom of expression in graffiti and campus order. As we can see, studies of "campus graffiti" in *universcapes* tend to recognize graffiti as university students' need for expression, and thus they advocate for governing bodies to adopt an inclusive approach, understanding graffiti as a communicative practice (rather than as vandalism), which requires a certain commitment from governing bodies to solve tensions within the social structure of the university.

Considering signs not just in isolation, but also as contributions to a whole that conforms the specific landscape of a community, as Blommaert and Maly (2015) suggest, we expect to find students' voices interacting with many different addressees, including governing bodies as well. An interesting question is how they construct their messages particularly when interacting with interlocutors at the top of the social structure. Equally interesting for the *universcape* is to explore how the governing bodies in control make their choices to construct their institutional identity, as well as to engage their addressees in the norms and values that the institution promotes. In this way, ULLS can provide a better insight into how universities fit into the picture of "schoolscapes" from a more comprehensive perspective.

This study aims to fill a gap in ULLS by presenting a study which compares the *universcapes* of two Spanish universities. As scholars as well as faculty members of the two institutions analyzed, we came to this research curious about how multilingualism would be present in the linguistic landscape of two universities which have different language policies, as one is located in a bilingual context (Lleida) and the other in a monolingual one (Salamanca). The complexity of signs we found during data collection and discussions deciding which of them were representative of each *universcape* made us move from a linguistic perspective into a semiotic one, as it became clear that cataloging the number of languages found would have been just a too partial and somehow superficial description of the landscapes perceived. This chapter presents an analysis of the language choices made by both universities, the signs found in them produced by the institutional voice as well as that of the students, and the ways chosen by governing bodies to persuade addressees about their norms and values. After a description of the methodology applied, we present a representative sample of our findings, illustrated with photographs from the two *universcapes*, together with a discussion about their relevance for ULLS.

Methodology

With an initial aim to explore the diversity of multilingualism in two Spanish universities, Universitat de Lleida and Universidad de Salamanca, our first decisions (after Backhaus 2006) were to delimit the geographical survey area, and to determine the survey items to analyze. We opted for looking into the faculties where language studies are carried out, which also receive international students, as we expected to maximize the range of languages present. An initial decision that we had to make was to choose a criterion for delimiting the geographical area from a comparable perspective. The structure of each university reflects a specific model of organization and evolution and, consequently, the buildings of different universities do not match in terms of the organization of their schools or faculties. We were convinced that our study should focus on the users of the environments rather than on the buildings per se, and so we opted for setting the geographical survey area to all the buildings comprising the departments, faculty offices and classrooms of the degrees of languages and of history (one building in the case of the bilingual university, and four in the case of the monolingual one).

After we collected our data, and as a result of our discussions about how to categorize them, we opted for a multimodal analytical approach, based on Halliday's (1978) comprehensive understanding of language as social semiotic and on Kress and Van Leeuwen's (2006, 2021) visual social semiotics. Two perspectives on multimodal analysis were particularly relevant for our study. We considered recent work on typographic landscaping (Curtin 2015; Järlehed 2015; Järlehed and Jaworski 2015; Screti 2015; Thurlow 2021), and on spatial discourse analysis (Ericsson 2023; Pennycook 2009; Ravelli and McMurtrie 2016), also developed from Hallidayan meaning-making semiotics and already mentioned in the previous section.

The fact that we are faculty members with personal experience in the chosen *universcapes* on a daily basis inspired us to adopt a methodology of "research walking," as proposed by Lamb, Gallagher and Knox (2019).[2] Hence, we took unscripted walks on three sessions visiting all the accessible spaces in the buildings of the faculties studied, which allowed us "an opportunity for reflection whilst simultaneously participating in the embodied experiences of the field[,] [r]ather than undertaking observation from the periphery" (Lamb, Gallagher and Knox 2019,

58). Thanks to the possibility of capturing data with two technological devices (mobile phone and iPad), these walks allowed us to experience the different environments and observe the linguistic variety and diversity present in them. Hence, the data collected attests and represents our own interactions with the environments and our immediate, affective experience of the messages in the semiotic signs found in them.

In order to scrutinize how power dynamics are established and enacted through language and other semiotic resources in the chosen *universcapes*, we decided to focus on the signs authored by two stakeholders. First, the governing bodies in control of the semiotic space, or institutional voice, which is associated with a top-down position in the power control in this context; and second, the voice of the largest population at the university, or students' voice. Although we will be referring to them in this way throughout the chapter, we understand that each group embodies a variety of voices. For example, some of the signage choices are made by the governing bodies of the faculty and for the faculty, whereas others are made for the university as a whole; choices in students' messages can also derive from individual decisions but also from choices made by a student group.

Context

Universitat de Lleida

Universitat de Lleida is located in the city of Lleida, home to 120,000 inhabitants, being the "largest demographic, economic and cultural center in inland Catalonia."[3] The city is in the north-east of Spain, and 155 km west from Barcelona. Situated in a bilingual community (both Catalan and Spanish are official languages), Lleida has strong Catalan traditions and a national identity. In relation to linguistic policy of the university, the webpage of Universitat de Lleida states that both Catalan and Spanish receive the same respect, and that faculty as well as students "have the right to express themselves in the official language that they prefer."[4] The fact that the terms chosen by the institution talk about "respect" and "rights" anticipates tensions between the use of one or the other, and makes us wonder about whether one of them will be dominant in this universcape over the other or if they will share the semiotic space in some way.

The data available in 2023 shows that Universitat de Lleida had a total of 18,742 students and 1,959 employees (teaching staff, administrative staff, Predoc and Postdoc researchers).[5] In the academic year 2021–2022, it received 309 international students, with 6.8% of international students in MA studies and 17.7% of international students in Doctoral studies. A total of 8.4% of the research staff were also foreign scholars.

The university has five different campuses (one of them in a nearby location) and five affiliated centers. The present study focuses on Campus del Rectorat, comprising a nineteenth-century building in the historical center of Lleida. A total of twelve bachelor's degrees and four MA Degrees are taught in this campus. It is also where the Doctoral School is located.

Universidad de Salamanca

Located in the north-western part of Spain, Universidad de Salamanca, founded in 1218, is considered the oldest Hispanic university. Currently, it has around 30,000 students scattered between its five different campuses. It is situated in the city of Salamanca, a monolingual area where Spanish is the only official language. It is inhabited by around 140,000 people, and situated 180 km from Madrid and 123 km from the border with Portugal. The university has had historical international relationships with other cultures, some of them represented through institutions such as the Hispanic-Japanese Cultural Centre, the Centre for Brazilian Studies, or the Institute of Iberoamerican Studies. Both the city and the university claim their international referential position as a site for learning Spanish as an additional language, which is clearly reflected in the presence of numerous private language schools that offer this type of tuition. University of Salamanca is also responsible for elaborating DELE diplomas, official certifications for Spanish as an additional language.[6]

The present study collected data from two faculties situated in the Historical Campus: The Faculty of Philology (which offers eleven Bachelor Degrees and eight MA Degrees) and the Faculty of Geography and History (which offers five Bachelor Degrees, one double Bachelor Degree, and four MA Degrees). These faculties cover four buildings in total, located at very short distance from each other. Three different buildings of the Faculty of Philology were examined: Palacio de Anaya, a building from the eighteenth century, where the departments of Hispanic, Classical, and Hebrew and Aramaic language and literature studies are located; Hospedería de Anaya, contiguous part of the former and home of the Modern Philologies Department (French, German, Italian, Portuguese, and Oriental Asian Studies), and Juan del Enzina building, next to the other two, and a modern edification consisting mainly of classrooms for the faculty taught degrees.

At a short walking distance, the Faculty of Geography and History is situated in a building from the sixteenth century which underwent a serious renovation in the 1980s. It is home to History, Geography, Arts History, Music, and Humanities studies.

Data collection and categorization

The empirical data used in this study were collected in the first semester of 2023 through an exhaustive observation and photographing of the signs carried out with a mobile phone camera and an iPad device. In particular, the data from Universitat de Lleida were collected in a single round which consisted of a "research walk". At Universidad de Salamanca, as more buildings had to be covered, data were collected in two rounds: a general observation and collection of a few data and a second, more in-depth data collection at a later stage. Pictures were taken of all signs found and subsequently classified according to the building they were situated in.

Bilingual and monolingual univerpages 129

In this chapter, we understand "sign" as multimodal sign, which consists of a combination of visual and verbal and/or graphical resources "within a spatially definable frame," thus extending Backhaus's (2006) definition to cover signs constructed multimodally, as the ones found in the *univerpage*. Four categorizations are used in this study: (1) language choice (Spanish, Catalan, mixed, any other); (2) typographic choice (including color); (3) sign type (e.g., graffiti); and (4) authorship (institutional voice vs students' voice), to explore the involved power dynamics.

Findings: *Univerpages* at Universitat de Lleida and Universidad de Salamanca

From the perspective of spatial discourse studies, "navigational paths" contribute to "organizational meaning" in buildings seen as spatial texts, either by means of literal pathways or indicated by sequences of salient elements which guide the direction of the users' movements vectorially (Ravelli and McMurtrie 2016, 108). Interestingly, not only are those vectors understood as "spatial semiotic resources that facilitate movement" (Ravelli and McMurtrie 2016, 109), but they also function as an indicator of how the space is regulated semiotically. In the universities studied, the language chosen for navigating instructions is the first noticeable difference between the two. In the case of Universitat de Lleida, signs combine the choice of Catalan language together within the use of a sans-serif typography and grey and wine-red colors, as the combination chosen by Universitat de Lleida to represent the institution. Figure 5.1 shows one of the signs found. At Universidad de Salamanca, signage choices are the use of Spanish language together with a sophisticated typography, as explained below.[7]

In addition to language and color choices, the strategic use of typography by Universidad de Salamanca represents its most salient feature in relation to choices made to construct corporate identity and top-down communication. In this chapter we understand, along Nørgaard (2009), that typography involves all visual signifiers (handwriting, calligraphy, and printed typography) along a continuum, rather than as separate semiotic systems, so that typographic choices, together with language choice and the choice of the space used mark a contrast between top-down and bottom-up dynamics and can reveal how divergent voices are crafted in the *univerpage*.

Typographic choices as institutional identity

Vítor typography is the set of letterforms and typefaces designed for corporate identity to achieve distinctiveness and convey historical rootedness. The Latin language is used for honorific inscriptions, but "latinized" names printed with this typography are used for signs of facilities or services (for example, "Mercatus" is the name of the university shop). The use of Latin language showcases the image of rootedness and suggests that institutional signage is designed more "to be seen" than "to be read" (Järlehed 2015, 166) by tourists and visitors, as snapshots in

130 *Ethnographic Landscapes and Language Ideologies in the Spanish State*

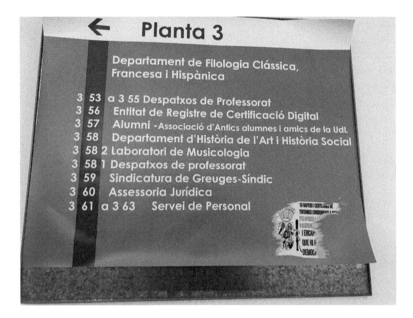

Figure 5.1 Signage choices at Universitat de Lleida.

Figure 5.2 suggest. Interestingly, *Vítor* typography has become an identity hallmark not just of Universidad de Salamanca, but also of the town itself. Shops, especially around the historical campus, often use this typography for brand labelling.

Graffiti at Universidad de Salamanca

A broad definition of "graffiti" is adopted here to approach the semiotic space, as the "words or pictures that are written or drawn in public places, for example on walls or posters" (Collins 2024). It is from this perspective that we can distinguish two types of graffiti: those regulated by the institution (top-down graffiti) and those that occupy any unregulated space, such as toilet doors or furniture (bottom-up graffiti), even trespassing these limits and making use of space devoted institutionally for official communication.

Top-down graffiti at Universidad de Salamanca

Similarly to other social institutions, universities constitute stratified and hierarchically structured semiotic spaces, and the use of traditional symbology contributes to make stratification overt. *Vítor* typography is based on a traditional symbol used at the Universidad de Salamanca (and extended to other universities) since Middle

Bilingual and monolingual universcapes 131

Figure 5.2 Vítor typography at Universidad de Salamanca.

Ages, consisting of a varying combination of the letters V-I-C-T-O-R painted in red (originally with a mixture of animal and vegetal pigments), together with the name of the student who has passed their PhD viva successfully. Vítor symbols are an institutional form of graffiti which populate semiotically regulated space on the walls of university schools or faculties, as Figure 5.3 shows, and represent institutional acceptance and academic recognition of scholar membership.

The specific locations where vítors are placed make them part of top-down communication. In the environment of the universities, top-down communication is found along the literal pathways designed with a variety of purposes in addition to guiding users' movements. As Blommaert and Maly (2015) contend, the location of signs "is not a random given, and neither is their 'syntagmatic' position relative to other signs" (194). As Figure 5.3 shows, signs point

132 *Ethnographic Landscapes and Language Ideologies in the Spanish State*

Figure 5.3 Vítors as top-down graffiti in semiotically regulated space at Universidad de Salamanca.

towards the "present" coexisting with other samples of top-down communication. Additionally, signs also point towards the "past," and very overtly in the case of vítors, which by highlighting their origins and modes of production, contribute to reify the institutional identity by pointing overtly to the past and history of the institution.

Bottom-up graffiti in unregulated semiotic spaces

The semiotically regulated space in the university designed environments corresponds in our research to the immediate environment of the main pathways in the buildings. Beyond that, graffiti covers any other kind of space, including toilets or furniture. According to Ferris and Banda (2018, 41), "[t]he confines of a toilet seem to disengage some social, political, racial and cultural inhibitions. It provides a rich site for discourses to be decontextualised from their known contexts and recontextualised in the toilet graffiti." So, while circulation of people typically sets the spaces that are semiotically regulated within university buildings, other spaces are occupied by a clutter of multilingual voices expressing dissent, emotion, or creativity from a bottom-up position.

Typographic, orthographic, and alternative spelling choices to normative practices are often present in semiotically unregulated spaces, such as the use in Spanish of the so-called "political <k>" (instead of <c> or <qu>) linked to the "politics of protest" from leftist voices of dissent (Screti 2015) and to other ideological symbolic meanings since the 1960s (Fuentes 2017), or word disemvowelling (eliding all the vowel letters in a word), as in the antifascist slogan FCK NZS, found in the linguistic landscape of both universities (Figure 5.4). These choices function as indexical tokens of social affiliation. However, the fact that the same slogan (in English) is reproduced in both environments points to an ideological expression of rejection that connects to a wider social arena, and not to the reaction to, or reflection of, a contextual socio-political situation, as was the case of the graffiti analyzed by Ferris and Banda (2018) in the University of the Western Cape, and also the one found at Universitat de Lleida shown in Figure 5.7.

Structures of student representation

Student representation in Spanish universities is regulated in such a way that students' delegates take part in the university governing bodies, also within schools or faculties. Their voices, therefore, are considered in this study top-down, as they have dedicated regulated space in the designed environment, and hence, a space where control is exerted by governing bodies. But in addition to those, there are also many students' associations involved ideologically in university life which try to make their voices heard from a bottom-up marginalized position. Lapyai (2003, 41) states that, among other reasons, university students become marginalized when they "lack access to mainstream communication outlets" or when they are "underrepresented members within their educational structures." Hence, having (or not) a dedicated space for communication marks a difference between who is considered a relevant voice in the university, and who is marginalized. When the organizational meaning of the environment is not "for all" (Ericsson 2023), marginalized groups find their outlets of expression somewhere beyond regulated space.

A closer look at how semiotic space is occupied by students reveals to what extent students' voices differ. We categorize as top-down students' voices those

Universitat de Lleida	Universidad de Salamanca

Figure 5.4 Bottom-up graffiti from voices of dissent.

with dedicated semiotically regulated spaces. Figure 5.5 shows the signboard of the Consell de L'Estudiantat (*Students' Council*) at Universitat de Lleida (picture a), and the door of the office of the Delegación de Estudiantes de Filología (*Philology Students' Delegation*) (picture b). Multimodal messages from both student representative structures combine visual and verbal resources to address other students for various purposes, such as promoting reusing resources: "Tria i remena. Emporta't tot el que vulguiss" (*Pick and mix. Take all you want with you*) or facilitating contact: "Contacta con nosotros" (*Get in contact with us*). The

Universitat de Lleida   Universidad de Salamanca

Figure 5.5 Top-down structures of student representation.

multimodal messages of these representative bodies resonate with the institutional voice, including the university logo as a token of institutionalized communication, or using *Vítor* typography in the Delegation logo in the case of Universidad de Salamanca, for example.

In contrast, students' associations and other voices expressing dissent tend to occupy other outlets. Figure 5.6 shows that, on one hand, the flexibility of space occupation in bottom-up communication is wide: any space is taken potentially as semiotic space, and so messages can be found anywhere (in the picture, a fountain is employed as a billboard). On the other hand, using stickers implies a difference with modes of expression like those shown in Figure 5.4. Texts constructed in stickers are concise, multimodal, and their stickiness allows them to be placed in any position and space with great versatility. The ones found in this university landscape correspond to bottom-up structures of student representation that raise voices of dissent, such as "¡Que paguen los ricos!" (*Let the rich pay!*).

Lacking a dedicated space, students often occupy spaces dedicated to other social actors. Figure 5.7 shows two samples of space occupation with different aims. The text at Universitat de Lleida is a protest demanding "llibertat persones preses i exiliades polítiques" (*freedom for imprisoned persons and political exiles*), addressing readers who are already familiar with the political contextual situation and the ideological implications of the demand. The message is constructed as a covert command (do liberate them!), and albeit using very economic resources, it stands out thanks to its strategical positioning at the center of the signboard, and to the choice of yellow color. The interpretation that this is a sample of bottom-up communication stems from the fact that the authorial voice is kept hidden, most likely to avoid social or legal negative consequences for such a controversial demand.[8]

The text at Universidad de Salamanca presents a protest against students' class schedules at the Faculty of Geography and History, calling for social action: "Ante los horarios partidos, organízate" (*In the face of split schedules, take action*). Below the command,[9] a statement provides the motivation for the protest: "Tenemos vida más allá de la Universidad" (*We have life beyond university*), implying that splitting

136 *Ethnographic Landscapes and Language Ideologies in the Spanish State*

Figure 5.6 Bottom-up structures of student representation.

the class schedule affects students' daily lives negatively. The visual resources effectively address readers by means of the direct gaze of the female character depicted, which also involves a command (Kress and Van Leeuwen 2006, 2021), and the class schedule split into two that she is holding. Even though the visual and the verbal resources present redundant information, the direct gaze engages readers effectively and the message is efficiently conveyed. The name of the faculty on top of the message, together with the authorial information of the students' association responsible for it, convey the effect that it represents a consistent voice, alternative

Bilingual and monolingual universcapes 137

Universitat de Lleida	Universidad de Salamanca

Figure 5.7 Occupation of regulated spaces.

to top-down voices, which aims to shape the university from below by calling to social action on specific aspects relevant to students.

Multimodal construction of institutional norms and values

When considering the multimodal resources employed by the universities to communicate stakeholders their norms of behavior and values, different approaches are observed. Figure 5.8 shows examples of the combination of visual and verbal strategies used by Universitat de Lleida in order to engage readers. A non-smoking policy is enforced by presenting the premises as an attractive environment where the absence of smoke, constructed verbally as "Universitat sense fum" (*University without smoke*), combines with the visual depiction of poppy flowers to create an emotionally positive effect. In contrast, a similar policy at the Universidad de Salamanca is constructed by means of the banning sign from the traffic regulation code, combined with the verbal message "Prohibido fumar" (*No smoking*), thus focusing on its warning effect instead.

Universitat de Lleida promotes a policy of water-consumption saving by means of a multimodal message in which the specific command "Utilitzeu l'aigua estrictament necessària" (*Use only the strictly necessary water*) is constructed verbally, thus addressing readers directly. The command is highlighted in green color (associated with ecology and environment) and accompanied with a statement addressing readers' awareness about their impact on the environment: "El Medi Ambient també depèn de tu" (*The environment also depends on you*). Visually, a tap leaking a water drop extends the verbal meaning by placing

138 *Ethnographic Landscapes and Language Ideologies in the Spanish State*

Figure 5.8 Top-down communication of institutional norms and values.

the focus on taking care of not leaving taps open when using the university lavatories. In terms of compositional choices, the command is placed at the top, the statement at the bottom, and the visual element is focalized at the center, thus keeping a balance between the command as an ideal and the statement as its real basis, with a salient central position for the visual element, all of which is coincidental with expected choices for an efficient communication maximizing multimodal interactional resources, according to Kress and Van Leeuwen's model (2006, 2021).

Universidad de Salamanca promotes a recycling campaign with the distribution of three containers for selective collection of recyclable material in all the university buildings. The campaign is endorsed by the university together with an externalized company responsible for this service so, even if it is uncertain who the actual creator of the message may be, we assume that their messages are representing the institutional voice of Universidad de Salamanca. As Figure 5.8 shows, the containers are accompanied by a message combining visual and verbal resources. Two commands: "antes de tirar nada, piensa en color" (*before getting rid of anything, think in colour*) and "mantengamos un entorno limpio" (*let's keep a clean environment*) are combined with a visual depiction of a male person looking down, smiling, and holding his head open to put into/take out of it the standard symbol for recycling in green color. Overlapping with this image, four containers of four different colors appear (one more than the three provided), labeled below indicating the kind of material that should go into each of them. Verbal choices point to an informal style imitating handwriting and ignoring writing norms in Spanish (capitalization and punctuation are missing), whereas letter size is used to highlight the command, which is further emphasized by writing the word "color" in red color and not in black, as the rest. The command promoting recycling appears in a smaller letter size at the bottom of the message, and hence not as an "ideal" to achieve but as something real already happening. The inclusive "mantengamos" (*let's keep...*) located next to the logo of the recycling company points to an intent to create affiliation between the readers and the company, rather than between the institutional voice of the university and the addressees. The effect then is an overall emphasis on focalizing readers' attention onto selecting the correct container for recycling, rather than on recycling itself, so the message does not seem to achieve effective engagement from addressees. All in all, a soft or passive construal of the addressees seems to be conveyed by placing the emphasis on thinking about choosing "the correct colors," rather than treating them as responsible social actors and demanding from them a more active course of action. There is no urgency or warning in the message, so mobilizing addressees for action is not needed; the environment is already clean and what has to be done is to keep it that way.

The two photos at the bottom in Figure 5.8 represent multimodal ways of conveying institutional values of responsible behavior by instructing addressees about how to wash their hands efficiently (frequent after COVID-19 pandemic in public spaces) and how to dispose of sanitary towels and tampons. These are two situated texts found in university lavatories. The choices made in each case point to addressees who are constructed multimodally in diverging ways. Universitat de Lleida's is a 'how to' text entitled "Com rentar-se les mans" (*How to clean one's hands*) and written in an impersonal style (there is no direct address), which details in ten steps how to achieve efficient hand washing. Visual elements depict hands and vectors indicating movement in a schematic style (Kress and Van Leeuwen 2006, 2021), while verbal sentences follow a pattern of infinitive structures instructing the successive steps to follow. Visual and verbal resources are coupled in such a way that the effect is clear thanks to the complementary information provided by each mode (typically the type of action is constructed verbally, whereas specific movement instructions are depicted visually).

The text at Universidad de Salamanca is constructed verbally but also makes use of *Vítor* typography for visually construing the message as institutional. It starts by describing the purpose of the container next to it: "Contenedor higiénico sólo para compresas y tampones" (*Hygienic container only for sanitary towels and tampons*). This continues with a command constructed impersonally (using an infinitive rather than an imperative verbal form): "No tirar papel higiénico" (*Do not throw toilet paper*). The emphasis is placed on the warning purpose and on indicating the addressees what not to do, so it involves an anticipation of undesired behavior.

Discussion and concluding remarks

Our study has attempted to provide a deeper insight into ULLS, by providing a comparative analysis of two universities in Spain with a different linguistic situation, in terms of what we have called *universcape*, or university semiotic landscape. Our data about signage choices has shown that, at Universitat de Lleida, even though there are two official languages in the community, only Catalan is chosen for the institutional voice. It is also the dominant language for communication in this *universcape* in general terms, as it is equally chosen for top-down and bottom-up communication, resulting in a monolingualism de facto that most likely corresponds with the mainstream ideological choices of the populating groups in that *universcape*, although toilet graffiti shows that other voices express dissent with messages in Spanish and as slogans such as FCK NZS, which attest that not all (left) ideologies are constructed from a nationalist perspective. At Universidad de Salamanca, as expected, the dominant language is Spanish, as it is the preferred language for top-down signage choices and also for bottom-up communication of university relevant issues. So, irrespective of the official bilingual (Lleida) or monolingual (Salamanca) contexts, both universities opt to resort to a single dominant language (Catalan and Spanish respectively). It is also interesting to note that, despite the sound presence of international students in both universities, English is not a language choice for signage purposes in any of two *universcapes*, unlike previous studies focusing on universities where internationalization policies have been adopted (Kadenge 2015; Legge 2015; Yavari 2012).

On the other hand, our study has also dealt with the users of the *universcapes*, and the signs they create. Previous work in ULLS has made a narrow connection between sign categories and population groups in such a way that top-down signs are assumed to correspond with the institutional voice, who exerts control regulating the semiotic space. Similarly, bottom-up signs are identified as corresponding to other stakeholders involved in communication in the *universcape* but who are not in control, namely students (both as individuals and as organized groups). Additionally, assumptions are made about graffiti being a type of bottom-up signage, as well as between different types of sign and specific locations within the semiotic space (e.g. graffiti expected to be found in toilets). By extension, top-down signs are expected to be located within officially regulated spaces and along main navigational pathways, whereas bottom-up signs are expected to be found, if existent at all, far from them.

Our analysis has revealed a somehow different picture. On one hand, a dichotomic division of power into two groups, those in control and those without, has been problematic. The data gathered has shown that, from a multimodal perspective on signage choices, the signs by students' delegates present features coincidental with top-down communication, namely corporative symbolic resources such as the university logo or the institutional typography. In addition, they are located within specifically devoted regulated space. These reasons lead us to conclude that it is not accurate to consider them bottom-up signs, so we consider them top-down instead accordingly.

On the other hand, the *universcape* of Universidad de Salamanca has shown that the automatic interpretation of graffiti as a bottom-up means of communication excludes other considerations that may apply to how people interact with them. A lay gaze on *vítors*, for example such as those of tourists, *see* them as an unusual form of graffiti: very symptomatically, a local newspaper called them "tattoos" (Europa Press Castilla y León 2017), thus constructing the built environment metaphorically as a "skin," and the *vítors* as leaving a historical "fingerprint" on it. In this way, *vítors* are seen as saliently pointing to the past, and to their origin and modes of production (Blommaert and Maly 2015, 193), while also pointing to the present, as new *vítors* are incorporated yearly to the semiotic regulated space with the involvement of the different stakeholders, including the affected doctorate student, who can start the process voluntarily.

In contrast with these symbolic signs that we interpret as top-down graffiti, the population of graffiti authored by students themselves in *universcapes*, for example, is recognized in the literature as students' need for expression, thus approaching them from an inclusive perspective which tries to showcase their value as a communication practice rather than vandalous forms of behavior.

In the *universcapes* analyzed in this chapter, we have found students' signs scattered everywhere within semiotic space, with walls, doors, and furniture used as billboards for stickers and graffiti. Yavari's (2012) analysis of a Swiss university is revealing for looking into ways how an inclusive perspective could be taken on, rather than banning or restricting the possibilities of expression. This could involve considering the possibility of providing or extending semiotic space in order to construct the "spatial text" of the university as an environment with organizational meaning potential for all, as suggested by Ericsson (2023). Yavari explains that, depending on the area in which the students' signs are located, they are under the control of the university authorities, but the author also adds that the university provides two types of noticeboards for students who are not controlled officially: those at student organizations offices and another two noticeboards at the main entrance that work independently, and are not controlled regarding the content and choice of language. Students are free to post their signs in these areas.

The suggested provision is not expected to affect the production of toilet graffiti as a means of individual expression of messages for initiating sexual contact, share testimonies about individual experiences, or express anger, among others, as attested by Ferris and Banda (2018). But providing the environment with semiotic spaces which may be said to recognize students' voices as a contribution to the conversations relevant to the university stakeholders involves necessarily that such spaces are ostensibly seen by them, and hence that they are located physically along main navigational paths in the buildings, and not in areas far from them or with difficult access. In this respect, devoting noticeboards at the main entrance of the building where students are free to contribute to them without top-down control, as in ETH Zürich University in Switzerland (Yavari 2012), seems to contribute to a more overt consideration of the students as relevant stakeholders who are visible within the organizational meaning potential of the university.

Finally, the comparison between the top-down messages in each *universcape* produced by the governing bodies to engage university members in the institutional norms and values may be taken as symptomatic of tendencies of the ways how members of those communities interact. This comparison yields a divergent view of how the institutional voice is employed for communicating in the *universcapes* studied. Our analysis suggests that Universitat de Lleida shows a richer and more efficient use of multimodal resources aimed at fostering community members' engagement with the university's norms and values, by presenting them as beneficial for the community. This is achieved through image choice with symbolic positive values, topic choice (e.g. by emphasizing the benefits to be achieved), and verbal choices that contribute to raising awareness about the global impact of single actions, or to instruct on how to act in a sustainable way. In contrast, the institutional voice of Universidad de Salamanca focuses more on impersonal banning or warning messages, does not rely on visual resources except for *Vítor* typography or conventional signs, so there is not a clear attempt to engage addressees in its values or norms efficiently, conveying a de-empowering effect on their capacity as social actors instead.

To conclude, although we feel that this study contributes to expand LLS by focusing on an under-researched area, that of the university, and also to the studies of linguistic landscapes in Spain and Catalonia, we are also conscious that the picture presented in this chapter has a limited impact. We hope that future studies can fill more gaps and shed light on the questions that still remain unanswered in the context of *universcapes*.

Notes

1 Research funding: This publication is part of the grant PID2021-124673NA-I00 funded by MCIN/AEI/10.130039/501100011033/ and by "ERDF A way of making Europe."
2 A similar approach is adopted by Badwan, Nunn and Pahl (2024) for a "listening walk" in a rural treescape.
3 Retrieved from https://www.udl.cat/ca/en/udl/city/. Accessed 11 July, 2023.
4 Retrieved from https://www.udl.cat/ca/en/udl/city/. Accessed 11 July, 2023.

5 Retrieved from https://www.udl.cat/ca/udl/figures/. Accessed 11 July, 2023.
6 Retrieved from https://www.usal.es/historia. Access 22 July, 2023.
7 Universidad de Salamanca introduced an alternative sans-serif typography in its corporate identity manual in 2021, to meet the demands of new media for more simplicity.Updates of signage choices of corporate identity features are not always possible in historic buildings due to preservation regulations.
8 The message alludes to a situation originated in October 2017, when an independence referendum banned by the Spanish government took place and the politicians responsible were accused of sedition (a crime that was later removed from the Spanish penal code). Exhaustive information about this can be found in Wikipedia, under the entry "Catalan declaration of independence."
9 "Command" and "statement" are used along Hallidayan systemic functional linguistics (e.g. Thompson 2014) and Kress and Van Leeuwen's (2006, 2021) visual social grammar. Commands aim to demand goods or services from the interlocutors, whereas statements provide them with information.

References

Abbas, Juhaid H., Binnor M. Abdul Samad, Mohammad Hussein M. Imam, and Annie Mae C. Berowa. 2022. "Visuals to Ideologies: Exploring the Linguistic Landscape of Mindanao State University Marawi Campus." *Lingua Cultura 16*, no. 2: 187–192. https://doi.org/10.21512/lc.v16i2.8406

Backhaus, Peter. 2006. "Multilingualism in Tokyo: A Look into the Linguistic Landscape." In *Linguistic Landscape: A New Approach to Multilingualism*, edited by Durk Gorter, 52–66. Clevedon: Multilingual Matters.

Badwan, Khawla, Caitlin Nunn, and Kate Pahl. 2024. "Working with/Beyond 'Language': Insights from a Listening Walk with Young Men from Asylum-Seeking Background in a Rural Treescape. *Language and Intercultural Communication 24*, no. 5: 497–510. https://doi.org/10.1080/14708477.2024.2373156

Blommaert, Jan, and Ico Maly. 2015. "Ethnographic Linguistic Landscape Analysis and Social Change: A Case Study." In *Language and Superdiversity*, edited by Karel Arnaut, Jan Blommaert, Ben Rampton, and Massimiliano Spotti, 191–211. New York: Routledge.

Bosworth, Yulia. 2019. "Gender Inclusivity in the Linguistic Landscape of Parisian Universities." *The French Review 93*, no. 2: 175–196. https://doi.org/10.1353/tfr.2019.0014

Collins. 2024. *Graffiti*. www.collinsdictionary.com/dictionary/english/graffiti

Chen, Hong. 2023. "Analysis of Marginal Discourse: Identity Construction in Campus Wall Graffiti." *English Language Teaching and Linguistics Studies 5*, no. 5: 28–49. https://doi.org/10.22158/eltls.v5n5p28

Curtin, Melissa L. 2015. "Creativity in Polyscriptal Typographies in the Linguistic Landscape of Taipei." *Social Semiotics 25*, no. 2: 236–243. https://doi.org/10.1080/10350330.2015.1010315

Ericsson, Stina. 2023. "Equality, marginalisation, and hegemonic negotiation: Embodied understandings of the built and designed environment." *Multimodality & Society 3*, no. 4: 313-335. https://doi.org/10.1177/26349795231178936

Europa Press Castilla y León. 2017. "Salamanca, una ciudad tatuada por la historia." *europapress.es*. Accessed December 6, 2017. www.europapress.es/castilla-y-leon/noticia-salamanca-ciudad-tatuada-historia-20171206180749.html.

Ferris, Fiona, and Felix Banda. 2018. "Recontextualisation and Reappropriation of Social and Political Discourses in Toilet Graffiti at the University of the Western Cape." *Stellenbosch Papers in Linguistics Plus 55*: 27–45. https://doi.org/10.5842/55-0-778

Fuentes, Juan Francisco. 2017. "Usos ideológicos de la letra "k" en la España contemporánea: sobre el cambiante significado de un símbolo." *Ariadna Histórica: Lenguajes, Conceptos, Metáforas 6*: 9–27.

Gorter, Durk. 2018. "Linguistic Landscapes and Trends in the Study of Schoolscapes." *Linguistics and Education 44*: 80–85. https://doi.org/10.1016/j.linged.2017.10.001

Halliday, Michael Alexander Kirk. 1978. *Language as Social Semiotic*. London: Hodder Arnold.

Im, Jae-hyun. 2023. "The Linguistic Landscape as an Identity Construction Site of a United States' Higher Educational Institution in the Time of COVID-19." *Education as Change 27*: 1–26. https://doi.org/10.25159/1947-9417/11405

Järlehed, Johan. 2015. "Ideological Framing of Vernacular Type Choices in the Galician and Basque Semiotic Landscape." *Social Semiotics 25*, no. 2: 165–199. https://doi.org/10.25159/1947-9417/11405

Järlehed, Johan, and Adam Jaworski. 2015. "Typographic Landscaping: Creativity, Ideology, Movement." *Social Semiotics 25*, no. 2: 117–125. https://doi.org/10.1080/10350330.2015.1010318

Kadenge, Maxwell. 2015. "Where Art Thou Sesotho?": Exploring the Linguistic Landscape of Wits University." *Per Linguam 31*, no. 1: 30–45. https://doi.org/10.5785/31-1-630

Kress, Gunther, and Theo Van Leeuwen. 2006. *Reading Images: The Grammar of Visual Design* (2nd ed.). London: Routledge.

Kress, Gunther, and Theo Van Leeuwen. 2021. *Reading Images: The Grammar of Visual Design* (3rd ed.). London: Routledge.

Lamb, James, Michael Gallagher and Jeremy Knox. 2019. "On An Excursion through ECI: Multimodality, Ethnography and Urban Walking." *Qualitative Research 19*, no. 1: 55–70. https://doi.org/10.1177/1468794118773294

Lapyai, Sirach. 2003. "Scratching Protest: A Study of Graffiti as Communication in Universities in Thailand." Unpublished Master's Thesis. Edith Cowan University. https://ro.ecu.edu.au/theses/1491

Legge, Nils. 2015. "A Survey of the Linguistic Landscape of Stockholm University." Unpublished Master's Thesis. Stockholm University. www.diva-portal.org/smash/get/diva2:897001/FULLTEXT01.pdf

Moghaddam, Mostafa M., and Neil Murray. 2023. "Linguistic Variation in Iranian University Student Graffiti: Examining the Role of Gender." *Journal of Psycholinguistic Research 52*: 721–742. https://doi.org/10.1007/s10936-022-09919-y

Nørgaard, Nina. 2009. "The Semiotics of Typography in Literary Texts: A Multimodal Approach." *Orbis Litterarum 64*, no. 2: 79–166. https://doi.org/10.1111/j.1600-0730.2008.00949.x

Pennycook, Allister. 2009. "Linguistic Landscapes and the Transgressive Semiotics of Graffiti." In *Linguistic Landscape: Expanding the Scenery*, edited by Elana Shohamy and Durk Gorter, 302–312. New York: Routledge.

Ravelli, Louise J., and Robert J. McMurtrie. 2016. *Multimodality in the Built Environment*. New York: Routledge.

Screti, Francesco. 2015. "The Ideological Appropriation of the Letter <k> in the Spanish Linguistic Landscape." *Social Semiotics 25*, no. 2: 200–208. https://doi.org/10.1080/10350330.2015.1010321

Spolsky, Bernard, and Robert L. Cooper. 1991. *The Languages of Jerusalem.* Oxford: Clarendon Press.

Thompson, Geoff. 2014. *Introducing Functional Grammar.* London: Routledge.

Thurlow, Crispin. 2021. "When *Globalese* meets *Localese*: Transformational Tactics in the Typographic Landscape -A Bernese Case Study." *Social Semiotics 31*, no. 1: 88–107. https://doi.org/10.1080/10350330.2020.1810544

Yavari, Sonia. 2012. "Linguistic Landscape and Language Policies: A Comparative Study of Linköping University and ETH Zürich." Unpublished MA Thesis. Linköping University. www.diva-portal.org/smash/record.jsf?pid=diva2%3A574524&dswid=6122

6 "Iruinkokoa" and the Basque semiotic landscape

Transgressive carnival voices taken to the streets

Agurtzane Elordui, Jokin Aiestaran and Samara Velte

> Chaos is the norm here. The social order that predominates throughout the year is reverted. This day gives an opportunity to young people to express their opinions through satire and in a public manner (...). It aims to be a big festival that takes over the streets, and this is illustrated through two opposing sides. And those two sides can represent different people, or they can represent the two sides that are present within the same person.
>
> Ihitz, dancer and participant in Iruinkokoa

Introduction

Since 2019, the city of Pamplona (Iruñea, in Basque) has had its own popular carnival, called *Iruinkokoa*. Ihitz – quoted above – was a member of the originally reduced group of cultural activists who first introduced and developed the event, based on the Northern Basque tradition of *libertimenduak*, on the other side of the Spanish-French border. Since then, it has been performed every year and has become increasingly popular within Pamplona's Basque community. Iruinkokoa is a combination of satirical play and parody, lyric oral improvisation or *bertsoak* (verses), live music, and a series of newly created dances that imitate traditional dances from the Basque Country as well as from other parts of Europe. A major trait of this "folkloric innovation" (Otaegi and Apodaka 2022) is that its whole process of creation and mise-en-scène is carried out solely in the Basque language by the local community, a rarity in an area in which Basque speakers are a clear minority. Most of the participants in Iruinkokoa are quite young – between 20 and 30 years old– and they live in a sociolinguistic context in which Spanish is the dominant language. In fact, in 2018, only 12.6% of the population in and around Pamplona was able to speak Basque (Euskarabidea – Euskararen Nafar Institutua 2020), and the current, everyday use of the language in the city may be as low as 2.9%, according to a report published in 2021 by the Basque Sociolinguistics Cluster (Altuna, Iñarra, and Basurto 2021). However, Ihitz's words illustrate how this annual carnival opens a brief window of exception into this reality. It alters both the linguistic and social status quo within a carnivalesque logic of parody

DOI: 10.4324/9781032687087-7

and satire, enabling an ephemeral semiotic landscape that becomes meaningful for those who participate in or feel identified with the local Basque community.

Our focus is on the ephemeral semiotization of space. We try to make sense of the *in place* meanings and discourses within the social and physical creative and performative world of Iruinkokoa. We are interested in exploring how the signs used in this *libertimendua* can demarcate spaces, cutting them up into precisely circumscribed zones in which identities are being defined and enacted, forms of authority can be exerted, and ownership and entitlement can be articulated (Blommaert 2012, 20–21). But, at the same time, by focusing on a carnivalesque performative frame such as Iruinkokoa, we also want to study how the creativity of this group of young people contributes to such semiotization process and helps to turn this space into an agentive zone that allows them to provide a public platform in which to showcase struggles about power and political conflicts involving the Basque language in Pamplona.[1]

According to Moriarty and Järlehed (2019), such agentive capacity is closely linked to the concept of creativity. Creativity is conceptualized as the playful reworking of semiotic resources in order to transcend existing social and material constraints with the intention of reconfiguring social meanings, relations, and structures. The *libertimenduak* are a good example of this attempt to creatively reconfigure and rework semiotic resources. In order to transcend the existing social and material constraints of a minority group, the participants in Iruinkokoa use carnivalesque humor to construct a different kind of frame that allows them to criticize or question ideologies rooted in society. They do so by relying mainly on the symbolic inversion typical of carnival. Parodic carnivalesque stylization introduces into the discourse a new semantic aim, contrary to the image that may be taken from an initial form, or often in opposition to it (Bakhtin 1981, 1984).

Focusing on the semiotization of space, this paper is guided by the following questions: what signs are used by these young people in Iruinkokoa? What do those signs do in space? And how does space become a non-neutral, even agentive zone, in which to bring ideological tensions into the public sphere? What is the role of carnival transgression in this agency? And how does it affect the interpretation of the signs? We try to answer these issues by focusing on the semiotic landscape, a landscape that includes, together with written texts, "verbal texts, images, objects, placement in time and space as well as human beings" (Shohamy and Waksman 2009, 314). We will focus on the verbal and written texts these young people display in the public square, but in general we pay attention to the whole sign apparatus in the social action of Iruinkokoa. We have employed direct observation and other ethnographic tools to analyze the action that takes place as well as its social actors and their habitus. We also focus on the embodied forms of discourse found in the interactional order. We try to explain how these young people's movements and positions are central to the production of meaning, and how they use their bodies to invert normative patterns of conduct through their attitudes, movements, and gestures. Furthermore, visual semiotics are part of our focus, or the visual signs created by this young community in and for the event. We finally consider place semiotics, that is, the *natural* landscape within which the action takes place (Scollon and Scollon 2003, 9). We focus on the old quarter of Pamplona: in particular, on the rules, possibilities, and restrictions of this spatial arena of the city, that is, the connection between space and normative expectations that makes this space historical.

Following this introduction, we will first provide an overview of the carnival transgressive frame created within Iruinkokoa in order to better understand how the carnival transgression can affect the interpretation of signs ("Performance and transgression: "Iruinkokoa," a carnival day for freedom"). In the "Method" section we will briefly introduce the methods used for collecting and selecting the corpus. In "Case studies: the means of transgression," we will explain the most significant results stemming from our analysis. In particular, we focus on the transgressive means used by these young people to create an agentive semiotic landscape. Subsequently, we give an example of how ideological tensions are addressed in the public sphere, in this case around the "Hand of Irulegi" (explained below). We will end with a few final remarks about the wider issues that this performative event reveals ("Final remarks").

Performance and transgression: "Iruinkokoa," a carnival day for freedom

Iruinkokoa is an adaptation of the Northern Basque traditional performance *libertimenduak* to the urban environment of Pamplona, south of the Spanish-French border. Libertimenduak have been revived in several inner-city/urban cultural areas in the last decade, following the model resurrected by Antton Luku in Donibane Garazi (Lower Navarre) which is explained in his work, *Libertitzeaz* (Luku 2014). Although the Iruinkokoa performance maintains most of its structural elements – such as the street dance in the morning and a satirical and parodic performance with two sides or groups interpreting opposing characters – it has also adapted the topics and forms to the political, historical, and sociolinguistic reality of Pamplona. These adaptations enable a redefinition of the city and its local community in terms of its own values and collective meanings, with Basque as a central but not exclusive element. Other values that can be identified through observing the visual semiotics and the oral and written discourses created by the participants are social critique, nonconformity, provocation, and transgression.

The libertimenduak are examples of playful and informal voices of young Basque speakers, innovative metalinguistic and metacultural creative activities. They connect Basque with other concerns and conflicts around gender, the environment, ethnicity, and class relations that Basque young people consider important nowadays. The young people taking part in the libertimenduak try to encourage audiences to see that the social world of today is not a predetermined *natural* reality, but, rather, one that is shaped by powerful forces in society and can, therefore, be reversed. Such a perspective shift is very significant. Performers and the audience alike realize that they can reinforce their agency to transform the social fabric. The whole performance establishes a continuous dialogue with the community. Those who join the parade and come to the square are not seen as mere spectators; instead, the public is expected to participate in the show by reacting to the discourses placed out by the performers and even entering the scene during specific dances. At the end, both performers and viewers have lunch together. This reminds us of Bakhtin's words: "Carnival is not a spectacle seen by the people; they live in it, and everyone participates because its very idea embraces all the people" (Bakhtin 1984, 7).

In this questioning and transformation of society, comic genres and the satires and parodies therein can be particularly effective. Performance provides a frame that invites critical reflection on communicative processes. "It opens up a reflexive space – it is language about language and culture about culture" (Bauman 1992): both the performer and the audience pay special attention to language esthetics and discourse. Furthermore, as Bauman and Briggs contend, "play frames not only alter the performative force of utterances but provide settings in which speech and society can be questioned and transformed" (Bauman and Briggs 1990, 63).

The participants in Iruinkokoa are aware of this transformative capacity: portraying a transgressive and buffoonish appearance of the city and its Basque community allows them to build an inverted interpretative frame. In fact, they consider that this symbolic inversion typical of carnivalesque humor provides "a route to knowledge" (Emerson 2002, 6), not simply a negation of the status quo. Actor Ilunber, who incorporates one of the buffoonish and provocative figures called Koko Beltzak or *black kokos*, reminds us that "it is healthy to make people feel uncomfortable and sometimes question your stuff." In this route to knowledge, Emerson notes that, as Bakthin emphasizes, ridiculing oneself can preempt another unfriendly response and, as such, "self-ridicule is a resoundingly healthy gesture, a profound form of self-affirmation and even of self-praise" (Emerson 2002, 6). The words of Oier, another participant in Iruinkokoa, lead us to a similar conclusion: "Carnival and disguise give us the freedom to revert the situation. That's the best lesson from Iruinkokoa: to learn to laugh at ourselves, and to laugh at others."

Method

Ethnography is at the core of our methodological approach, not as a mere compilation of contextual descriptive techniques, but as a paradigm, as a way to capture reality in all its kaleidoscopic, complex, and complicated nature (Blommaert and Dong 2010). Indeed, we share the view of Shohamy and Waksman (2009) and conceive the semiotic landscape as an ecological arena with fluid and fuzzy borders in which the public space is negotiated and contested. It is a landscape that includes all those "interwoven 'discourses' – what is seen, what is heard, what is spoken, what is thought" (Shohamy and Waksman 2009, 313), and one in which semiotic activity turns the physical space into social, cultural, and political space (Blommaert 2012, 20). The integration of the ethnographic perspective allows us to understand how these processes develop.

Our ethnographic fieldwork was carried out around the Iruinkokoa performances of 2023 and 2024. The techniques employed in our research include direct observation, interviews with participants and organizers, and group interviews. Chronologically, the fieldwork was divided into three main phases: before the performance day, during the performance day, and after the performance day. Below, we provide a general outline of this fieldwork.

Evidence of the rehearsal process and the performance itself was collected, so that a more detailed stylistic and discursive analysis could be performed. Photographs were also taken to document banners and all kinds of written texts, the participants' costumes, their hairstyles, the places in which the performances were carried out, and many other kinds of symbols. Moreover, we carried out individual interviews with eight participants and held two group discussions with another nine, including dancers, actors, and members of the organizational structure. Interviews were scheduled during the rehearsal period prior to the performance and afterward. In both cases, we conducted semi-structured interviews. The pre-performance interviews with the participants aimed to explore the actors' habitus: their personal and sociolinguistic context, as well as to gather their motivations and expectations around the performance. The post-performance interviews revolved around some extracts from the videos and audios recorded, and they sought to promote metalinguistic reflections about the narrative and stylistic choices made by the interviewees and the rest of the group, as well as their roles in the performance. Moreover, in the initial phases of the rehearsal period, we conducted interviews with two of the external organizers, in order to gather a general understanding of the performance.

The oral data recorded in these encounters, as well as in the public performances on February 19, 2023 and February 11, 2024, were subsequently analyzed through the theoretical-methodological lens of both Semiotic and Linguistic Landscape literature, in particular Blommaert (2012), Jaworski and Thurlow (2010), and Scollon and Scollon (2003), as well as through Discourse Analysis. The latter was especially relevant in that we wanted to study the relationship between concrete linguistic utterances and their social, political, and historical background (Van Leeuwen and Wodak 1999). Questions about legitimacy and the power to establish social meanings are disputed within the public space, and can be identified in the different linguistic or semiotic expressions that arise in these spaces. Although the main focus of Discourse Analysis has been on text, we adhere to multi-modal approaches (Kress 2009, 2011; Van Dijk 2001), treating different types of *signs* as constitutive elements of certain *social discourses* that emerge and compete within situated semiotic landscapes.

Case studies: The means of transgression

For the purpose of this chapter, the public performances displaying some discourse or thought on Pamplona's linguistic landscape were chosen as examples. As has already been mentioned, Basque is a marginal language in the usual linguistic fabric of Navarre's capital city. Its status is semi-official, meaning that its use "may be promoted" (Provincial Decree 103/2017) by the local authorities voluntarily, but it does not have the legal protection that possessing the status of co-officiality would grant. Furthermore, the question of linguistic rights and national/ethnic identities is entangled within a context of political polarization. Iruinkokoa is a creative attempt to transcend these social and material constraints of a young Basque-speaking minority group with the aim of reconfiguring social meanings, relations, and structures. In what follows, we will illustrate how this reversion of the social status quo takes place. First, by the resemiotization of space created by the festive practice. A performative framework takes over the streets of the old quarter of Pamplona. Starting with the *kalejira* or parade, they use carnival strategies – such as ambiguity, the grotesque, the hyperbolic and masks – to create a transgressive and buffoonish semiotic framework. This allows for the construction of a new and inverted interpretative frame that facilitates revealing ideological tensions. Such tensions arise in discourse during the theatrical parodic performance (as we will see in "Ideological tensions in the square: parody and the 'Hand of Irulegi'").

The creation of an agentive zone through the carnivalesque semiotization of space

With the concept of *emplacement*, the Scollons come to the most fundamental issue of geosemiotics: where in the physical world is the sign located in the concrete and material world? (Scollon and Scollon 2003, 145) In the case of Iruinkokoa, this issue also makes a difference. In fact, there is a meaningful symbolic link between Iruinkokoa and the Old Town of Pamplona: "Iruinkokoa and the Old Town are synonymous," explains Maddi, a member of the event organization, in a focus group. According to the participants, this connection between Iruinkokoa and the old quarter of Pamplona has to do, above all, with the critical spirit they both share. Endika explains the reasons: "I believe that the old quarter has a small-town feel about it. We connect with them because they also want another Iruñea. They've had a lot of problems and I think they're willing to make that criticism."

In the aforementioned focus group, the participants remind us of the common ordered patterns of normative conduct and expectations to which one should adhere in the Old Town during the whole year. They describe a context in which Basque is very unusual and not always socioculturally authorized. By putting up signs, Iruinkokoa actors revert these common ordered patterns of normative conduct, and mark their presence and authority over parts of the shared space in this particular area of the city. Iruinkokoa declares power over these spaces, at least for one day. In fact, a recurrent discourse among them is that Iruinkokoa is a day to "take over the streets," namely, the centrality of public space that otherwise functions mainly in Spanish. The itinerary of the *kalejira* itself, for instance, is not trivial. In fact, it can be interpreted as a tribute to the Basque-speaking nuclei and places in Pamplona's Old Town that evokes a sort of demarcation. This demarcation has led to a clear self-consciousness of the Basque-speaking community and its usual *safe spaces*.[2]

Iruinkokoa usually takes place on Carnival Sunday, which can be either in February or in March, depending on the year. The day begins with a group breakfast at the gastronomic and cultural association *Zaldiko Maldiko*, a central meeting point for most cultural initiatives in favor of Basque in the greater area of Pamplona. Participants, organizers, and voluntary helpers eat *churros* with chocolate while the dancers dress up. At 9.30 a.m. a rocket is set off, and Iruinkokoa officially begins. It kicks off with a street dance by all the participants, including members of the organization and the public, accompanied by their own brass band. The ensemble undertakes an itinerary through the streets of Pamplona's Old Town, stopping at four specific sites to perform their so-called *asalduak* (assaults). These brief visits usually happen in front of meaningful places that vary each year, such as the headquarters of social movements, local stores with a well-known history of supporting the Basque language, or simply streets in which a neighborhood association has shown interest in welcoming the parade. All in all, there is a clear visual and auditory occupation of the spaces through which they transit. By doing so, the group – which becomes larger as the morning progresses, because many spectators join the march – *marks* an itinerary of places they consider *theirs*, that is, close or sympathetic to the Basque carnival. The itinerary ends in Santa Ana Square, a semi-hidden place within Pamplona's Old Town, but well-known to the local community. The square has a meaningful connotation of *belonging to the neighborhood*, inter alia because it is home to a number of communitarian vegetable gardens and many popular events take place there: "It's a square made by the residents," explains dancer Itxaso in the focus group. As such, it is no coincidence that the final performance of Iruinkokoa is carried out there: it is a *safe space* for the community, in which satire and criticism can be freely expressed.

Participants in Iruinkokoa bring their real bodies into play in this spatial area, upon which they act semiotically. In this semiotization, bodies take on a great significance. They have very marked esthetics that do not go unnoticed on the streets and at work as an agent in itself. Their movements and positions are also central to the production of meaning. The bodies are semiotically enskilled (Blommaert 2012, 38) and trained during the previous months. The performers in Iruinkokoa can be classified into four major groups, each of which represents a collective voice within the multi-directional social dialogue that constitutes the practice of Iruinkokoa. On the one hand, there are the black kokos (*koko beltzak*, originally *zirtzilak*, meaning *rags*); they represent the buffoonish and grotesque side of the collective body. On the street, they are accompanied by the *fauna,* similar figures who will thereafter disappear from the performance, and who are often portrayed by former participants. Their forms are vulgar and loud; their clothes are decadent and tattered versions of old urban clothing, and their faces are usually dirty with ashes, in a clear gesture toward factories and the urban lower classes.

During the focus group, participants reported that their esthetics were initially inspired by the *zirtzil* of Lower Navarre, but that these esthetics were not, in their view, appropriate for an urban context like Pamplona. They considered the *zirtzils* to be "wilder," and felt the need to adapt the esthetics of their clothing and their attitudes to a more urban context. "They have nature, we have factories," explains the actor Akier. In fact, the British TV show *Peaky Blinders* was taken as an esthetic reference for the clothing they wear, but they share many things with the *zirtzils*.

Figure 6.1 Koko beltzak during an *asaldua* in the *kalejira* (February 19, 2023).

Most of their attitudes and movements, as in the Lower Navarrese case, are rife with *grotesque realism* (Bakthin 1984) and its associated degradation: "the lowering of all that is high, spiritual, ideal, abstract; it is a transfer to the material level, to the sphere of earth and body in their indissoluble unity" (Bakthin 1984, 19–20). The grotesque imagery in Iruinkokoa includes references to the body, in particular to the "lower stratum of the body" (Bakthin 1984, 20) and they all suggest that the world within Iruinkokoa is a way to break away from the norm. At the same time, these esthetics serve to refract the world through a lens that encourages the audience to critically engage with it (see Figure 6.1).

Next, there are the white kokos or *koko xuriak*, the group of dancers who, at first glance, represent the *good* side of the collective body. They are all dressed in a mix of traditional Basque carnivalesque, although gender-neutral, dancing outfits, and each of them carries two wooden sticks on their shoulders, which they use in most of their dances. However, the dancers are anonymous and uniform: their faces are covered with a mask that imitates a metallic fox. Through their coordinated movements and upright walking, they evoke the image of an army (Figure 6.2).

Figure 6.2 Koko xuriak dancing in Santa Ana Square (February 19, 2023).

If we focus on the constant confrontations between *koko xuriak* and *koko beltzak* during the *kalejira*, a binary scheme springs to mind. Likewise, in the performances in Santa Ana Square, both groups take turns taking over the plaza, as in a constant struggle for space. Ihitz, who trains them during the rehearsals, warns that the *good vs bad* schema should be questioned: "Don't get too close to the *koko xuriak* – they don't have words, but they do have their bodies and movements to defend themselves." Her statement reveals their desire to avoid essentialist and binary relationships between the two groups, but also the importance of the body and movements in the semiotic landscape created by Iruinkokoa. The mask also takes on a special role in the abolishment of binary connections between the two groups, insofar as it represents an inner duality and establishes a distance with its surroundings. Finally, *Zaldikoa* – "the Rider" – represents the same kind of ambivalence, but unlike anyone else. The leading figure in the group of dancers represents a horse and carries an inflated pig bladder, a popular element in Navarrese festivities that is mostly used to tease children. Ihitz draws our attention to the importance of colors and shapes in their clothes: *Zaldikoa* is the ambivalent figure between the bright and dark sides of the collective body, and that is why its jacket shows a tree with black and white branches on the back.

There are other actors in the libertimendua who lay outside such binary configurations: two *bertsolari* or oral improvisators and the musical band. The former sing verses at each other in the *asalduak* and thereby comment on whatever current event or issue may have caused the *asaldua* to take place there. In 2023, for example, the parade decided to stop in front of a well-known local stationery store whose owners had historically been involved with pro-Basque language initiatives and who were about to retire. The verses sung in that *asaldua* honored their history of activism and their role within the neighborhood. As a general rule, the job of the bertsolariak (plural form) is to regulate the discourses of the black koko group: if they think that they are too extreme, they will moderate or respond; or, on the contrary, if they perceive that the satire is too soft, they may also sing in an even more provocative tone. And lastly, the brass band plays music throughout the parade, playing a major role during the walking/dancing itinerary. According to the participants interviewed, the songs are a mixture of local *charanga* (fanfare) and jazz music, with some comic gestures such as the inclusion of a fragment of North Korea's national anthem. Thus, the music is an important semiotic element, insofar as it constructs a frame of reference to interpret the cues of Iruinkokoa as a space in which ambiguity and irony prevail.

Ideological tensions in the square: Parody and the "Hand of Irulegi"

"The aim of the Libertimendua is to provoke, to bring our dirty linen to the center of the square, so that the community washes it clean," explains Oier, the director of the acting group. The theater itself represents a trial or a revision of the common attitudes of anyone in the square: the topics that emerge are often linked to the sociolinguistic and political identities of the area, delimitating clear in- and out-groups and mocking primarily their own collective identity. The polarized character of Pamplona helps in constructing this bilateral scheme, according to Iker, a former black koko and nowadays member of the *fauna*: "We live in a continuous conflict, and the fact that we do this in Basque allows us to do things we wouldn't otherwise."

In the following section, we will show how these political and ideological discrepancies and tensions that exist within Navarrese society are addressed in Iruinkokoa. We will focus on those around the presence and social role of the Basque language by explaining how this issue was represented in the satirical sketches of 2023 and 2024. In both years, the acting group within Iruinkokoa chose to comment on the discovery of the Hand of Irulegi, making fun of the social reactions it generated. By analyzing the multimodal signs used in their sketches, we aim to illustrate how the establishment of these discursive norms or of this semiotic landscape is achieved through concrete linguistic means.

New symbolic means: the discovery of the Hand of Irulegi and its symbolic power for the Basque community of Navarre

The Hand of Irulegi is a late Iron Age bronze object that was discovered in the summer of 2021 during excavations in the archaeological site of Irulegi, just 15 km from Pamplona. The sheet is in the shape of a right hand with extended fingers, and its most remarkable feature is a four-row inscription engraved on the back. The conspicuous similarity between the first word in the text, *sorioneku*, and

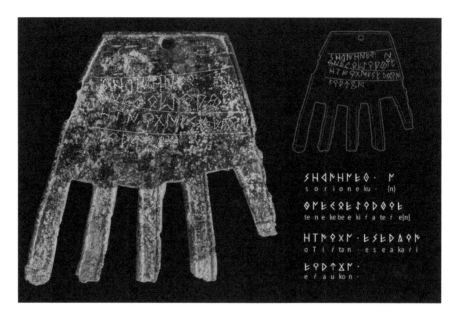

Figure 6.3 The Hand of Irulegi.

the contemporary Basque word *zorioneko* ("of good fortune"), the fact that the object was unearthed at the heart of Vasconic territory (the land of the Vascones), and its antiquity led the experts who first examined the piece, namely Velaza and Gorrochategi, to deduce that the text was written in the Vasconic language, and that there is a continuous historical line that connects Vasconic to the modern Basque language. These experts – and many others – maintain this conviction to this day, and defend the notion that the "script represents a graphic subsystem of Palaeohispanic that shares its roots with the modern Basque language and constitutes the first example of Vasconic epigraphy" (Aiestaran et al. 2024, 66).

The official presentation of the piece (Figure 6.3) took place on November 14, 2022 with the intervention of the President of the Government of Navarre, and it provoked an immediate social and academic earthquake. The news spread all over the local as well as international media and in scholarly circles. Particularly in Navarre, the claim that the roots of Basque in the area dated back to more than 2000 years ago reinforced the conviction that "Navarre is the land of Basque. Basque hasn't come from anywhere, it was here and it will remain here," as put by the recently created association to support Basque *Sorionekuak* ("the fortunate ones") in opposition to those who believe that the Basque language is not originally from Navarre. Such nationalist discourses of pride mesh with capitalist discourses of profit, once again in the Basque case (Järlehed 2020). The Hand of Irulegi and the script itself have become iconic objects in the last two years, and today there is a vivid market for t-shirts, necklaces, bracelets, posters, and many other formats, depicting its image as

"*Iruinkokoa*" *and the Basque semiotic landscape* 157

a good example of the commercial appropriation and commodification of a minority culture and language (Heller and Duchêne 2011).

More recently, some highly influential experts who have analyzed the piece in detail have alleged that it cannot be guaranteed that the text on the hand is written in a language related to Basque. These conclusions were published in a special issue of the academic journal *Fontes Linguae Vasconum* (Gorrochategi and Santazilia 2023). They all accept the authenticity of the piece, but they emphasize that the text on the hand cannot be understood – even the interpretation of the word *sorioneku* proves to be controversial – with what is known about the languages of the time. This has led to some confusion and bewilderment in society and has fueled heated debates, sometimes with obvious political overtones. At any rate, the Hand of Irulegi, with all its symbolic power, is already part of the Basque collective imaginary.

Discursive and semiotic analysis of the gags

Iruinkokoa is fundamentally a satirical revision of deeds that are considered meaningful for its community. As such, its aim is not to inform about something that has occurred, but to comment on it. As was expected, in the theatrical representation of 2023, the Hand of Irulegi became a major focus. At no time during the *kalejira* or the performance did we see the image of the hand. But in the *kalejira*, a big black banner on which you could read an inscription that reproduced the first word, *Sorioneku*, in the Vasconic epigraphy of Irulegi, introduced us to the issue. Underneath, one could read *Zirioneku, Irrian Federatu* or "good trick, federate in laughter" (see Figure 6.4). This banner, interpreted through the filters of parody, is a good example of Bakhtin's *double-voicedness*, the chief feature of parodic

Figure 6.4 Iruinkokoa *kalejira* (parade) in Pamplona (February 19, 2023).

stylization (Bakhtin 1981, 324). In this case, the banner paid tribute to the Irulegi discovery by bringing its iconic expression, *Sorioneku*, to the performance. Yet, at the same time, it inverted the meaning through the parodic word *Zirioneku*, proposing a reading that invited spectators to take as a joke or relativize the importance of the archaeological discovery and probably to mock the importance that was given to it at institutional levels and in the press.

During the performance, Iruinkokoa mocked the collective hype that arose following the discovery of the ancient site, making fun of several expressions of banal nationalism and exploitation that emerged in its aftermath. Four black kokos entered the scene, each of them singing their own national anthem: *Gernikako Arbola* (The Tree of Gernika), *Ikusi mendizaleak* (Look around, mountaineers), *Eusko Gudariak* (The Basque Combatants), and *Topa dagigun* (Let's have a toast). There was a discordant effect that made us think about a dismembered Basque community; in fact, the gag refers to an existing dispute within Basque nationalist circles about what the consensual national anthem should be. Suddenly, they all met in the middle of the square and ended up chanting a song from the popular commercial music group Zetak: *Mendikate honek lotuta / Zure zauria nirea da / Ta kantu hau DENONA*[3] ("Tied by this mountain chain / Your wound is mine / And this song is that of all of us"). Immediately, the scene changed. The movements of the participants reminded us of an archaeological discovery. Some *koko beltzak* were mimicking digging in the ground in search of something. But, instead of a metallic hand, they found an ancient lubricant at the archeological site, and took it as a sign of the natural and inherent fondness for sex of Basque people:

1.

Koko Beltz 1:	I found something, I found something!
	[Zerbait aurkitu dut, zerbait aurkitu dut!]
Koko Beltz 2:	What, what is it?
	[Zer, zer da?]
Koko Beltz 1:	I don't know!
	[Ez dakit!]
Koko Beltz 3:	It's an ancient lubricant! [shows the pot to the public]
	[Garai bateko lubrikante bat!]
Koko Beltz 2:	And it has an inscription on it. In Basque!
	[Eta inskripzio bat dauka. Euskaraz!]
All three [reading loudly]:	"Of-good-sex".
	["Sexuoneku"]
Koko Beltz 1:	"Of good sex". This proves that ancient Basques enjoyed sex!
	["Sexu oneku". Honek erakusten du aitzinako euskaldunek sexua maite zutela!]

The wordplay between the original inscription (interpreted as "of good fortune") and their own version ("of good sex") and the hyperbolic interpretation of the characters formed a parodic version of the overreaction of Basque society regarding the conclusions that could be extracted from the archaeological item. Such ambiguity was then repeated in several different situations in the sketch, comparing collective and public events that are organized in support of the Basque language – such as the biannual Euskaraldia or initiative to promote the use of the language in everyday life – with orgies. "In the Libertimenduak, we are always using transpositions and metaphors," explains Oier: "The aim is to place a mirror in the middle of the arena, so that people can look at themselves."

Although Iruinkokoa uses no fixed atrezzo and the actors change their appearance only minimally, it is easy for the audience to understand what is being talked about. Gestures, speech styles, and objects function as contextualization cues (Gumperz 1982) that guide the meaning-making process and generate immediate laughs. The explicit and hyperbolic representation of sexual acts by the *koko beltzak* in the plaza takes us to that grotesque and ambiguous world of carnival and satire. All those intertwined oral expressions refer to Irulegi in sexual terms, such as "Stick it in my Irulegi!" and expressions such as "It's been proven that ancient Basques loved sex!" and "They used to bang nonstop!" Ultimately, they all guide us to the final question posed by one of the actors: "But… is Basque of any use for anything?" To which another actor responds: "Yes, of course, for fucking!"

As Bakthin points out (Bakthin 1981, 1984), parody is by definition intertextual, requiring constant cross-reference between the parody itself and its model: between the present text and a variety of other texts. In the case of the 2023 sketch, the repetition and exaggeration of some slogans that had been used in pro-Basque campaigns were re-contextualized as orgasms, an effect achieved by intonating them in the form of sighing and moaning:

2.

- 24/7!
- Get out of the closet! [Atera armairutik]
- More, with more people, more often! [Gehiago, gehiagorekin, gehiagotan]

These slogans had originally been used in institutional campaigns with almost identical wordings, but of course in a different tone. Besides this, the group included references to the Basque-language learning process by intonating as orgasms typical exercises that are usually done while studying Basque grammar:

3.

- I'm… fond… of… you! [Zu… niri… gustatzen… zatzaizkit!]
- I… to you… eh… can… lick it! [Nik zuri hura, e, diezazuket! Zurrupatu!]
- Fill in the voids! [Bete hutsuneak!]
- There, there, precisely on the genitive! [Hor hor, justu genitiboan!]

This ambiguity – the fact that any of these utterances can be applied to two completely different contexts – is what generates the satirical effect and constitutes one of the major discursive rules of Iruinkokoa. Its underlying discourse poses the notion that *we*, the ingroup, can exist in both these interpretative frames, that both are familiar discursive areas for the community involved. It thus opens a window of possibility for new kinds of identities – usually built around rather nasty, malicious, and shameless attitudes.

Another critique within this gag was aimed at the attempts to make commercial or self-marketing profit of the Hand of Irulegi. In order to do so, a well-known singer and entrepreneur from Navarre, Pello Reparaz, the leader of the group Zetak, was subsequently parodied. His character appeared three times during the sketch, filming himself in selfie mode and urging his online followers to both get to know the discovery of the "lubricant of Irulegi" and to buy tickets for his concert: "We are in a new time for the Basques, and we want to share it with you. Give me a 'like.'" This figure was characterized through code-switching, alternating Basque and Spanish; thus, he was presented as someone who attributes to himself the symbolic value of the archaeological discovery and tries to make profit out of it by converting it into a spectacle to the outside world. His use of Spanish indicated this commercial aspect, as it is a widely perceived assumption that majority languages open up more doors than their minority counterparts. It was also a nod to balanced bilingualism in order to highlight the hypocrisy of the official authorities and media with respect to Basque. Those who were initially separated by contradictory national aspirations suddenly united in the face of the archaeological finding and the possible commercialization and manipulation of the discovery.

Reparaz's character functioned as a parodic element not because of its ambiguity, but because of its hyperbolism. At the same time, it represented a broader attitude in the face of the discovery of the hand: the reaction of all those who tried to make it a personal attribute or mark of true Basqueness. It also ridiculed gatekeeping attempts to keep Basque unchanged and rooted in the past. By doing so, the actors in Iruinkokoa relied on a shared cultural background they expected their community to be aware of. This allowed them to construct further interdiscursive meanings. In the case of the *Hand/Lubricant* of Irulegi, they were responding to socially established foundational myths (Assmann and Czaplicka 1995) about Basqueness as being *pure*, an idea that is linked to the stereotype of the Basque as fundamentally not interested in sex. It was also a clear interdiscursive gesture toward the social debate on the role of Basque in Navarre.

Questions about who forms the Basque community and what kind of attributes characterize it are a recurrent topic in the satirical performances of Iruinkokoa. The Hand of Irulegi was again addressed the following year, during their 2024 performance. The main topic of the gag was prompted by the declarations of a local politician who had complained about the *privileges* of Basque-speaking children because they could participate in ludic activities both in Basque and in Spanish. Iruinkokoa heavily ridiculed this discourse and constructed a satirical situation in which they interpellated everyone present in the square to recognize their *privileges* as speakers of a minority language and to express penitence. This satirical frame of *the world upside down* was created through an *in crescendo* exchange of absurd statements:

4.

Koko Beltz 1: Wait a minute. All of you speak Basque?
[*Ei, geldi, geldi! Hemen guztiok dakizue euskaraz?*]

Rest of koko beltzak and the audience: Yes!
[*Bai!*]

Koko Beltz 1: Me too, me too. Well, then, I have to warn you that the events organized in this square violate language rights. Because those who know Basque understand Spanish, but Spanish speakers don't know Basque.
[*Nik ere bai, nik ere bai. Ba orduan ohartarazi beharrean nago plaza honetan egiten diren ekitaldiek hizkuntza eskubideak urratzen dituztela. Izan ere, euskara dakitenek gaztelania ulertzen dute, baina gaztelania hiztunek ez dakite euskaraz.*]

Rest of koko beltzak: She's right!
[*Egia da!*]

Koko Beltz 2: Man! How did I not realize earlier? I have so many privileges! I'm a man, oh! White, gosh! Middle class, and Basque!
[*Tio, nola ez naiz lehenago konturatu? Ostiaren pribilegio pila ditut! Gizona, ai! Zuria, oh! Klase ertainekoa, eta euskalduna!*]

Koko Beltz 3: Fuck, I have even more privileges! White, Basque, without any disabilities, middle class, Basque [sic], English- and French-speaking, and also handsome!
[*Ostia, nik are pribilegio gehiago ditut! Txuria, euskalduna, desgaitasunik gabea, klase ertainekoa, euskalduna, ingeles eta frantsesduna, eta gainera guapoa!*]

At the end of each gag, one figure or character was symbolically killed. This *conviction* was represented through a pile-up of the rest of the actors on that individual. In the above quoted gag, a local philologist appeared on scene with a special issue of the academic journal *Fontes Linguae Vasconum* (Gorrochategi and Santazilia 2023) in his hand, incorporating the voice of linguistic authorities. Suddenly, the *koko beltzak* group ceased its discussion and looked at him, expectantly, and asked "So, is it or is it not Basque?", in a clear reference to the inscriptions found on the Hand of Irulegi a year prior. The philologist hesitated and made a gesture of doubt: "Meh." He hesitated again: "Well…" And then he concluded with a gesture of defeat. The furious group ran toward and piled on top of him, symbolically sentencing or *killing* the philologist.

Two weeks later, the actors reflected on that gag during a group interview with us. They acknowledged that it was not easy to decide which figure to sentence. "In a gag, you can make all the jokes you like, but to me, the most important thing is on whom you will pile up, because in the end, that's the message: who are we *judging*? It's a carnival, a satire: who do we want to target?" explained Oier: "It wasn't so much that we wanted to kill him [the philologist] personally, but last year we had done a whole sketch out of '*sorioneku.*' So, now it may not even be Basque? No discovery of good fortune?" The actor Ilunber clarified the issue: "We will always pile on those who, in one way or another, foil our dreams. They're neither friends nor enemies – they are the irritating people who take away our happiness."

Final remarks

Humor and parodic strategies are particularly worthy when overt critique is not permissible (Hill 1993) and that seems to be the case of Basque speakers in Pamplona. Participants in the Iruinkokoa festivity spoke to us about their desire for another possible Iruñea and how, through creativity, they construct a framework of *freedom*. Iruinkokoa is a creative attempt to transcend the social and material constraints of a young Basque-speaking minority group. Among other things, the libertimendua allows this young group from Pamplona to question and put an end to stigmatized language uses they experience as Basque speakers.

Throughout this chapter, we have illustrated some semiotic means through which this reversion of the social status quo takes place. Iruinkokoa introduces new carnivalesque signs in a public space: Zaldiko, the banner evoking the hand of Irulegi, the masks, the clothes, the dances, the music and the grotesque movements and gestures of the *zirtzilak*, they all are signs that request, ask, demand and inform people within that spatial zone, and in that way, introduce new forms of agency. By means of those signs, Iruinkokoa demarcates spaces during the itinerary of the *kalejira*, in the old quarter of Pamplona in which different social groups and social orders compete over rights of ownership. Such demarcation reveals a clear self-knowledge of the places that the Basque-speaking community considers *their own*. But in general, the public space of the Old Town is renegotiated and contested through carnival strategies and its resemiotization gives way to an inverted and critical interpretative frame. Iruinkokoa turns the physical space of the Old Town in Pamplona into a transgressive social, cultural, and political space for a day. Spots such as the Santa Ana Square, for instance, become arenas in which those who are usually voiceless become judges, and in which attitudinal norms and conventions are transgressed and mocked. The resemiotized spaces also reorganize and invert the communicative behavior and the orders of indexicality; what people can and cannot do, and the value of their sociolinguistic repertoires; Basque, for instance, has become for them a relevant tool for transgression.

The analysis also provides interesting insights into the role of carnival in terms of agency, and how it affects the interpretation of the signs. In fact, the study of the playful reworking of semiotic resources in Iruinkokoa reveals that framing an action in a humorous and carnival semiotic grants the performers in Iruinkokoa the potential to break with social conventions of politeness and respect that would otherwise restrict stigmatized cultural stereotypes in Pamplona's Old Town. The use of grotesque imagery confirms the idea that Iruinkokoa is an escape from the norm, and also that it refracts the world through a perspective that encourages the audience to engage critically with it. Iruinkokoa speaks as a single, collective voice and thus engages in a provocative dialogue with its community. "People often ask who writes this," explains Iker: "And it's always: 'Iruinkokoa.' If you want to get mad, you'll have to get mad at all of us."

The ambivalent semiotics of carnival, moreover, serve to reveal established social hierarchies and to create an agentive frame that allows bringing those hierarchies to debate, competition, and review. In fact, these carnivalesque semiotics invite us to look inside ourselves and to abolish opposites through a much more fluid vision of social structures. All these creative semiotics lead to an agentive frame that facilitates a field in which to address ideological tensions in the public sphere, mainly during the theatrical parodic performance. Focusing on the last sketch about the discovery of the Hand of Irulegi, for instance, the grotesque body semiotics and oral discourses displayed in the square make us question the importance of being "true" Basque speakers by origin or not, and also encourages the audience to take up a critical distance toward what we would otherwise consider *our own* discourses. This double meaning, typical of the carnival semiotics, is used to criticize the hypocrisy that often accompanies initiatives in favor of the Basque language. Through carnival ambivalence, they show us how such nationalist demands intertwine in a sex orgy with the capitalist discourses of profit.

Notes

1 We understand agency as "the capacity for socially meaningful action" (Parish and Hall 2021, 1). As Parish and Hall (2021, 1) suggest, this definition pays attention to meaning and to the social semiotic mechanisms that mediate action, in particular to indexicality. In fact, social meaning and agency are co-constitutive through the mechanism of indexicality. Indexicality points towards the actions that bind agents in Iruinkokoa together as a "we," while at the same time imbuing those actions with meaning and thereby agency.
2 The term *safe space*, which dates to the late twentieth-century women's movement, was originally associated with keeping marginalized groups free from violence and harassment (The Roestone Collective, 2014), and it has since been used in many different contexts. For example, in the Basque context Hernández and Altuna (2021) analyzed different communities of practices (CofPs) and conceived them as safe spaces in which young people could attempt to modify their linguistic practices at different levels. Likewise, Ortega et al. (2021) consider Participatory Action Research (PAR) methodology a safe space for new speakers of Basque to try out new forms of speakerhood.
3 In the original song *biona*, "of both of us."

References

Aiestaran, Mattin, Javier Velaza, Joaquín Gorrochategui, Carmen Usúa, Pablo Pujol, Euken Alonso, Eneko Iriarte, Josu Narbarte, Dani Ruiz-González, Oihane Mendizabal-Sandonís, Jesús Sesma, Jose Antonio Mujika-Alustiza, Jesús García Gazólaz, Berta Balduz, and Juantxo Agirre-Mauleon. 2024. "A Vasconic Inscription on a Bronze Hand: Writing and Rituality in the Iron Age Irulegi Settlement in the Ebro Valley." *Antiquity* 98 (397): 66–84. https://doi.org/10.15184/AQY.2023.199

Altuna Zumeta, Olatz, Maialen Iñarra Arregi, and Asier Basurto Arruti. 2021. *Hizkuntzen erabileraren kale neurketa. Euskal Herria, 2021. Laburpen txostena*. Andoain: Soziolinguistika Klusterra.

Assmann, Jan, and John Czaplicka. 1995. "Collective Memory and Cultural Identity." *New German Critique* 65: 125–133. https://doi.org/10.2307/488538

Bauman, Richard. 1992. "Performance." In *Folklore, Cultural Performances, and Popular Entertainments*, edited by Richard Bauman, 41–49. New York/Oxford: Oxford University Press.

Bakhtin, Mikhail. 1981. "Discourse in the Novel." *The Dialogic Imagination*, edited by Michael Holquist, and Caryl Emerson, 259–422. Austin: University of Texas Press.

Bakhtin, Mikhail. 1984. *Rabelais and His World*. Bloomington: Indiana University Press.

Bauman, Richard, and Charles L. Briggs. 1990. "Poetics and Performance as Critical Perspectives on Language and Social Life." *Annual Review of Anthropology* 19: 59–88.

Blommaert, Jan. 2012. *Chronicles of Complexity. Ethnography, Superdiversity and Linguistic Landscapes*. Tilburg: Tilburg Papers in Social Studies.

Blommaert, Jan, and Jie Dong. 2010. *Ethnographic Fieldwork: A Beginner's Guide*. Bristol: Multilingual Matters.

Emerson, Caryl. 2002. "Coming to Terms with Bakthin's Carnival: Ancients, Modern, Sub Specie Aeternitatis." In *Bakthin and the Classics*, edited by R. Bracht Branham. Illinois: Northwestern University Press.

Euskarabidea – Euskararen Nafar Institutua. 2020. *Nafarroako datu soziolinguistikoak, 2018*. Iruña: Nafarroako Gobernua.

Gorrochategui, Joaquín, and Ekaitz Santazilia (eds.). 2023. "La mano de Irulegi: reflexiones desde la paleohispanística y la vascología [Dosier]." *Fontes Linguae Vasconum* 136: 485–637.

Gumperz, John J. 1982. *Discourse Strategies*. Cambridge: Cambridge University Press.

Hernández, Jone Miren, and Jaime Altuna Ramírez. 2021. "Communities of Practice and Adolescent Speakers in the Basque Country. Research and Transformation Face-to-Face." *Journal of Multilingual and Multicultural Development* 43, no. 1: 321–344. https://doi.org/10.1080/01434632.2021.1998078

Heller, Monica, and Alexandre Duchêne. 2011. "Pride and Profit Changing Discourses of Language, Capital and Nation-State." In *Language in Late Capitalism. Pride and Profit*, edited by Alexandre Duchêne, and Monica Heller. London/New York: Routledge.

Hill, Jane H. 1993. "Hasta La Vista, Baby: Anglo Spanish in the American Southwest." *Critique of Anthropology*, 13, no. 2: 145–176. https://doi.org/10.1177/0308275X9301300203

Järlehed, Johan. 2020. "Pride and Profit: Naming and Branding Galicianness and Basqueness in Public Space." In *Names in Writing*, edited by Maria Löfdahl, Michelle Waldispühl, and Lenna Wenner. 147–176. Göteborg: Meijerbergs arkiv för svensk etymologisk forskning. https://doi.org/10.13140/RG.2.2.28400.81922

Jaworski, Adam, and Crispin Thurlow (eds). 2010. *Semiotic Landscapes: Language, Image, Scape*. London: Continuum.

Kress, Gunther. 2009. *Multimodality: A Social Semiotic Approach to Contemporary Communication*. London: Routledge.

Kress, Gunther. 2011. "Multimodal Discourse Analysis." In *The Routledge Handbook of Discourse Analysis*, edited by James Paul Gee, and Michael Handford, 35–50. London: Routledge.

Luku, Antton. 2014. *Libertitzeaz*. Iruñea: Pamiela.

Moriarty, Máiréad, and Johan Järlehed. 2019. "Multilingual Creativity and Play in the Semiotic Landscape: An Introduction." *International Journal of Multilingualism*. https://doi.org/10.1080/14790718.2018.1500256

Ortega, Ane, Jone Goirigolzarri, and Estibaliz Amorrortu, 2021. "Participatory Action Research to Promote Linguistic Mudas Among New Speakers of Basque: Design and Benefits." *Journal of Multilingual and Multicultural Development* 43, no. 1, 55–67. https://doi.org/10.1080/01434632.2021.1968877

Otaegi, Kepa, and Eduardo Apodaka. 2022. "Iruinkokoa: A Case of Folkloric Innovation in an Urban Environment." *European Public and Social Innovation Review* 7, no. 2, 70–83. https://doi.org/10.31637/epsir.22-2.6

Parish, Ayden, and Kira Hall. 2021. "Agency." In *The International Encyclopedia of Linguistic Anthropology*, edited by James Stanlaw, 1–9. New Jersey: John Wiley and Sons.

The Roestone Collective. 2014. "Safe Space: Towards a Reconceptualization." *Antipode* 46, no. 5, 1346–1365.

Scollon, Ron, and Suzie Wong Scollon. 2003. *Discourses in Place. Language in the Material World*. London: Routledge.

Shohamy, Elana, and Shoshi Waksman. 2009. "Linguistic Landscape As An Ecological Arena: Modalities, Meanings, Negotiations, Education." In *Linguistic Landscape: Expanding the Scenery*, edited by Elana Shohamy, and Durk Gorter, 313–331. New York: Routledge.

Van Dijk, Teun A. 2001. "Multidisciplinary CDA: A Plea for Diversity." In *Methods of Critical Discourse Analysis*, edited by Ruth Wodak, and Michael Meyer, 95–120. London: Sage.

Van Leeuwen, Theo, and Ruth Wodak. 1999. "Legitimizing Immigration Control: A Discourse-Historical Analysis." *Discourse Studies* 1, no. 1, 83–117. https://doi.org/10.1177/1461445699001001005

Wong Scollon, Suzie, and Ron Scollon. 2004. *Nexus Analysis. Discourse and the Emerging Internet*. London: Routledge.

7 Ethnographies to localize (in)visibility and complexity

A collaborative study in higher education to explore the Bengali linguistic landscape in Madrid

Adil Moustaoui Srhir and Carlos Aliaño Pérez

Introduction: Project presentation

This chapter is the result of a collaborative action-research study,[1] understood as a way of improving pedagogical practices in the classroom, solve problems, and transform realities in which social and linguistic inequalities are present. In addition, it aims to foster a greater critical sociolinguistic and metalinguistic awareness of multilingualism among university students by mapping the LL, both in their educational and other spaces attended by students. To do so, the principles of Critical Linguistic Education (CLE) have been followed (Prego Vázquez and Zas Varela 2018; Gorter et al. 2021; Martín Rojo et al. 2023). The objective is to develop students' interpretative capacity and a critical reflexivity on the political and sociocultural factors that interact with multilingualism, especially those related to the use of both local and migrant languages within the public linguistic landscapes (Sabaté-Dalmau 2023). A further objective is to "mobilize language pedagogy" (Cenoz and Gorter 2023; Chesnut et al. 2013; Malinowski et al. 2020; Rowland 2013; Sayers 2010). In these works, LL mapping is used as a pedagogical tool to document the visibility, competences, and ethnolinguistic vitality of language varieties in a given space. We consider it a useful pedagogy that enables students to acquire creative techniques for self-learning and the acquisition, production, and transmission of sociolinguistic knowledge. This engaged pedagogy aims to develop awareness-raising strategies oriented towards a citizenship that is more committed to sociolinguistic, intercultural, political, and social issues. This pedagogical intervention is also intended to involve learners by creating and opening up debates on how multisituated multilingualism operates in society and the immediate environment. In this sense, it is an action through which knowledge generated at university is shared, transferred, and disseminated beyond the classroom. This implies epistemological and methodological changes in which students are not merely passive recipients but active co-participants and producers of knowledge and transformative actions.

DOI: 10.4324/9781032687087-8

Pedagogical tasks

During the course of the project, the collaborative research tool applied a pedagogical intervention aimed at converting LL into a window on the practices of citizens, social groups and ethnic minorities that generate demographic, sociocultural, and linguistic changes in the contact areas they reside in. To this end, both Lavapiés area, where the student and co-author of this chapter was living, and the Bangladeshi community were chosen as the objects of study. The main reason for this choice is the process of gentrification and touristification it has undergone and the notable effect on its LL and the businesses of the local migrant population (Saiz de Lobado 2021). Lavapiés area is part of the Central District of Madrid and is located southeast of the centre of the city. Like its neighbouring districts, its steep streets, narrow and irregularly wooded and conserve still their medieval origin as a suburb that extended outside the downtown. Lavapiés has always been a humble neighborhood, inhabited until the 1980s by the working class and the elderly. However, from the 1990s it became a neighbourhood where immigrants, mostly Moroccans, began to live. Lavapiés is also one of the most multicultural and multilingual areas in Madrid and had been the object of several studies (Moustaoui 2013, 2018; Saiz de Lobado and Revilla Guijarro 2019), where a considerable sample of signs and LL in Arabic and other languages were collected. Furthermore, the Bangladeshi community was found of interest for several reasons. First, because both the community and the language have the minority and migrant status, and especially Bengali is not among the top 10 minority languages spoken in the Madrid region. Second, this community is one of the most numerous in the Lavapiés area. Third, this pedagogical intervention is also oriented towards sociolinguistic issues regarding globalization, indexicality, and scales, due to the status of the community and the language under investigation.

The tasks and activities carried out in this action-research were designed to develop critical linguistic awareness of the use of Bengali in the LL of Lavapiés. For this purpose, ethnographic work was carried out over an 18-month period, focusing on the observation of this language, its dynamics, and the languages it is in contact with in the context and spaces in which it is used in (Gorter et al. 2019; Gorter 2021; Migge 2023; Rasinger 2018). Furthermore, the intervention was drawn up in line with recent studies on language teaching through LL beyond the educational settings of the classroom (Gorter and Cenoz 2021; Niedt and Seals 2020). Likewise, by choosing Lavapiés and Bengali, the pedagogical intervention attempted to observe the visibility and presence/non-presence of minority languages in an urban space. On the one hand, this can provide information about the linguistic communities represented in this contact zone through the analysis of LL (Barni and Bagna 2009; Marten, Van Mensel and Gorter 2012), as well as the underlying motivations for using Bengali, a language other than the dominant one(s). On the other hand, it will help to understand the communication patterns and dynamics of Bengali speakers, but also to identify its symbolic and social function in this area (Blommaert 2010). Therefore, the intervention focuses on the linguistic-communicative, socio-identitarian, ethnic, and economic function or place-making (Scollon and Scollon 2003) of Bengali in a sociolinguistic regime and landscape that is hierarchical and indexicalized.

Theoretical framework in the study of LL

Different theoretical approaches and methodological tools have addressed the study of space in the rapidly expanding framework of Linguistic Landscape Studies (LLS) (Backhaus 2007; Blommaert 2013; Gorter 2006; Shohamy and Gorter 2009) to explore the sociolinguistic and semiotic dimension of space. These approaches have shown that the study of LL does not merely involve counting and describing the languages contained in it, but also contextualizing the analysis and combining its methods through the diachronic historicist approach, ethnography, and the observation of the space itself. Such contextualization and analysis have recently been developed in works on the LL that address globalization and other socio-economic phenomena (Ben-Rafael 2009; Ben-Rafael and Ben-Rafael 2015); issues of identity (Blackwood et al. 2016); sociolinguistic regime (Blommaert 2013; Blommaert and Maly 2015); language policy in relation with spatial features (Du Plessis 2012; Shohamy 2015); issues related to political and social conflicts (Martín Rojo 2014; Pavlenko 2009; Rubdy and Ben Said 2015); and multilingualism (Hatoss 2023) or gentrification in multilingual areas (Saiz de Lobado 2022). Furthermore, the analysis of landscape dynamics regarding the sociolinguistic stratification and inequality invites us to address the category of minority languages in the study of LL. The pioneering work of Cenoz and Gorter (2006) focused initially on the relationship between LL and the sociolinguistic context based on the case of Euskera in the Basque Country. In this work, both authors highlight how LL reflects the power and status of some languages present in the space. The LL approach focused on minority languages helps to understand the struggles between languages, speakers, and power structures and, ultimately, empowers minority groups by giving visibility and recognition to their languages. Therefore, it was important to include the notion of minority languages such as Bengali in the analysis of Lavapiés' LL in this case study. According to Marten et al. (2012, 7), Bengali can be considered in this case as migrant (or "new") and "local-only" minority language. This sheds light on the distinction that might exist in the construction of the LL between what is local/dominant, on the one hand, and what is legitimate/illegitimate, on the other. The implementation of these categories provides an understanding of the power relations involved in the use of the Bengali language, as well as their respective identities at local and transnational status. So, both the contact between languages in the LL – regardless of their status – and linguistic simultaneity and hybridity can intervene in approaching language varieties as a set of resources that could be equally or hierarchically stratified (Moustaoui 2019). Consequently, according to Blommaert (2013) and Silverstein (2003), there is a multiscale indexicality connected to the varying roles of the speakers themselves and to different functions (Jüssen 2014) for the language under analysis. We thus consider that these spaces of indexicality contain different scales of authority/legitimacy and restrictions for participating in the semiotic construction of the space (Maly 2016; Zas Varela and

Prego Vázquez 2016) and that pedagogical intervention through LL would help map and highlight these phenomena.

In addition, our pedagogical intervention considers that no site is linked to a single community, language, or identity in the sense that space is not a single geosemiotic and material arrangement, but rather a scale of spaces with varying configurations, assemblages, and narratives that refer to different experiences of language use. Thus, spatiality is also a multiplicity of scales and micro-spaces and regimes. With this in mind, the methodological and conceptual innovation in language mapping consists of not only conceiving the city as a text or discourse, but also of understanding how individuals experience their multilingual/scalar area, how they give meaning to these practices and how they use their resources in the cityscape. Consequently, the analysis of space and its LL as a scalar phenomenon will allow us to offer interpretations and insights into the linguistic, social, and political stratification that might occur between Bengali and other languages and varieties in the space in which it interacts. Indeed, as Hatoss (2023, 9) points out, "the LL also helps us understand social change and transformations. It provides a diachronic insight into the changing language ecology, as the linguistic mapping of public places becomes a historical record of gradual social and linguistic change."

Methodology and data collection

The methodology of this action-research focuses on the exploration in situ of the LL of Bengali in Lavapiés, complemented by the virtual exploration derived from the use of Google Street View, used in previous research in the Spanish context (Gómez-Pavón and Quilis Merín 2021), and other virtual tools developed by Google that will be discussed below. At the beginning of our intervention, the observation of LL revolved mainly around signs posted on the facades of migrant businesses. Thereafter, the study of signs adjacent to these, such as the associative, socio-cultural, and political signs produced by the community under study, became increasingly important. These types of signs were mentioned at the beginning of the research (Aliaño 2022), albeit without addressing the crucial role they play in the place-making of this migrant group. Consequently, the initial phases of observation focused on the production of space and how Bengali as a minority language was utilized. In addition, monolingual practices were frequent in this type of signs and established dynamics that invert the fixed linguistic hierarchies reflected in other types of signs studied. The reason for extending the typology of the sample is due to a growing linguistic awareness and perception of students as active subjects in the exploration of LL. The student's immediate access to Lavapiés area was also very positive. The continuous ethnographic exploration of the place has allowed us to delve deeper into the sociolinguistic dynamics present in the day-to-day life of this area. It guaranteed the students' observational and investigative eye development, giving them self-initiative and criterion during the fieldwork. Furthermore, the students became familiar with the Bengali script in order to be able to identify its signs. It was also extremely gratifying to observe how the trends that were identified at the beginning evolved throughout our intervention. Over time, multilingual, translingual, and hybrid signs of interest appeared and disappeared around the spaces and businesses managed and run by the Bangladeshi community. As a result, these trends and dynamics became increasingly evident to the student through the development of the competences required in the implementation of the intervention. Likewise, the initial exploration phase of the fieldwork in situ was carried out intensively in 2021. The in situ exploration was complemented by the student on January 10 and February 3, 2023 to reassess the situation of the Bengali LL and identify new dynamics of change.

A key factor in the development of the methodology was the use of tools for the virtual exploration of the LL, focusing especially on the use of Google Maps, including Google Street View (hereafter GSV) and Google Reviews (hereafter GR), as well as Google Lens (hereafter GL). Gorter (2018, 7) mentioned that "Google Street View is a tool that can offer interesting new ways to conduct LL studies," and it has been used already to combine LLS and digital ethnographies (Maly and Blommaert 2019). These tools have helped the learner delve into the migrant business owners' background, examine customers' perceptions and attitudes about the identity of these businesses, and translating from Bengali. It was also possible to extract the written language present in the signs studied, regardless of their writing system. The use of these virtual tools implies a delocalized methodology and depends directly on the characteristics implicit in the agreed object of study.

Finally, the signs studied focus on the facades of businesses, including the peripheral signs. Our analysis focuses on Bangladeshi community restaurants/business's signs and other signs of socio-cultural, religious, and political nature. Therefore, a multiscale analysis was carried out, allowing different sets of signs to be classified and analyzed either as a whole unit or separately. Both virtual and physical places were explored and more than 130 samples were collected, including in situ photographs taken by the student and the professor involved in this research, and screenshots taken by the student from GSV and GR. These samples were collected and classified based on their geolocation and included monolingual Bengali signs, bilingual Bengali-Spanish signs, and bi-multilingual signs, mostly Spanish-Bengali-English signs.

Lavapiés as language learning and critical linguistic awareness environment

Despite having its own identity within the urban imaginary of Madrid, Lavapiés area (see Map 7.1) is located within the administrative neighborhood of Embajadores, part of the Central District of the city of Madrid. Lavapiés is one of the most densely populated areas in Madrid. Despite the population's decline, Lavapiés area maintains its high population density with 432 inhabitants per hectare, compared to 53.3 in the rest of Madrid (Reichborn-Kjennerud, Ruano and Sorando 2021), and almost doubling the Central District's population density, which is 257 .

The processes of touristification and gentrification are reflected in the new businesses that are appearing in terms of property rental or purchase prices. Since 2013, rents have increased by 47% and sales by 38.5% (Aunión and Medina 2018).

Ethnographies to localize (in)visibility and complexity 171

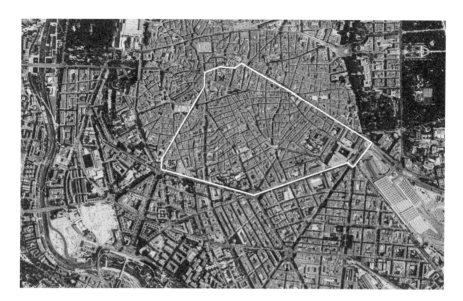

Map 7.1 Map of the Lavapiés area extracted from participabarrio.es.

Likewise, in 2018 there were more than 2,000 tourist flats in active use, aggressively limiting the supply of housing and restricting residence to citizens with a higher level of purchasing power. Due to gentrification, several groups of migrant origin began to abandon the neighborhood as a place of residence (Barañano-Cid and Uceda-Navas 2021). At the same time, these new conditions led to an increase in the number of cultural leisure activities on offer and a rise in the general cost of living in the neighborhood, causing processes of Anglicization of the LL (see Figure 7.1) and of the social semiosis of the neighborhood (Saiz de Lobado 2022).

These processes are accompanied by the securitization of the area, where 48 video surveillance cameras have been operating since 2009 (Ruiz Chasco 2014, 315), a figure that represents a third of the cameras present in the Central District. The neighborhood is under constant surveillance through video surveillance and police presence.

As for the demographic and migratory matter, it is significant to mention that foreigners accounted for 35% of the neighborhood's population in 2018, with Ecuador, Bangladesh, Morocco, China, Colombia, Senegal, and Bolivia as the most represented countries (Aunión and Medina 2018). At that time, no fewer than 88 nationalities were present in the neighborhood, making it an example of coexistence and superdiversity, largely thanks to the associations that aligned themselves with the local authorities to rebuild and structure this very central area. Superdiversity is also reflected in the economic structure, as ethnic businesses have a strong presence in the cartography and everyday life of the neighborhood. These businesses represent highly relevant enclaves in the transnational activity

172 *Ethnographic Landscapes and Language Ideologies in the Spanish State*

Figure 7.1 Bilingual Spanish/English sign of a cafeteria in Miguel Servet Street.

and sociability of migrant communities. To a certain extent, the emergence of a new immigration economy and its subsequent consolidation has resulted in an ethnicization of economic activities and the space (Pérez-Agote et al. 2010; Riesco Sanz 2010). This economy also flourished thanks to the social, ethnic, linguistic, religious, and spatial conditions offered by the neighborhood. In this sense, it is worth highlighting Lavapiés' significant value as a space for socialization, leisure, consumption, and work for many other migrants who are not residents of the neighborhood and are attracted by the opportunities offered by this area. Lavapiés represents a plurality of spaces and subjective experiences, which refer to different and increasingly heterogeneous groups and identities. From this reality, migratory

Ethnographies to localize (in)visibility and complexity 173

Figure 7.2 Multilingual sign in a Bangladeshi hairdressing salon facade in Lavapiés Street.

movements and the models that organize their location are characterized by the capacity for feedback.

As for multilingualism, it should be noted that it is visible in all the streets and the LL is more diverse and multilingual, as can be seen in Figure 7.2, and in more detail in Figure 7.3, due to the presence of a greater number of shops per square meter and of other groups of immigrant origin.

Bangladeshis in Lavapiés

According to data from the National Register, in 2021 there were 19,865 Bangladeshi residents in Spain. The Bengali diaspora in Spain is concentrated mostly in the province of Barcelona, with 8887 Bangladeshis (44.74%), and in the province of Madrid, with 7229 Bangladeshis (36.39%). Ninety-two percent of the Madrid Bengali community resides in the capital, which hosts 6716 Bangladeshis

Figure 7.3 Bilingual Arabic/Spanish sign in a Bangladeshi hairdressing salon.

(Spanish EAPS 2021). Thus, the community continues to grow steadily. It is also worth noting the possibility that this community may be larger, due to the presence of migrants who have not been able to regularize their status. As for their country of origin, the official language of Bangladesh is Bengali. However, there are 40 additional languages, including 36 languages native to the region, that are spoken as a minority. Ninety-eight percent of the country's population is ethnically and linguistically Bengali, although there are other ethnic groups such as the Garo, Marma, Chakma, and Santhals. The most spread religion is Islam, with 89.7% of the population being Muslim, followed by Hinduism (9.2%), Buddhism (0.7%), and Christianity (0.7%) (Spanish Ministry of Foreign Affairs, European Union and Cooperation 2024). Although their Muslim identity is not strongly perceived by the local population, the role of Muslimness in shaping the Bangladeshi identity is remarkable. Regarding their presence in Lavapiés, it should be noted that in 2018, the percentage of foreign population in the neighborhood stood at 25%, and among the nationalities with the highest population were Bangladesh, Morocco, and Senegal, along with Italy, France, the United States and the United Kingdom (Aunión and Medina 2018). Although the Bangladeshi population in Spain is smaller than that of Pakistan and India, it comes as no surprise that their segregation is stronger than in the case of the migrant population of these countries (Garha, Domingo and López Sala 2016; Méndez 2019). Lavapiés area could be considered the socio-ethnic, religious, economic, and even political enclave for the Bangladeshi community in Madrid, being one of the communities with the greatest presence in the neighborhood. To a lesser extent, this community is also

Ethnographies to localize (in)visibility and complexity 175

concentrated in other areas, with different socio-demographic characteristics. Moreover, the locals mistake Bangladeshis for Pakistanis and Indians (Jüssen 2014, 707), due to the historical processes of domination by England, India, and later Pakistan. Also worth noting are the precarious conditions and sociability towards the "community" (Méndez 2019), street vendors and their visible presence in Madrid's festivals, celebrations and holidays as hawkers of a variety of products and drinks. In addition, the shops, the mosque or Bangladeshi groups act as nuclei of sociability and thus allow the expansion of transnational networks and socialization around Bangladeshiness. This justifies why most of the population and activity of the Bangladeshi community is concentrated in Lavapiés, where mosques run by the Bangladeshi community can be found. Therefore, both tourism and migration are factors that influence the remarkable and changing multilingualism with the presence of Bengali in the area (Castillo Lluch and Sáez Rivera 2011). This multilingualism is reflected in the LL and embodies a new hierarchy in the use of the written language and semiotic artifacts.

Results of the collaborative action-research

Restaurant and business signs

In this section, the construction of Bangladeshi identity and its mimicry or non-mimicry towards other more prestigious identities will be discussed. Furthermore, special emphasis will be placed on how this construction of the Bangladeshi identity navigates between invisibility and the repositioning of semiotic elements that recognize this identity and its presence in the public space. To analyze this process of invisibility, we will focus on the signs used in Bangladeshi-run restaurants and businesses.

Figure 7.4 shows a Bengali-English bilingual sign, where only the Latin alphabet is used. The Bengali element that implicitly dominates this sign is the word "SHAPLA" (শাপলা), which refers to the national flower of Bangladesh, and to the name of this restaurant. Although it should be noted that the word Shapla exists in both Bengali and Hindi (शापला) to name this flower, commonly called water lily, the review below confirms the Bengali identity, which has been made invisible to the non-Bangladeshi clientele.

The review says that it is a "Bangladeshi restaurant disguised as Indian restaurant" (see Figure 7.5) and sheds light on the culinary differences between Indian and Bengali cuisine. This review was located by using the word "Bangladeshi" in the GR search engine on the restaurant's Google Maps profile, along with two other reviews pointing to the Bangladeshi identity of the business. The case of this restaurant serves as an example of the role of this type of business in the expansion of the Bangladeshi economy, given that there is a second restaurant called "Shapla 2" on the same block. Opposite the first restaurant, there is also a phone shop with the same name.

In order to delve deeper in our virtual mapping, the GR profile of the user who reviewed the Shapla restaurant was explored, and another similar review of the

Figure 7.4 Bilingual Bengali/English sign of the Shapla restaurant facade in Lavapiés Street.

★   Hace 4 años

This is a Bangladeshi restaurant disguised as Indian restaurant. Food was horrible. Owner was so disinterested and rude that it is unbelievable. If they had even a basic decency to claim as Indian restaurant, they would not carry beef when they carry Halal. Avoid them at all costs.

Figure 7.5 Review extracted from GR.

Ethnographies to localize (in)visibility and complexity 177

Figure 7.6 Multilingual Bengali/Spanish/English sign of the Baisakhi restaurant facade in Lavapiés Street.

Indian Baisakhi restaurant was found, which is located between the Shapla and Shapla 2 restaurants. In it, the user expresses his disappointment, since he thought it would be run by migrants from Punjab, whose historical territory is divided between an Indian state and the second largest province of Pakistan, both of which have the same name. On the facade of this restaurant (Figure 7.6), there is a multilingual Bengali-English-Spanish sign.

The word Baisakhi has been considered as a Bengali word due to its transcription "Baiśākhī" (বৈশাখী), although such transcription is not too far from the Hindi (बैसाखी-Baisaakhee) and Punjabi (ਵਿਸਾਖੀ-Visākhī) transcriptions. On this sign, we can see how the English word "Indian" is superimposed over the Spanish word "*restaurante*" as a consequence of the contact between these languages, and their dominant presence in the linguistic indexicalization of the construction of the semiotic space of these restaurants.

Following the trail of reviews, we entered words such as "Punjab" or "Bangladesh" in the GR search engine and found the review (Figure 7.7) of an Indian user from the Punjab region who confirms the Punjabi origin of the food, but comments on how the workers of the restaurant revealed their Bangladeshi identity and their lack of knowledge about the preparation of Punjabi dishes.

Of interest here is the owner's response to the review (Figure 7.8): written in Spanish, he clearly lacks a fluent command of the language.

The response appears to be an apology, claiming that the unique taste of Punjabi food can only be found in India.

Following the aforementioned tracking patterns, we used keywords, such as Bangladesh, Bangladeshi or Bangla, to find testimonies that may give some

178 *Ethnographic Landscapes and Language Ideologies in the Spanish State*

Rashi
6 reseñas

Hace 5 meses

As an Indian person from Punjab (they serve Punjabi food) I can say this, this is the worse food I've ever had in 1 year of being in Spain.
I ordered 3 different curries, two of which were the exact same with different toppings which also didn't match the description on the menu. They don't use any spices, it was all cream and tomatoes.

When I complained to the staff, he explained that they all hail from **Bangladesh** and have no idea about cuisine from Punjab (quite obviously).

All I can say is that this food is as far from Indian food as possible.

Figure 7.7 Review and owner's response extracted from GR.

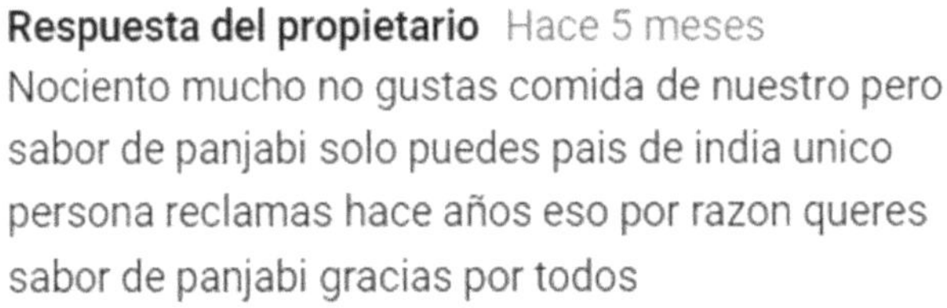

Respuesta del propietario Hace 5 meses
Nociento mucho no gustas comida de nuestro pero sabor de panjabi solo puedes pais de india unico persona reclamas hace años eso por razon queres sabor de panjabi gracias por todos

Figure 7.8 Review and owner's response extracted from GR.

evidence in order to reveal the Bangladeshi identity of other restaurants located on the same street. We found testimonies pointing out to the Bangladeshi identity of the following restaurants on Lavapiés Street: "Calcuta," "Tam Mijaem," "Anarkoli," "Döner Kebab Comida Turka," "Delhi Express," "Shapla," "Baisakhi," "Sonali," and "Kebap and Biryani House." The restaurant "Sonali" also has a Bengali name, since this word (সোনালী) means golden in Bengali and is used as a proper noun. As in the case of the "Shapla" restaurant, there is a process of invisibility of their Bengali identity and their language to the non-Bangladeshi public through the use of the Latin alphabet on their signs. Furthermore, the presence of Bangladeshi

Ethnographies to localize (in)visibility and complexity 179

Figure 7.9 Istanbul Doner Kebab restaurant facade in Miguel Servet Street.

kebab shops and the mimicry towards Turkish identity for commercial purposes, which is discussed below, is also remarkable.

In Figure 7.9, the dominance of the Spanish language can be seen on this sign, although we also find neologisms such as "Döner Kebap" and the name of the famous Turkish city "Istanbul," which has not been adapted to Spanish. On this sign, we find semiotic elements that reveal hints of a possible concealed Bengali identity. First, the signs' letter colours on the left and above, which contain the name of the restaurant and have a white background, are dark green and red, present in the Bangladeshi flag. The words "Doner Kebap" are written in dark green and the words "Istanbul" and "Turkish Food," in red. According to our exploration, this semiotic element is a frequently used resource in Bangladeshi businesses. For example, in Figure 7.2, the door of the hairdresser's shop is green, while the main sign has a red background. Likewise, in Figure 7.14, the presence of these colours is much more explicit, and the Bangladeshi flag can be seen framed in the outline of the map of Bangladesh. Moreover, we perceived the presence of samosas, a kind of dumpling typical of the Indian subcontinent, on the menu of this establishment. These elements point out the underlying Bengali identity in the production of the space, although, unlike in the previous cases, we were unable to find any reviews that confirm this due to the lack of reviews in the Google Maps profile of Döner Kebap Istanbul. Regarding the use of colour, Otsuji and Pennycook (2019) argued there is a semiotics of colour that emerges in normative discourses to contribute to the assemblages of time, place, people, and discourse. In addition, there is also a symbolic layer through the use of colour which –at the same time – is in a

180 *Ethnographic Landscapes and Language Ideologies in the Spanish State*

Figure 7.10 Tazim Food Corner restaurant facade in La Fe Street.

dialogical relationship (Rasinger op.cit), form a "semiotic aggregate" (Scollon and Scollon op. cit. 12) and multimodal artifacts.

Trough the analysis of these examples, we have seen how Indian and Turkish identity (Jüssen op. cit.) play a key role in the invisibilization of the Bangladeshi identity and the community's commercial discourse, as can be seen in the list of restaurants mentioned above, whose Bengali identity is highlighted in the reviews.

Figure 7.10 shows an English-Spanish bilingual sign, in which the use of English is dominant. In contrast, Figure 7.11 depicts three posters, acknowledged as monolingual signs produced by the same Bangladeshi restaurant.

From top to bottom, the first sign is a job offer that translates as follows: "A waiter and a male or female kitchen assistant are needed," followed by the word "contact" and a telephone number. On the second sign, we find the opening hours of the restaurant. The third sign advertises bengali food offered by the restaurant.

This example (Figure 7.11) displays how the restaurants and other businesses opened in the last two years show a new trend in the indexicalization of the languages involved in the construction of the space, in which the Bengali language started to become more visible. As far as we have been able to observe, there is a tendency towards monolingualism in Bengali businesses with the use of very few words in Spanish, usually regarding to the address. Unlike the rest of the "Indian" restaurants that are concentrated in Lavapiés Street, this is a type of business targeted exclusively at the community. Therefore, the communication pattern and the symbolic and practical function of the language is completely different from businesses whose services, products and information target a non-Bengali clientele. This is also noticeable on other signs, such as those in Figure 7.12.

The signs on these posters belong to a food shop called Lavapiés Cash and Carry. The translation of the top sign reads, "On the occasion of the month of Ramadan. Special price discount." The word written in larger letters, next to "Cash and Curry," is the transcribed Arabic word Halal (حلال), which shows the Muslim identity of the majority of the Bengali population (Salguero Montaño 2018) and is found mostly in Bengali food shops. At the bottom right, there is a poster for an organized pilgrimage, and on the left, a poster about the sale of lambs slaughtered

Ethnographies to localize (in)visibility and complexity 181

Figure 7.11 Monolingual Bengali signs displayed in *Tazim* Food Corner restaurant facade.

in the Muslim halal way. These Bengali-dominant multimodal signs are mostly found inside the shops and provide very specific information aimed exclusively at the community, even though there are other Muslim communities in the neighborhood. The functions of the use of Bengali on these signs are socio-pragmatic and identitarian in nature, and therefore require not only linguistic but also situated socio-cultural competences to understand them.

In addition to restaurants, we also encountered other types of businesses in the Bengali community: bazaars, travel agencies, internet cafés, print shops, phone shops, clothing shops, money remittance shops, Islamic goods shops, crafts shops,

182 *Ethnographic Landscapes and Language Ideologies in the Spanish State*

Figure 7.12 Bengali signs found inside the Lavapiés Cash and Carry food shop in Sombrerete Street.

convenience stores, mini-markets, and hairdressers. Sometimes the services provided in these businesses are concentrated in the same store: this is the case of the Darul Jannat Islamic shop, located at Sombrerete 10, which also has a sign that reads "Jannat Money Exchange," and sells other goods beside Islamic ones (see Figure 7.13).

During the exploration of these shops, mainly concentrated in Amparo, Caravaca, Lavapiés, and Tribulete streets, we found a tendency towards the invisibility and indexicality of Bangladeshi identity and language, although not as marked and constant as in the case of the restaurants whose customers are not Bangladeshi. We understand that these are physical spaces shared by different Muslim communities that mainly acquire Muslim products which can also be found in Bangladeshi shops.

Figure 7.13 Darul Jannat store facade in Sombrerete Street.

Nevertheless, the following image of a recently opened Bangladeshi supermarket shows how this trend seems to be changing towards a greater use and visibility of Bengali and Spanish-Bengali bilingualism.

As stated before, the facade of this new Bengali supermarket combines the red and green of the Bangladeshi flag. Another semiotic resource is the use of images referencing the history of Bangladesh, such as the February 21 Martyrs' Monument (Figure 7.14) (শহীদ মিনার, *Shaheed Minar*), created to commemorate those killed by the Pakistani police during the Bengali Language Movement demonstrations in 1952, and the National Martyrs' Memorial, which commemorates those killed during the Bangladesh Liberation War, which ended in 1971.

These examples (Figures 7.11, 7.12, and 7.13) show how Bengali signs serve as outward emblems, providing not just a visible but also a semiotic, cultural, and linguistic demarcation of the community presence in a given place-space (Rasinger op. cit.). In addition, these examples demonstrate that language is understood not only as a cognitive object but also as a set of resources and semiotic artifacts which are distributed, repositioned and capitalized in specific temporalities/spaces and with explicit purposes.

Figure 7.15 shows how this type of monolingual political, social, religious and cultural posters is clustered together at the entrance or around the business premises

184 *Ethnographic Landscapes and Language Ideologies in the Spanish State*

Figure 7.14 Bilingual Spanish/Bengali sign of the Bangladeshi supermarket facade in Lavapiés Square.

Figure 7.15 Signs in Bengali and Spanish at the entrance of a business.

of the Bangladeshi community, in such a way that they are often superimposed and cover up those that were previously there at the same spot. At the top, there is also a monolingual Spanish sign that directly concerns the Bangladeshi community, as it announces the event "LENGUA O MUERTE" (LANGUAGE OR DEATH): recognition of the Citizen Network of Mediating Interpreters in homage to Mohammed Abul Hossain, a member of the community who died during the pandemic due to the language barrier present in the health system of the Community of Madrid (Museo Nacional Centro de Arte Reina Sofía 2020). Below this sign, there is a duplicate poster of a discussion meeting with cultural programming, organized by the Bangladesh Association in Spain. The reason for this meeting is to celebrate a Bangladeshi bank holiday, called Victory Day, which commemorates the country's independence from Pakistani rule, in 1971. As we scroll down the image, we can see a political poster with photos of the committee members of a Bengali association. At the bottom right of the image there is a poster for a trip to Malvarrosa beach in the city of Valencia, organized by the Gran Noakhali Association of Madrid. The poster also includes telephone contact numbers and retail outlets where the trip can be paid for. These outlets are migrant businesses and they helped in locating businesses of the Bengali community that do not reveal their origins. It is also important to remark the presence of these associations on social media, as several Facebook groups, pages, and profiles related to them were found during this action-research, along with similar poster images.

Figure 7.16 shows a poster announcing the inauguration of the Sylhet District Association in August 2022, held at the Bangladesh Association in Spain, Jesús y María Street, 32. It can therefore be assumed that these associations tend to share their spaces. Our action-research also revealed that these associations also use restaurants as meeting places. As for the function, or place-making, of the monolingual posters analyzed, it differs paradoxically from the function of the Bangladeshi businesses commercial signs. These signs are aimed exclusively at the community and contain information that requires a great deal of linguistic and cultural knowledge of the community itself. Therefore, the intention is not business oriented, but specifically cultural, social, political and religious. Moreover, it should be stressed that the remarkable presence and diversity of these posters is characteristic of the Bengali LL. This also indicates how the communication pattern of the Bengladeshi diaspora remains visual, through writing, suggesting that a large part of the Bengali diaspora can read Bengali. The emergence of future generations may bring about changes in this communication model. For the time being; however, Bengali LL continues to play a key communicative role within the Bengali diaspora. In comparison, other migrant communities in the neighborhood, such as the Senegalese and Moroccan communities, do not produce such signs with the same frequency or to the same extent as the Bangladeshi community. This practice creates what Rasinger (op.cit. 16) call a "'Bangla-ness' that serves to underline the 'exotic-ness' of the spaces."

Furthermore, the signs analyzed so far were from a bottom-up level, due to the lack of top-down directional signs. However, during our research, we found one example (Figure 7.17) that presented a monolingual top-down sign, issued by the Central District of the Madrid City Council and written in Bengali.

186 *Ethnographic Landscapes and Language Ideologies in the Spanish State*

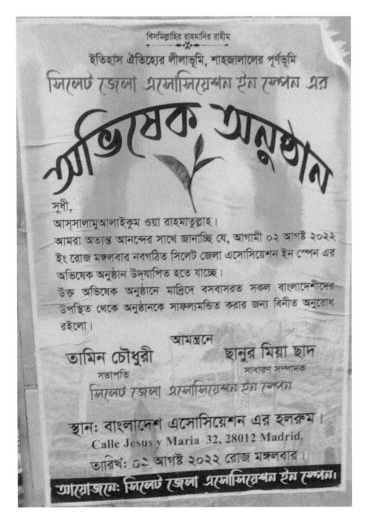

Figure 7.16 Advertising in Bengali announcing the inauguration of the Sylhet District Association.

Although it also includes Spanish words, we assume that this is due to the use of a template, as it does not affect the content. The title of the poster reads "Parenting group" and advertises three workshops which have been translated as "healthy newborn," "early stimulation," and "parenting guidelines." It also announces that there will be a Bengali translation service and that it will be held at the Casino de la Reina Community Center, located in Lavapiés. We assume that the reason for this sign is that this social center has several networking tables, including the Bangladesh Table (Madrid City Council, n.d.).

Ethnographies to localize (in)visibility and complexity 187

Figure 7.17 Monolingual poster in Bengali produced by the Central District of the Madrid City Council.

Conclusions

The action-research presented in this chapter synthesizes the results obtained since the beginning of the project, focusing on the evolution of the LL of the Bengali diaspora in Lavapiés area in Madrid. We have broadened the work carried out in the co-author's degree thesis as a result of action-research and pedagogical practice, including new findings and conclusions that stem from in situ fieldwork and virtual exploration. The latter has allowed us to explore the LL in greater depth, and find testimonies about the Bengali identity behind these migrant businesses. We have also been able to explore the contact and support networks stemming from the associations of the Bangladeshi community in Madrid. The pedagogical exploration of LL can thus be defined as a new way of understanding the sociocultural, ideological, and historical role of communication practices and experienced lives within Bangladeshi community in Lavapiés in a transnational and globalized world.

The analysis of the examples suggests, first, that linguistic landscapes are translocal spaces well suited to exploring social and linguistic changes in superdiverse contexts. In this sense, the translingual practices of the Bangladeshi community are part of everyday multilingualism in Lavapiés as a multiscalar urban setting. As a result, migrants operate in translocal spaces, maintain transnational identities, and nurture their social (and even political) relations across national boundaries. These engagements can be physical or virtual through the formation of "cyberspora" (Hatoss 2023, 7).

Secondly, through the analysis and results of ethnographic work, we have seen how the language choices and uses within the Bangladeshi community represent a complex web of interconnected factors. In such network spatial repertoires are instrumentalized, in order to adapt to the spatial-temporal demands and possibilities offered by the social, cultural, economic, and political context for the construction of LL and space (Pennycook and Otsuji 2015).

Thirdly, according to the sign typology and place-making, two trends have been identified. We find restaurants and some businesses where there is an indexicality and invisibility of Bengali. This indexical order is a conceptual tool which, as Silverstein (2013, 193) points out, is "necessary to showing us how to relate the micro-social to the macro-social frames of analysis of any sociolinguistic phenomenon." In addition, this indexical order in linguistic landscapes is also shared by wider processes of social change and urban development. Furthermore, our analysis points out that there is a shift in this trend in recent years to a more prominent use of Bengali in terms of both quantitative distribution and its location in the signs. Yet, according to the new scales used in the creation of space, as shown in the example of the Tazim Food Corner restaurant (Figures 7.10 and 7.11) and the Bangladeshi supermarket (Figure 7.14) and other businesses, Bengali is gaining prominence and visibility, "which function as outward markers of their character" (Rasinger op.cit. 14).

Our work has also highlighted how the non-correspondence between demolinguistic and LL data should be examined with caution. Even if Bengali is invisible and indexicalized in some spaces and during some temporalities, it is present and visible and fulfill other functions; social, political, economic, and even religious. Indeed, the ethnographic work has shown that the prominence or not of Bengali signs is not necessarily a good indicator of language (in)vitality (Shohamy 2012).

Finally, we consider that our action-research has mobilized the pedagogy in which both teachers and learners have been involved outside the traditional space of the classroom. Through this pedagogy, competences have been developed and applied for the exploration of LL as a research and pedagogical task for the development of critical linguistic awareness. This has allowed us to discover how "linguistic landscape can enable the learning mobilities that epitomize the contemporary age, giving us impetus to reconsider the places of learning, possibilities for culturally and historically rich trajectories of apprenticeship, and the actualization of new networks of learning" (Malinowski et al. 2020, 5–6). The active engagement of the learner who participated in this study with urban LLs provided an opportunity to reflect on the construction of identities and space. Identities that are represented or invisibilized, of the Bengali community and its socio-economic, cultural, historical, and political conditions in Lavapiés, Madrid. These conditions intervene in the creation of signs, semiotic and multimodal practices in public spaces that the student and co-author will continue to investigate in future research. More specifically, the professor's expertise and guidance on the topic, along with the student's self-initiative and growing interest in the Bengali LL and other related issues, were carefully integrated in this action-research. The interaction between the professor and the student was inspiring and allowed us to transcend the hierarchical boundaries between teacher and pupil. This pedagogy also placed sociolinguistic studies in their natural context and guaranteed learning opportunities beyond the traditional higher education environment.

Note

1 The action-research and data in this chapter were developed within the framework of the R+D+I projects: (1) *Towards a new linguistic citizenship: action-research for the recognition of speakers in the educational field in the Community of Madrid (Madrid)* of the National R+D+I Plan FEDER / Ministry of Science, Innovation and Universities – National Research Agency (PID2019-105676RB-C41).

References

Aliaño, Carlos. 2022. "Exploración virtual del Paisaje Lingüístico de Lavapiés y sus signos: El caso del árabe y el bengalí." Unpublished Bachelor's Thesis, Universidad Complutense de Madrid.
Aunión, J.A., and Miguel Ángel Medina. 2018. "Del mestizaje a los turistas en bicicleta." *El País*. March 16, 2018. https://elpais.com/ccaa/2018/03/16/madrid/1521224323_066 578.html
Backhaus, Peter. 2007. *Linguistic Landscapes: A Comparative Study of Urban Multilingualism in Tokyo*. Clevedon: Multilingual Matters.
Barañano-Cid, Margarita, and Pedro Uceda-Navas. 2021. "Embajadores/Lavapiés, ¿un barrio con vulnerabilidad o gentrificado?" *Ciudad Y Territorio Estudios Territoriales* LIII (M): 83–100. https://doi.org/10.37230/CyTET.2021.M21.05
Barni, Monica, and Carla Bagna. 2009. "A Mapping Technique and the Linguistic Landscape." In *Linguistic Landscape: Expanding the Scenery*, edited by Elana Shohamy and Durk Gorter, 126–140. London: Routledge.
Ben-Rafael, Eliezer. 2009. "A Sociological Approach to the Study of Linguistic Landscapes." In *Linguistic Landscape: Expanding the Scenery*, edited by Elana Shohamy and Durk Gorter, 40–54. London: Routledge.

Ben-Rafael, Eliezer, and Miriam Ben-Rafael. 2015. "Linguistic Landscapes in an Era of Multiple Globalizations." *Linguistic Landscape* 1–2: 19–37. https://doi.org/10.1075/ll.1.1-2.02ben

Blackwood, Robert, Elizabeth Lanza, and Hirut Woldemariam. 2016. *Negotiating and Contesting Identities in Linguistic Landscapes*. London: Bloomsbury.

Blommaert, Jan. 2010. *The Sociolinguistics of Globalization*. Cambridge: Cambridge University Press.

Blommaert, Jan. 2013. *Ethnography, Superdiversity and Linguistic Landscapes: Chronicles of Complexity*. Bristol: Multilingual Matters.

Blommaert, Jan, and Ico Maly. 2015. "Ethnographic Linguistic Landscape Analysis and Social Change: A Case Study." In *Language and Superdiversity*, edited by Karel Arnaut, Jan Blommaert, Ben Rampton, and Massimiliano Spotti, 191–211. London: Routledge.

Castillo Lluch, Mar, and Daniel Sáez Rivera. 2011. "Introducción al Paisaje Lingüístico de Madrid." *Lengua y Migración* 3, no. 1: 73–88.

Cenoz, Jasone, and Durk Gorter. 2006. "Linguistic Landscape and Minority Languages." *International Journal of Multilingualism* 3, no. 1: 67–80.

Cenoz, Jasone, and Durk Gorter. 2023. *A Panorama of Linguistic Landscape Studies*. Bristol: Multilingual Matters.

Chesnut, Mary, Victoria Lee, and Jonathan Schulte. 2013. "The Language Lessons around Us: Undergraduate English Pedagogy and Linguistic Landscape Research." *English Teaching: Practice and Critique* 12, no. 2: 102–120.

Du Plessis, Theodorus. 2012. "The Role of Language Policy in Linguistic Landscape Changes in a Rural Area of the Free State Province of South Africa." *Language Matters* 43, no. 2: 263–282.

Garha, Nachatter Singh, Andreu Domingo, and Ana María López Sala. 2016. "Surasiáticos en Madrid y Barcelona: Encarnando la Diversidad." In *Inmigración y Diversidad en España. Crisis Económica y Gestión Municipal*, edited by Andreu Domingo, 211–236. Vilassar de Dalt: Icaria.

Gómez-Pavón Durán, Ana, and Mercedes Quilis Merín. 2021. "El Paisaje Lingüístico de la Migración en el Barrio de Ruzafa en Valencia: Una Mirada a Través del Tiempo." *Cultura, Lenguaje y Representación* 25: 135–154. https://doi.org/10.6035/CLR.2021.25.8

Gorter, Durk. 2021. "Multilingual Inequality in Public Spaces: Towards an Inclusive Model of Linguistic Landscapes." In *Multilingualism in Public Spaces: Empowering and Transforming Communities*, edited by Robert Blackwood and Deirdre A. Dunlevy, 13–30. London: Bloomsbury.

Gorter, Durk, ed. 2006. *Linguistic Landscape: A New Approach to Multilingualism*. Clevedon: Multilingual Matters.

Gorter, Durk. 2018. "Methods and Techniques for Linguistic Landscape Research: About Definitions, Core Issues and Technological Innovations." In *Expanding the Linguistic Landscape: Linguistic Diversity, Multimodality and the Use of Space as a Semiotic Resource*, edited by Martin Pütz and Neele Mundt, 38–56. Bristol: Multilingual Matters.

Gorter, Durk, and Jasone Cenoz. 2021. "Linguistic Landscapes in Educational Contexts: An Afterword." In *Linguistic Landscape and Educational Spaces*, edited by Emilee Krompák, Víctor Fernández, and Stephan Meyer, 277–290. Bristol: Multilingual Matters.

Gorter, Durk, Jasone Cenoz, and Katrijn Van der Worp. 2021 "The Linguistic Landscape as a Resource for Language Learning and Raising Language Awareness." *Journal of Spanish Language Teaching* 8, no. 2: 161–181. https://doi.org/10.1080/23247797.2021.2014029

Gorter, Durk, Heiko F. Marten, and Luk Van Mensel, eds. 2019. *Linguistic Landscapes and Minority Languages*. London: Palgrave Macmillan.

Hatoss, Anikó. 2023. *Everyday Multilingualism: Linguistic Landscapes as Practice and Pedagogy*. London: Routledge.

Jüssen, Lara. 2014. "Ethnic Business in Whose Name? Translocality of Belongings and the Case of Bangladeshis in a Barrio of Madrid." *Estudios Geográficos* 75, no. 277: 707–716.

Madrid City Council. n.d."Casino de la Reina Community Social Centre." Accessed February 19, 2024. www.madrid.es/portales/munimadrid/es/Inicio/Servicios-sociales-y-salud/Direcciones-y-telefonos/Centro-Social-Comunitario-Casino-de-la-Reina/?vgnext fmt=default&vgnextoid=086dff20c703b110VgnVCM1000000b205a0aRCRD&vgnext channel=2bc2c8eb248fe410VgnVCM1000000b205a0aRCRD.

Malinowski, David, Hiram H. Maxim, and Sébastien Dubreil, eds. 2020. *Language Teaching in the Linguistic Landscape: Mobilizing Pedagogy in Public Space*. Cham: Springer.

Maly, Ico. 2016. "Detecting Social Changes in Times of Superdiversity: An Ethnographic Linguistic Landscape Analysis of Ostend in Belgium." *Journal of Ethnic and Migration Studies* 42, no. 5: 703–723. https://doi.org/10.1080/1369183X.2015.1131149

Maly, Ico, and Jan Blommaert. 2019. Digital Ethnographic Linguistic Landscape Analysis (ELLA 2.0). *Tilburg Papers in Cultural Studies* 233: 1-26.

Marten, Heiko, Luk Van Mensel, and Durk Gorter, eds. 2012. "Introduction: Studying Minority Languages in the Linguistic Landscape." In *Minority Languages in the Linguistic Landscape*, 1–15. London: Palgrave Macmillan.

Martín Rojo, Luisa. 2014. "Taking Over the Square: The Role of Linguistic Practices in Contesting Public Spaces." *Journal of Language and Politics* 8, no. 3: 1–22. https://doi.org/10.1075/jlp.13.4.03mar

Martín Rojo, Luisa, Clara Molina, and Camila Cárdenas. 2023. *Lenguas Callejeras. Paisajes de las Lenguas que Nos Rodean*. Barcelona: Octaedro.

Román Méndez, Juan. 2019. "Nos Tocan a Uno, ¿Nos Tocan a Todos? Políticas de lo Colectivo en Torno a lo 'Bangladesí' en Lavapiés." *PhD diss.*, Universidad Nacional de Educación a Distancia.

Migge, Bettina. 2023. "Assessing the Place of Minoritized Languages in Postcolonial Contexts Using the Linguistic Landscape: The Role of Ethnographic Information." *Linguistic Landscape* 9, no. 4: 329–356. https://doi.org/10.1075/ll.22027.mig

Moustaoui Srhir, Adil. 2013. "Nueva economía y dinámicas de cambio sociolingüístico en el paisaje lingüístico: el caso del árabe en Madrid." *Revista Internacional de Lingüística Iberoamericana* 11, no. 21: 89–108.

Moustaoui Srhir, Adil. 2018. "Recontextualización Sociolingüística y Superdiversidad. El Árabe en el Paisaje Lingüístico del Barrio de Lavapiés en Madrid." *Lingue e Linguaggi* 25: 197–225. https://doi.org/10.1285/i22390359v25p197

Moustaoui Srhir, Adil. 2019. "Migración, Contacto de Lenguas y Paisaje Lingüístico: El Caso del Árabe en la Ciudad de Madrid." In *Zonas de Contacto en el Mundo Hispano: Estudios Interdisciplinares*, edited by Marco Thomas Bosshard and Laura Morgenthaler García, 145–172. Berlin: Peter Lang.

Museo Nacional Centro de Arte Reina Sofía. 2020. "Lengua o muerte." www.museoreinaso fia.es/actividades/lengua-o-muerte

Niedt, Greg, and Corinne A. Seals. 2020. *Linguistic Landscapes Beyond the Language Classroom*. London: Bloomsbury.

Otsuji, Emi, and Alastair Pennycook. 2019. "Sydney's Metrolingual Assemblages: Yellow Matters." In *Multilingual Sydney*, edited by Alice Chik, Phil Benson, and Robyn Moloney, 40–50. London and New York: Routledge.

Pavlenko, Aneta. 2009. "Language Conflict in Post-Soviet Linguistic Landscapes." *Journal of Slavic Linguistics* 17, no. 1–2: 247–274.

Pennycook, Alastair, and Emi Otsuji. 2015. *Metrolingualism: Language in the City.* London: Routledge.

Pérez-Agote, Alfonso, Benjamín Tejerina, and Marta Barañano, eds. 2010. *Barrios Multiculturales. Relaciones Interétnicas en los Barrios de San Francisco (Bilbao) y Embajadores/Lavapiés (Madrid).* Madrid: Editorial Trotta.

Prego Vázquez, Gabriela, and Luz Zas Varela. 2018. "Paisaje Lingüístico: Un Recurso TIC-TACTEP para el Aula." *Lingue e Linguaggi* 25: 277–295. https://doi.org/10.1285/i2239 0359v25p277

Rasinger, Sebastian. 2018. "Constructing Banglatown: Linguistic Landscapes in London's East End." *Linguistic Landscape* 4, no. 1: 72–95. https://doi.org/10.1075/ll.16015.ras

Reichborn Kjennerud, Kristin, José Manuel Ruano de la Fuente, and Daniel Sorando Ortín. 2021. "Ways to gain influence for residents in two gentrifying neighbourhoods. A comparison between Tøyen in Oslo and Lavapiés in Madrid." *Papeles de población.* Vol.27(10): 109-137.

Riesco Sanz, Alberto. 2010. "Inmigración y Trabajo por Cuenta Propia: Economías Inmigrantes en Lavapiés (Madrid)." *PhD diss.* Universidad Complutense de Madrid.

Rowland, Laura. 2013. "The Pedagogical Benefits of a Linguistic Landscape Project in Japan." *International Journal of Bilingual Education and Bilingualism* 16, no. 4: 494–505. https://doi.org/10.1080/13670050.2012.708319

Rubdy, Rani, and Selim Ben Said, eds. 2015. *Conflict, Exclusion and Dissent in Linguistic Landscape.* London: Palgrave Macmillan.

Ruiz Chasco, Sonia. 2014. "Videovigilancia en el Centro de Madrid: ¿Hacia el Panóptico Electrónico?." *Teknokultura: Revista de Cultura Digital y Movimientos Sociales* 11, no. 2: 301–327.

Sabaté-Dalmau, Maria. 2023. "'Localizing English in town': A Linguistic Landscape Project for a Critical Linguistics Education on Multilingualism." *International Journal of Bilingual Education and Bilingualism* 25, no. 10: 3580–3596. London and New York: Routledge. https://doi.org/10.1080/13670050.2022.2067978

Saiz de Lobado, Ester. 2022. "Multilingualism and Gentrification in Lavapiés' Linguistic Landscape." *Kamchatka Revista de Análisis Cultural* 20: 381–402. https://doi.org/10.7203/KAM.20.21379

Saiz de Lobado, Ester. 2021. "Construcción Identitaria de la Inmigración en el Paisaje Madrileño: Lavapiés y San Diego." *Migraciones Internacionales* 12: 1–24. https://doi.org/10.33679/rmi.v1i1.2358

Saiz de Lobado, Ester, and Almudena Revilla Guijarro. 2019. "Analysis of Lavapiés through its Linguistic Landscape and the Press." *Open Linguistics* 5: 466–487. https://doi.org/10.1515/opli-2019-0025

Salguero Montaño, Óscar. 2018. "Baitul Mukarram: el islam en el espacio público del barrio de Lavapiés." *Revista De Estudios Internacionales Mediterráneos* 25: 118–138. https://doi.org/10.15366/reim2018.25.007

Sayers, Philip. 2010. "Using the Linguistic Landscape as a Pedagogical Resource." *ELT Journal* 64, no. 2: 143–154.

Scollon, Ron, and Suzanne Wong Scollon. 2003. *Discourses in Place: Language in the Material World.* 1st ed. London: Routledge.

Shohamy, Elana. 2012. "Linguistic Landscapes and Multilingualism." In *The Routledge Handbook of Multilingualism*, edited by Marilyn Martin-Jones, Adrian Blackledge, and Angela Creese, 538–551. London: Routledge.

Shohamy, Elana. 2015. "LL Research as Expanding Language and Language Policy." *Linguistic Landscape* 1, no. 1: 152–171. https://doi.org/10.1075/ll.1.1-2.09sho

Shohamy, Elana, and Durk Gorter. eds. 2009. *Linguistic Landscape: Expanding the Scenery*. New York: Routledge.

Silverstein, Michael. 2003. "Indexical Order and the Dialectics of Sociolinguistic Life." *Language and Communication* 23, no. 3–4: 193–229.

Spanish EAPS. "Padrón de Bangladesíes en España." Accessed April 19, 2021. https://epa.com.es/padron/bangladesies-en-espana/

Spanish Ministry of Foreign Affairs, European Union and Cooperation. 2024. "Ficha país: Bangladesh." Accessed February 5, 2024. www.exteriores.gob.es/Documents/FichasPais/BANGLADESH_FICHA%20PAIS.pdf

Zas Varela, Luz, and Gabriela Prego Vázquez. 2016. "Las Escalas del Paisaje Lingüístico en los Márgenes de la Superdiversidad." *Cescontexto Debates* 15: 6–25.

8 Street Languages

An insight into linguistic landscapes for critical language education

Luisa Martín Rojo, Camila Cárdenas-Neira and Clara Molina

Researching and contesting language-mediated inequalities

Speakers are recurrently immersed in situations in which the management and valuation of languages play a fundamental role in the production, reproduction, and reinforcement of social inequalities, whether based on class, gender, age, ethnicity, nationality, or place of origin.[1] As sociolinguists, we can investigate how language-mediated situations of injustice arise by analyzing how linguistic aspects are intertwined with the social axes of inequality. This occurs when linguistic resources are not evenly distributed in society, or when the use of some languages or varieties is imposed, while others are marginalized in a specific context. Thus, for example, the monolingual imposition of normative Spanish in a public institution or service, such as a school or a hospital, may prevent minorities who do not have this linguistic resource within their repertoires from accessing and fully participating in these social domains. Generally, this unequal distribution of linguistic resources is justified based on prestige, correctness, or usefulness, and ends up privileging some languages and speakers over others. When some varieties are considered cultured or better than others, a scale of value is created that contributes to disseminating social representations that legitimize certain speakers and marginalize others as less competent speakers or as non-speakers. In this context, speakers whose language is not valued will probably not feel socially recognized, their voice will not be heard, and they will face obstacles to full participation in society, which translates into unequal participation and a questioning of their linguistic citizenship. The same is true for those who speak with an "accent" considered local, "small-town," "vulgar," "valid only for comedy," associated with racialized groups, or who are excluded because of their gender identity and/or sexual orientation (Bourdieu 1982; Martín Rojo 2020).

This is, de facto, a daily reality in the Madrid region, despite the diversity of languages and speakers it hosts. The Spanish capital attracts both national and international populations and, according to data published on the city's official statistics website *Portal Estadístico* (2023), 26.3% of Madrid's inhabitants were born abroad (a figure that does not include the not inconsiderable number of visitors and tourists). Therefore, the linguistic diversity of the city is remarkable, and so is the complexity of the linguistic repertoires of its residents. However, not all of these languages and varieties are equally recognized, nor do they enjoy the same prestige, nor do they allow equal access to services or social spaces. The region is officially monolingual and, given the supremacy of Spanish in the legal framework of the State, its prevalence is not even questioned. This shapes the linguistic behavior and expectations of speakers and is evident in their practices and even in their perception of the sociolinguistic order. Such dissonances between the sociolinguistic order and the perception of it were one of the triggers that led us to include the Linguistic Landscapes (LL hereafter) approach in our teaching, intending to reflect with the younger generations on their social consequences and to try and envision other possible sociolinguistic orders. In doing so, we align ourselves with an emerging trend within sociolinguistics that is not content to simply analyze situations of language-mediated injustice but has become more committed. Part of this commitment encompasses the involvement of multiple agents in research, along the lines of citizen sociolinguistics (Rymes 2020; Svendsen and Goodchild 2024), inspired by citizen science (Irwin 1995) and connecting with recent research on linguistic citizenship (Hyltenstam and Kerfoot 2022; Stroud 2023). Thus, it seeks to establish links with society through alliances with citizen and professional groups, with social movements, and with all those interested in the task of understanding, challenging, and transforming situations of inequality in which language plays a fundamental role.

This is the framework for the research carried out by a joint participatory action-research project carried out in different sociolinguistic contexts in Spain, *EquiLing* (https://www.equiling.eu/en/), whose main objective is to develop a theory, a method, and a sociolinguistic practice to address situations of language-mediated injustice. In pursuit of this goal, and with a vocation of transformation, we try to identify how speakers can exercise their agency to reverse these injustices and explore how we, as researchers, can be part of this transformation, accompanying speakers and trying to mobilize their desire for change. To this end, we generated theoretical and methodological tools that, although designed to respond to the needs of our environments, can be replicated in other contexts where the management of languages generates social inequality. In line with the transformative objective of the EquiLing project as a whole, the work in the Madrid site is oriented towards the construction of new linguistic citizenship through action research for the recognition of speakers in the educational environment. We work, therefore, with students, in particular with university students of language degrees, with whom we try to respond to our sociolinguistic context, marked by hybridization and also by the hegemony of Spanish and, academically, of English. We, therefore, coexist with discursive practices that, institutionally, impose a monolingual and standardizing perspective, but also with transformative practices through which citizens express their identity in very diverse languages and varieties. We pay attention to this together with our students, whom we wish to accompany on an emancipatory journey that brings them closer to a more inclusive sociolinguistic order.

The transformative goal we have set for ourselves is not easy to achieve. One of the many factors that make it difficult is how our linguistic socialization takes place. In primary and secondary education, everything that has to do with language tends to maintain a normative character through which a hierarchy of values of languages and speakers is naturalized. Often, in the educational environment, people are linguistically disciplined based on these values that prioritize some varieties, stigmatize others, and homogenize forms of speech (Martín Rojo 2023). These values and norms are integrated into the *habitus* and form part of our disposition towards language. Thus, it is not difficult to find ourselves reproducing these linguistic canons, even embodying them, for instance, by preferring silence to intervening using a non-legitimized linguistic variety. Although it is difficult to control this initial inclination, a reflexive and critical analysis of the situations we experience, particularly those involving social injustice, can change these dispositions. For Bourdieu (1999), for example, critical sociology, and similarly, in our view, the LL approach presented in this chapter, can contribute to altering our perception and, therefore, our reaction, enabling us to somehow monitor some of the determinisms that operate through the relationship of immediate complicity between social position and dispositions.

If, as researchers, we want to get involved in the transformation of situations of sociolinguistic injustice, we need to contribute in some way to a modification of the *habitus* of those with whom we work. To achieve this, and from our position as teachers, we adapted the critical pedagogy of the Brazilian educator Paulo Freire, who seeks *conscientization* through three stages (i.e. discussion of oppressive social structures, reflection on their causes, and action aimed at challenging and transforming them). We believe that it is the speakers themselves who must identify situations of linguistic injustice; understand how they are rooted in other social inequalities; and awaken their desire to transform and transform themselves to respond to such injustices. This requires a reflective and critical approach that seeks not only to understand but also to actively improve the underlying linguistic dynamics and power structures. In terms of teaching, this implies transforming the pedagogical approach, advocating for an education that does not normalize and discipline, but rather enables and empowers to try to achieve the goal of fostering a more inclusive and just linguistic citizenship that does not discriminate against anyone based on their speech or accent, nor limits their participation or excludes them from socially relevant spheres.

Drawing on Freire's educational philosophy, we adopted the concept of "conscientization spaces." Conscientization (*conscientização* in Portuguese) implies a dialectical relationship between reflection and action that guides participants to transcend naïve or passive understandings of social inequalities (Freire 1970). Applied to the linguistic sphere, Freire's critical proposal encompasses reflection on the sociolinguistic order, acknowledgment of the unequal distribution of linguistic resources and the misrecognition suffered by non-legitimized speakers, and problematization of the existing norms. This would be, in Freire's terms, the magical stage, in which experiences of inequality are identified and shared. As we analyze below when presenting and exemplifying the different phases of Freire's proposal, this is followed by the naïve stage, in which the socioeconomic causes of inequality are analyzed; and finally, by the critical stage, in which the desire to transform the conditions of inequality and its causes is awakened (Freire 2004).

In our research, we applied this perspective by creating conscientization spaces in university classrooms and changing the educational dynamics to facilitate the development of Freire's phases. To this end, over the last decade, we designed LL practices for groups of students to conduct ethnographic explorations both at Universidad Autónoma de Madrid and in different neighborhoods of the city, often their own, observing their landscapes and detecting the experiences of their inhabitants. Through these landscapes, our university students analyzed situations of inequality, such as the contrast between the prevailing institutional monolingualism and the linguistic diversity of the population, or the marked differences between rich neighborhoods, with a notable presence of English in their streets, and poorer ones, with no presence of English but many languages of migration. Thus, assisted by a set of guidelines, our students analyzed in teams how linguistic processes are intertwined with sociocultural and urban processes. Afterward, each team shared their observations and analysis with the rest of the class, and, to move towards transformation, they formulated proposals for change targeting the university and other relevant institutions in Madrid.

In addition, in an attempt to transcend our research site and even the Madrid region itself, we created teaching materials so that people in different sociolinguistic contexts could replicate and adapt these conscientization spaces to their environment. These resources are accessible even to non-specialists in the field, which facilitates their adoption in a variety of locations, educational or otherwise, as they are designed to facilitate collaboration with organizations of all sorts that wish to replicate our experience. A key resource in this regard is our book *Street Languages: Collective landscapes of the languages that surround us. A guide to promote critical sociolinguistic awareness* (Martín Rojo, Cárdenas-Neira and Molina 2023). This volume departs from the tradition of LL in that it does not seek to compile a corpus of signs to offer an image of the dominant landscape in a neighborhood or institution, but rather aspires to be an instrument for reflection and action. In the following pages we will first present our approach to LL, then how the practices implemented in our classrooms contributed to unfolding the awareness-raising process, and finally, we will describe the *Street Languages* resource and conclude with a brief assessment of the impact of our proposal, based on the testimonials of our students.

Linguistic landscaping as a tool for conscientization

The analysis of the LL can be approached in many different ways. In fact, over the last few decades, both the focus of interest and the working methodology have varied. At an early stage, the LL was conceived of as an eminently quantitative vantage point from which to observe the vitality of languages in contact. Although it was sometimes more descriptive than analytic, it revealed a new way of understanding what happened around us, and, gradually, LL studies began to integrate qualitative aspects to explore the how and why, instead of focusing only on the what. Today, it includes broader elements of analysis such as semiotic landscapes, soundscapes, and other spaces such as school-scapes and body-scapes.

The *Street Languages* proposal invites to analyze how linguistic and spatial practices are co-constructed, that is, the "spatial turn," which involves examining how communicative and spatial practices (reterritorialization, self-management, privatization, etc.) are co-constructed. In this way, the interrelationship between linguistic processes (such as hybridization or the multiplicity of languages in use), sociocultural processes (such as the integration of migrant populations), and urban processes (such as gentrification, which can displace communities to the periphery and away from intercultural neighborhoods) is highlighted (for an introduction to this approach, see Martín Rojo (2016 [2014]); Alonso and Martín Rojo 2023; Martín Rojo forthcoming).

In our case, we understand LL as a springboard from which to explore what happens to the people who inhabit them, as well as the social, demographic, and urban processes that explain, and at the same time shape, those landscapes. It is an invitation to understand, and also to take sides, not to be a mere spectator. Our purpose, rooted in our teaching practice, is to learn and teach to discover how LL provides us with a daily opportunity to become aware of how languages are linked to society. We do not, hence, pursue the creation of a corpus from which to extract statistics to describe but to qualitatively analyze how LL relate to the myriad of the processes that explain them and from which they emerge. It is, therefore, a situated reflection that transcends linguistic boundaries. We do not analyze decontextualized images, however striking they may be, because doing so does not help us understand. Nor do we tend to focus exclusively on images in which language is the sole focus of interest, because the scope of our project includes all semiotic manifestations, linguistic or otherwise, with which people create meaning, express themselves, and relate to and with their environment.

In approaching the LL with the purpose of learning and teaching to try to understand the reason for the messages of all kinds that surround us daily, we want to analyze the landscape as a critical activity that helps to awaken awareness. The LL is never a blank canvas, it is never neutral. It always reveals what happens to the people who inhabit it, whether we recognize ourselves and see ourselves reflected in it, or not. The space that surrounds us is a symbolic terrain, often contested, that lends itself to struggles as well as to coexistence, and that always takes sides: at times, it is in favor of those who make it theirs while others allow it. On other occasions, it is in favor of those who, in the face of usurpation, reappropriate the space they claim as their own and, by making it theirs, reaffirm their identity. The walls then become a backdrop against which to exercise agency, and it is then that landscapes powerfully call our attention and make us realize what happens to those who live there. But it is not always necessary for landscapes to reveal struggles and debates: just stopping and observing what is around us, and also what is not, to begin to take the pulse of our societies.

In an attempt to trigger awareness-raising processes in our classrooms, we seek to harness the descriptive and analytical potential of the LL as a tool that indexes social, cultural, and political patterns (Blommaert 2013). Our approach, therefore, goes beyond merely capturing the diversity of languages and inhabitants, but rather we emphasize what landscapes reveal about our environment, a densely multilingual metropolis like so many others around the globe. Our approach also allows us to trace and understand the material and symbolic transformation involved in urban processes, and it is precisely this relationship between the material and symbolic transformation of cities, exercised by their inhabitants, and the urban processes that we set out to study through the educational action presented in this chapter. Over the years, this has allowed us to accompany our students and help them discover a different experience of the city in which they live, establishing relationships between the configuration of the landscape and the presence of social processes.

Seeking an alignment between academic programs and daily life, and thus trying to promote meaningful learning of complex processes, we adjusted the practices to the profiles of the groups. Sometimes we worked in neighborhoods, sometimes at the university, or in the protest movements that are part of everyday life in the big city. The objective was always to encourage the understanding of how languages play a role that often goes unnoticed, but which, once discovered, activates many other discoveries. To achieve this, in addition to ensuring the appropriateness of the activities, another key element has been the application of a longitudinal methodology. Thus, from 2011 to the present, in several courses, we made the landscape a lever with which to set in motion processes of awareness, making students revisit the landscape at different moments in their maturation process. Thus, students were introduced to LL during their first year, later they analyzed it firsthand (Figure 8.1), and finally, in the last year of their degree, they proposed transformative actions or even carried out interventions to transform the LL of the university (Figure 8.2). Thus, accompanied by the teaching team, they discovered the field of study, made it their own with inquiries that led them to create and share knowledge, and finally exercised agency by intervening in the landscape. Figures 8.1 and 8.2 below attest to this transition.

As mentioned above, our action-research project seeks to promote speaker agency. Taking the role of facilitators, we act as mediators to propose activities that give voice to participants' experiences and discoveries, support them with concepts and tools, mobilize their agency, and try to remove any obstacles that may arise. To do this, the first step is for them to learn to identify linguistic inequality, to then address it. Landscapes provide an optimal platform for this, as our streets allow us to observe the extent to which citizens exercise agency in the construction and transformation of the LL. Learning to analyze how we link with our environment is learning to become aware of the social processes with which we coexist, and only if we are aware of their existence will we be able, if necessary, to act to promote or try to eradicate them. Therefore, from our teaching perspective, we not only want students to learn to look around: the ultimate goal is that, if they find something they think should be different, they do something to change it. Therefore, we want them to detect, explain, and present proposals for transformation. Very often, admittedly, this does not happen, and we must be content with them becoming aware of the messages that the environment incessantly throws at us, which they had not noticed until then.

In any event, we realize that most learning does not occur inside the classroom, but outside. Therefore, our desire to mobilize the agency of speakers has led us to

200 *Ethnographic Landscapes and Language Ideologies in the Spanish State*

Figure 8.1 Proposal for transformative action in the Lavapiés neighborhood, produced as coursework by Aída Cajaraville, Elena González, Jasmín Soto, and Raquel Oviedo (UAM 2nd-year students taking the BA course "Multilingualism and Languages in Contact"). The image names and describes proposals such as including the languages of migration in public services or controlling gentrification, among others.

Figure 8.2 Intervention in the LL of the Faculty of Philosophy and Arts to challenge linguistic prejudice and glottophobia. The sign in the picture reads: "Learn how to pronounce if you want to work here. What about you, would you disguise your accent to get a job? Take part in our survey!" Photograph by Lucía de León and Laura Marino (4th-year UAM students taking the BA course "Intercultural Pragmatics").

expand the scope of LL observation beyond the educational environment. We all place ourselves in very diverse contexts daily, and in all of them, we interact with the environment. Looking closely at what the walls of our streets, the signs on our public transport, the windows of our stores, the advertisements in public and private establishments, the messages on the clothes we wear, etc., tell us, makes us aware of the processes of a very different nature, all of which are crucial to our existence. The tensions that affect the citizenry as a whole are exposed with singular clarity in our urban landscape, which is why citizens need to become aware of them and learn to analyze them critically. In this endeavor, the *Street Languages* guide that we present as a didactic resource invites citizen associations, grassroots movements, and protest collectives to learn to read and work with the LL. Through this approach, we aim to advance in the construction of a more inclusive, more livable, and sociolinguistically fairer society, thus aligning ourselves with the tenets of participatory action research and citizen science.

Applying the LL approach in our teaching has enabled us to identify striking similarities in the sociolinguistic structures across diverse regions, suggesting the existence of shared axes of inequality despite varying contexts. However, not everyone feels adequately prepared to engage in LL analysis, whether due to a lack of familiarity with the field or feelings of inadequacy in linguistics or sociology. In response, we developed a guide aimed at empowering individuals of all expertise levels to navigate the LL domain with confidence and independence. We aim to democratize participation, ensuring it is accessible to all, not just those already well-versed in the subject matter, both within and beyond academic environments. This principle underpins EquiLing, with the *Street Languages* guide serving as a tangible manifestation. Furthermore, in line with our commitment to inclusivity, we created an English version of the guide (available at https://octaedro.com/libro/street-languages-collective-landscapes-of-the-languages-that-surround-us/) in addition to the original one in Spanish (available at https://octaedro.com/libro/lenguas-callejeras-paisajes-colectivos-de-las-lenguas-que-nos-rodean/).

The *Lenguas callejeras "Street Languages"* step-by-step guide for linguistic conscientization

Description of the internal structure of the guide

Once we had tested in class didactic materials with which to use the LL as a lever for raising awareness, we published an open-access guide providing step-by-step guidance to all those who wish to put into practice a popular education exercise for building knowledge collaboratively and dialogically. This is why *Street Languages* was designed as an instruction manual to reflect on the uses and distribution of languages in public spaces, sharing experiences, ideas, and reflections. The role assigned to the interlocutors, as well as its structure and the register used in its design, respond to the purpose of fostering the agency of those who work with the guide. In the first place, the text constructs its potential users as co-researchers, not as passive readers. Like any exercise in critical pedagogy, its development requires encouraging a horizontal relationship between whoever facilitates the workshop and the participants, to re- and co-construct learning without hierarchies or biases about who dominates what knowledge. Therefore, the guide encourages to capture, analyze, and discuss findings collectively, through data collections, presentations, and debates. Furthermore, to mobilize agency through the adoption of empowering roles, the guide promotes the use of simple but transformative tools, such as observation, contextualization, photography, and critical analysis of signs in urban space. Finally, to reinforce the desire for change, the guide requires, as part of the active learning activities, designing proposals with which to transform the inequalities detected. Thus, by acquiring the tools, participants exercise their sociolinguistic citizenship and even become activists. That is, through situated learning (how to do research) and shared learning (of the results of teamwork) they move towards a greater awareness of how language creates and perpetuates power inequalities in society, and collective agency is fostered to actively address them.

Secondly, in the interest of popular education, the structure of this free guide encourages participants to appropriate the tools of analysis following the "do-it-yourself" philosophy. We propose an itinerary with different steps, questions, and clues with which to explore the LL, as well as instructions for observing, photographing, and analyzing it. To guide the route, *Street Languages* consists of five chapters. The *Introduction* contextualizes the action-research work of the EquiLing project, explaining the need for the guide, its use, and its audience. In the chapter *What is the Street Languages workshop about?* an approach to the LL and the processes examined are provided, along with a summary of the workshop stages. *The workshop step by step* details the activities and materials for each stage, with a focus on neighborhood LL. *Let's go for more: Ideas for implementing other workshops* proposes adaptations for educational centers and protest demonstrations. The final chapter, *Toolbox*, compiles examples of implementation, provides access to downloadable templates via a QR code, displays a glossary of key concepts, and collects additional resources to enrich the workshop experience. Thus, the guide aims to orient participants in the execution of a workshop which consists of three stages, structured in six steps that involve a day's work. This structure is similar regardless of whether the workshop is applied to the study of the LL of neighborhoods, educational centers, or protest demonstrations. In the latter two cases, however, we propose some variations, so that their distinctive features can be captured more adequately.

In the first of the three stages in the workshop, the first out of six steps takes place: *What are we going to observe?* Two central activities are carried out here, an introduction of the workshop by the facilitator, and the organization of each group to decide which neighborhood to visit and in which specific area to photograph. The introduction seeks to imbue the work with an experiential and situated sense from a critical perspective, for which it is recommended to pose some guiding questions that lead the participants to recognize the presence or absence of languages in the streets they frequent every day and to elaborate a first reflection on what this means. However, the organization leaves it up to the participants to decide what neighborhood to explore according to their interests and accessibility, while clarifying some basic guidelines on how to obtain more information on the demographic and linguistic characteristics of each district, what participants can photograph (e.g. graffiti, posters, stickers, signs, advertisements or bulletin boards, brochures, shop windows, advertising, mailboxes, etc.), and what they should pay more attention to (e.g. the presence or absence of languages in the streets, which languages are more visible than others, which speakers they represent and what they are used for, which languages would be expected and do not appear, which languages are erased or crossed out, etc.).

In the development stage, the following three steps are carried out. The second step, *To the street!*, provides a series of practical recommendations about planning, mapping (to select the perimeter and what streets to visit), distribution (to assign streets to a person, pair, or team), and notetaking (to record the name, street number and site to which each photograph corresponds, e.g. residential building, restaurant, school, store, etc.). The third step, *Look again*, consists of completing a contextualization sheet for each photograph, identifying whether the LL is monolingual or multilingual, which language is the main one and which is secondary, where the message is located, its format, its purpose, and its most outstanding characteristics, as well as comments on what other written or visual elements. The fourth step, *What do the streets tell us?*, is divided into four activities and includes questions to unpack and deepen into the linguistic, sociocultural, and urban processes observed: (1) a review of the data incorporated in all the files to find shared or differentiating features, as well as possible relationships between the photographs; (2) the creation of a presentation for each group to makes their results known; (3) the viewing of all the presentations; and (4) a joint discussion of the findings surveyed by the other groups and the formulation of conclusions about what was learned from the presentations and the workshop dynamics itself.

In the closing stage, the last two steps are carried out. The fifth step, *Let's move on to action!*, seeks to encourage the mobilization of collective agency. For this, each group reflects on what they would modify in the language policies and practices detected, suggesting collective actions to make the neighborhoods more livable and inclusive, with greater social and linguistic justice. With this purpose in mind, each group completes a transformational proposal sheet where they define what the specific problem is that the proposed action would contribute to solving, how this action would be executed step by step, when and where it would be carried out, and who could be involved in its implementation. The sixth and final step, *Let's show what we have learned*, aims to raise awareness among other people and groups and encourage them to act based on the transformational horizon already outlined. To meet this objective, each group is invited to disseminate its presentation through the internet and social networks, and/or to choose a different format (e.g. infographic, poster, mural, documentary, etc.) that, by exploiting creativity, helps to enhance the scope of the results and reflections agreed upon.

We must conclude this section by stressing the impact that our citizen science approach had on the register and semiotic design of the guide. We tried to avoid overly technical terms and to explain them plainly. In addition, we opted for a full-color visual composition with a diverse representation of both the places to approach and those who, we believe, can use it. There are also dialogues in speech bubbles, icons that illustrate the actions to follow, and a wide selection of landscape images collected by the authors. With these design decisions, we tried to make the book not only look friendly and dynamic but also serve as a pedagogical tool for anyone to become familiar with the study of LL and to encourage them to undertake it. In this sense, we believe that opting for plain language, an easy-to-follow organization, and rich visual content favors this popular education exercise, as it allows all those involved in this study to contribute, on equal terms, to the compilation and analysis of the data collected and to the generation of new viewpoints, questions, and knowledge that nurture a critical understanding of the languages around us.

LL as a gateway to the study of linguistic, sociocultural, and urban processes

Our guide adapts the three Freirean phases described above to the critical analysis of LL. Thus, first, it helps identify processes of inequality associated with language; second, it encourages to analyze their causes and consequences; and finally, it tries to develop a willingness to take transformative action. From now on, we will link each of these phases of the conscientization process to the study of the LL in further detail.

Since the first phase involves the identification of situations of inequality, we endow our practice with a reflexive component. This search for reflexivity implies a change of position since the research is carried out by those participating in the workshop, while the researchers only act as facilitators. Another key aspect in critical pedagogy, the use of the experiences of the participants themselves as a departure point, is also present in our proposal, which chooses the city's neighborhoods, each with its distinct identity, as the setting. This decision not only facilitates the analysis, by delimiting the field and inviting comparative reflexivity but also brings an experiential and situated component to the work. In the neighborhoods, moreover, community relations and solidarity are established that foster collective behaviors, for example, resistance to building in green areas, which illuminate the analysis of the processes that take place in them. Neighborhoods, the epicenter of the step-by-step workshop proposed in the guide, do not only exist in cities: they can also be found in towns and peri-urban areas all over the world, making it possible to replicate the workshop and explore the differences that depend on geographical, linguistic, ethnic, cultural, political, and urban factors.

In addition to the workshop on neighborhoods, the guide outlines two other workshops also tested in our classrooms, one on landscaping an educational center and the other on protest movements. All three scenarios are familiar to anyone wishing to participate in LL activities, but each confronts participants with realities that tend to go unnoticed. Thus, in all cases, questions that trigger reflexivity are proposed, as seen in Figures 8.3 and 8.4.

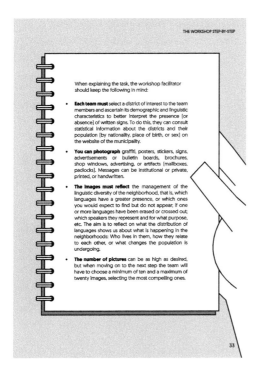

Figure 8.3 Questions in the *Street Languages* guide to steer observation and analysis.

Source: Martín Rojo, Cárdenas-Neira, and Molina (2024, 33).

Once the situations of inequality have been identified, the second phase of the conscientization process requires (re)learning how to look at places and acquiring a critical awareness of the role that languages play in social, economic, political, and cultural changes. Thus, to reflect on neighborhoods we propose several questions:

The questions serve as a stimulus to trigger reflection and critical analysis on three types of processes that, in one way or another, will be linked to the production of inequality: (i) linguistic, to determine whether a hierarchy of languages is taking shape in the LL and whether communities are being linguistically homogenized, despite their *de facto* diversity; (ii) sociocultural, to determine whether the management of linguistic diversity is oriented towards assimilation, segregation, marginalization or integration of the population and its diversity; and (iii) urban, to assess whether the territory is being commodified and transforming the reality of neighborhoods and the lives of neighbors. To facilitate the exploration of these three types of processes, the volume includes a glossary that presents essential notions in a plain but critical way.

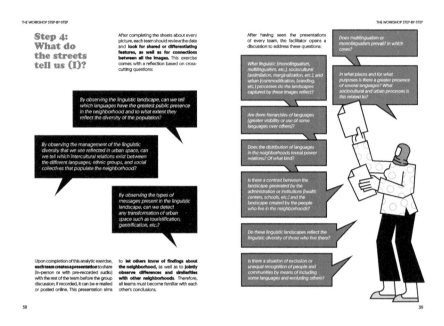

Figure 8.4 Questions to guide reflection on what was previously observed and photographed in the neighborhoods, from the *Street Languages* guide.

Source: Martín Rojo, Cárdenas-Neira, and Molina (2024, 38–39).

Discovering linguistic processes in town

Since the basic premise of the guide is that language is involved in the production, reproduction, and legitimization of social inequality (although this crucial role is seldom recognized), the landscaping we propose begins with the observation of linguistic processes: how linguistic diversity is managed in the explored areas, whether monolingualism or multilingualism predominates, what language hierarchies can be observed in the LL, and how they are linked to linguistic ideologies. This observation of linguistic phenomena is carried out by seeking a connection with the urban space in the neighborhoods, investigating which languages are mobilized or completely erased in monolingual or multilingual landscapes, and who mobilizes them (for example, whether it is the administration or the residents), how citizens combine different resources, different writing systems, and semiotic resources from their repertoires, and where (institutional, commercial, or recreational spaces). Thus, observing linguistic processes reveals, firstly, the unequal distribution of languages in spaces that are more or less valued or vital for people. Second, the outcome of landscaping highlights the differences in the value assigned to these linguistic resources, undoubtedly generating inequality among those who use them. Finally, this leads to questioning what kind of intercultural relationships different social actors want to establish, whether it be the administration or the residents, as we address in the next section.

Discovering sociocultural processes in town

The second major block of processes that the guide helps detect and analyze is that of sociocultural processes, which are also connected with the issue of social inequality. To learn to connect the languages observed in the streets with the sociocultural processes that reveal the presence of certain policies, ideologies, and daily practices, two questions are proposed: Are the maintenance of minority cultural and linguistic identities and characteristics facilitated? and Are inter-group relations promoted? To answer these questions, it is essential to explore whether embracing linguistic and cultural diversity is imperative for fostering intercultural relations. Based on the answers to these two questions, four possibilities open up. The first of these, *assimilation*, occurs when intergroup relations between minority groups and the host society are promoted, but only if all differences are erased. In the sociolinguistic order, this assimilation process involves the imposition of monolingualism, with the local language as the dominant or sole language in services and public life. Assimilation is thus linked to a set of cultural and linguistic patterns considered inherent or essential to the nation, of which the local population is considered the quintessential representative. This is the case in many neighborhoods of Madrid, although today it is difficult to find areas in the city that show complete assimilation, since, because of gentrification, the presence of English is notable in areas where Spanish dominates.

Nor is it common to find the second alternative, *segregation*, which occurs if the identity and cultural and linguistic characteristics of minority groups are maintained, but intergroup relations with the host society are not promoted. Instead of spaces for coexistence, spaces reserved for different groups emerge (schools, differentiated medical or justice services, separate commercial and leisure areas, etc.) This is the difference between interculturalism (coexistence) and multiculturalism (separate groups), and at the linguistic level it does not lead to a situation of multilingualism, but of compartmentalized monolingualism, since people maintain the use of their languages of origin in the private space, but also in some public spaces. In Madrid, no ghettos or "small cities within the city" are formed, and only some areas of neighborhoods, situated in peripheral areas or the poor or even degraded downtown areas of the city such as Usera (known as Madrid's Chinatown: Figure 8.5) or Little Caribbean in the Tetuán neighborhood might show some signs of ghettoization.

The third possibility, *integration*, occurs if the maintenance of the identity and cultural and linguistic characteristics of minority groups is facilitated while promoting intergroup relations with the host society. This is the case in multilingual neighborhoods, where intercultural competencies are developed and the linguistic diversity of the population is accepted, especially in medical services, libraries, schools, etc., but also in commerce, leisure spaces, etc. In other words, where there is coexistence and no one is required to renounce

Figure 8.5 Photograph of the LL of the Usera neighborhood by Sara Gómez, Constantino Settino, Lidia Sola, Lucía Villegas, and Edward Wills (UAM students). The image shows a storefront with traditional Chinese paraphernalia and signs advertising fortune cookies in Chinese and Spanish.

his or her language or customs, which is reflected in posters, shop windows, specialized stores, advertisements for religious services in several languages, etc. In Madrid, this occurs in the neighborhood of Lavapiés (Figure 8.6), which has achieved intercultural features with a population of North Africans, Bangladeshis, Senegalese, etc.

The last possibility, *marginalization*, occurs if the maintenance of the identity and cultural and linguistic characteristics of minority groups is not facilitated, nor are intergroup relations with the host society promoted. In these cases, there is no coexistence in the different sectors, and some are excluded. This is the case in areas of illegal settlements or shanty towns, such as the Cañada Real, where different migrant populations and minorities coexist in situations of extreme poverty and without public services. The four possibilities described above occur today not only in the city of Madrid but in many other cities around the world. Their existence highlights different approaches to addressing the relationship between minority groups and the host society, all of which come to light when analyzing the LL by following the steps detailed in the guide.

Figure 8.6 Photograph of the LL of the Lavapiés neighborhood by Luisa Martín Rojo. The image shows graffiti in which the word "freedom" can be read in Spanish and Arabic.

In previous experiences implementing the pilot version of this LL practice, despite encountering some difficulties in identifying the various processes, the participants even managed to detect their simultaneous presence in the Madrid neighborhood of Lavapiés. First, they detected a greater diversity of languages in the streets and stores than in other neighborhoods: Arabic, Chinese, Urdu, Romanian, as well as Latin American varieties of Spanish. In this case, the sociolinguistic order characterized by monolingualism is reconfigured, as also occurs in peripheral neighborhoods such as Parla, reflecting the willingness of migrant communities to maintain cultural differences and create their own spaces. Thus, the images collected showed how migrant communities tend to reproduce (using their languages and writing systems) different aspects of their culture of origin in the urban space, thus avoiding the loss of their identity, creating a welcoming space for newcomers, and articulating resistance and defenses against assimilation and discrimination.

We refer to *reterritorialization* as the process in which signs of national identity, customs, festivals, or religious celebrations from the place of origin are preserved, reintroduced, and ritually recreated in the host country's space. This includes the use of flags, the original language, writing systems, etc., in the streets, businesses, and recreational spaces of the host country within the host community. The trend towards integration is evident when residents show a willingness to maintain spaces for coexistence and intercultural relations. However, this diversity is scarcely visible in institutions or services such as educational or health centers. The administration's policies demonstrate the prevalence of the assimilation trend, making it difficult for some residents to access these services. As a result of assimilation and the lower presence of the migrant population in other neighborhoods, diversity may not be as evident. Spanish dominates, often accompanied by English, particularly in commercial spaces catering to elites or tourists in residential and luxury areas such as the Salamanca district. Additionally, due to segregation, there may even be a certain degree of ghettoization. In neighborhoods with a high percentage of residents from the same community of origin, the language of the migrated community becomes notably prevalent. Thus, sociocultural processes cannot be separated from the urban processes we examine next.

Discovering urban processes in town

Of the three types of processes that are revealed by an exhaustive analysis of the landscape (linguistic, sociocultural, and urban), it is undoubtedly the latter, urban processes, that tend to go unnoticed. These processes are also linked to the construction of social inequality, particularly with the distribution of economic resources, as urban land, a necessary space for everyday life, becomes a commodity. Lefebvre's work, as outlined in his 1974 publication, applies economic concepts such as surplus value, value, capital, and labor power to analyze urban spaces, not just a physical entity but intricately linked to economic processes and power dynamics within society. Neoliberal globalization has strengthened and intensified the commodification of space, elevating the influence of economic interests in shaping spatial organization. The circulation of capital and people means that cities must increasingly compete to attract tourism and investment. The displacement of former inhabitants, branding (urban rehabilitation and renovation, urban landscaping, tourist circuits, etc.), and price speculation not only mean the return of the wealthy classes to city centers (gentrification) and the displacement of those who lived there when they were degraded areas (often migrants or minorities) or the sale of that center to tourism (*touristification*) but also transform the experience and life experiences of their inhabitants. Shows, cultural goods, and landscapes become symbolic capitals of cities, objects of consumption, and merchandise. For their part, the inhabitants can resist these processes, be displaced, and see their neighborhoods transformed into international shopping malls, etc. The production of space is therefore not only a process of material transformation of the city, but also a symbolic one.

Thus, the neighborhoods in which our participants found the greatest cultural and linguistic diversity were marked by the commodification of space. The neighborhoods where they found the highest concentration of migrants, from other parts of Spain and other countries, were neighborhoods, such as Lavapiés, where housing was cheaper. However, discussions revealed processes that went much

Street Languages 211

further and showed the constant evolution of LL. Specifically, the reterritorialization that we pointed out in Lavapiés in the previous point has become a hallmark of the neighborhood, "the most multicultural in Madrid," and, recently, also a lure for the neighborhood's commodification. Thus, lower housing prices, together with *Airbnbinization*, are encouraging the touristification of the neighborhood, and rehabilitation policies are increasing the price of rents and home purchases. Residents are being displaced to peripheral areas, to make way for more affluent social classes, commercial chains, luxury stores, or art galleries (see Alonso and Martín Rojo 2023). This abandonment of the neighborhood generates changes, such as the substitution of migrant languages (Arabic, Urdu, etc.) for English, the language of tourism. This substitution is fully consolidated in some of Madrid's more fashionable neighborhoods with residents from other European countries, such as Chueca and Malasaña (Figure 8.7), where English has become the language of commerce and restaurants.

In short, the critical reflexivity mobilized by the LL workshop questions processes with which we coexist, such as touristification or the imposition of

Figure 8.7 Photograph of the LL of the Malasaña neighborhood by Andrea Pérez, Celia Moreno, Carlota Martínez, and June Lacoste (UAM students). The image shows a gentrified food market, where many of the food stalls have been replaced by bars and restaurants. The use of English reveals this orientation towards tourism and leisure, and not towards the needs of the neighborhood.

monolingualism, and raises questions about hegemonic ways of understanding and living in the city. So, the three types of processes are intertwined, and the way they intertwine is linked to the construction of inequality. For example, the selection of languages refers to sociocultural processes that impose, integrate, segregate, or marginalize residents. These processes cannot be separated from the value of the territory in the neighborhoods they inhabit, which may be subject to speculation, sale, or transformation. In those cases, the distribution of residents and languages may change, as both can be displaced for the economic benefit of those who trade with the territory.

It is from this point that the third phase of Freirean conscientization, the mobilization of agency, can be approached. This point, however, is reached after other steps: it starts by encouraging active learning and the assumption of researcher roles by students/participants; also, by making learning a shared experience in which the joint acquisition of new knowledge and reflection on what has been discovered is shared. Two preconditions must arise from this collective learning before the will to propose actions to reverse situations of injustice materializes: first, some consensus must be reached on how and why the current situation is perceived as unjust, thus generating the desire to change it. Secondly, a critical position that motivates one to act in a dissident and innovative way against the realities that are rejected. The will to change and the agency of speakers are complex and difficult phenomena to mobilize. For this reason, in *Street Languages*, we proposed the formulation of proposals in different social settings where agency is mobilized in different ways.

In fact, in our activities, we observed that participants tend to propose changes in social contexts where they have a position that allows them some leeway and access to resources. For instance, they feel more capable of proposing changes in social spheres in which they participate and have a role in the organization and development of activities, such as the educational centers where they study. In this area, they dare to propose transformative actions and try to carry them out (for example, by incorporating languages other than Spanish into the Faculty's signage). On the other hand, in the neighborhoods, faced with the assimilationist policy of the local government, they come up with proposals for improvement, such as making public services accessible in other languages, but they do not even imagine themselves carrying out these transformations. By addressing LL in protest movements, we seek to empower participants by showing the power of action of citizens and how they manage to prefigure other possible worlds.

Assessing the impact of our participatory action research

As part of our action research, we asked the students with whom we piloted the workshop to share their impressions of the work carried out. A preliminary analysis of their testimonies reveals that students go through the three phases (magical, naïve, and critical) identified by Freire. This transit is described, metaphorically, as an experience that consists of "opening their eyes" and "never looking at their surroundings in the same way again" (see Sabaté-Dalmau 2022 for similar testimonials). As exemplified by the quote below, students interpret the practice as a "process of awareness" that irreversibly changes their ways of observing the neighborhoods and the university, noticing the presence or absence of languages and trying to explain the reasons for such unequal representation.

> When we took the photos of the Linguistic Landscape, we were looking at every detail of the neighborhood: the walls, the posters, signs, lampposts, and any surface that could hold a written text. We paid attention to every corner, every person, and every language that could be spoken. This work has made me start to look around me in a very different way than before. Now I notice these characteristics of the neighborhoods wherever I go (...) I would also say that with this work I have learned to be more critical about the selection of languages that are represented and those that I think should be represented.
> (UAM student testimony; in all cases, translated from the Spanish original by the authors)

From this point of view, the testimonies show that the LL workshop has helped them "learn more than I would have imagined," allowing them to "realize," "understand," "reflect" and "adopt a more analytical and critical attitude" regarding the linguistic, sociocultural, and urban processes involved in situations of inequality, as the quote below:

> I have learned that every detail has its explanation and responds to the interests of a certain group or community. I have also learned to appreciate the linguistic diversity that exists in Spain, specifically in Madrid. Yes, there is discrimination of the co-official languages, but I think I had never paid attention to the existence of communities that speak languages other than Spanish.
> (UAM student testimony)

This awareness is also assimilated as "reality shock" that turns into empathy and solidarity with "some groups of the population that are having a really hard time adapting [linguistically]," motivating them to "appreciate the linguistic diversity that exists in Spain, specifically in Madrid." Along these lines, several testimonies, such as the one below, value the opportunity to get closer to the reality of the speaker communities in the neighborhoods analyzed:

> Thanks to the tour we took to take the photos we had contact and were able to talk to people of different nationalities, as well as learn many curiosities and aspects of their culture, which in my opinion is quite an enriching and fun experience, [which occurs] at the same time that we are gaining knowledge and becoming aware of the injustices that exist, and [we feel] the desire to want to avoid such injustices to [achieve] a more integrated society and with greater coexistence.
> (UAM student testimony)

214 *Ethnographic Landscapes and Language Ideologies in the Spanish State*

In summary, these testimonies highlight that the workshop fostered situated learning, the result of which was a newly awakened social awareness. In this sense, students support the idea that languages create community and sustain or resist power relations. They also point out the axes of reproduction of inequality and propose measures to combat it, aspiring to a more equitable distribution of linguistic resources, full recognition of all speakers and their languages, and equal visibility in neighborhoods and educational institutions. They agree that "solutions must focus on the inclusion of these groups and on valuing their identity, linguistic and cultural characteristics." For example, "facilitating accessibility to the languages spoken by the entire [neighborhood] population through QRs to [provide translations into] various languages in the administration and public services" or carrying out "activities organized by volunteers that promote artistic production in the languages of migration, such as theater, music, dances, readings, exhibitions, festivities, films, etc." are proposals for transformation suggested by the groups.

As one student expresses below, formulating these actions for change forced him to take the time to critically analyze the effects of the processes observed and how people can fight against them, which increased his awareness of sociolinguistic dynamics and the challenges that communities and institutions must face to change them. The testimony illustrates how the transit through the magical, naïve, and critical phases ends up articulating them after the workshop:

> The Linguistic Landscapes (...) revealed several problems of sociolinguistic injustice. One of the main issues observed was linguistic hierarchies and the privileging of dominant languages, such as Castilian Spanish and English, over minority languages, such as Bengali and Arabic in Lavapiés. This led to a marginalization and devaluation of the minority linguistic communities and their cultures. This phenomenon was visible in various neighborhoods throughout Madrid. To tackle these problems, it is crucial to promote linguistic inclusivity and equality. One proposal for change is to increase language support and resources for minority language speakers. This would include offering language classes, providing translation and interpretation services, and encouraging the use of multiple languages in public spaces. Additionally, creating platforms and spaces for linguistic and cultural exchange can foster understanding and appreciation of different languages and cultures. This would lead to increased visibility of these minority cultures and provide a better space for the coexistence of multiculturalism. Another aspect to address is the commodification of language and culture. It is important to ensure that the representation and use of languages in the Linguistic Landscape go beyond commercial interests and marketing strategies. Encouraging authentic representations and empowering local communities to participate in shaping the Linguistic Landscape can contribute to a more just and inclusive sociolinguistic environment.
>
> (UAM student testimony)

We hope to have shown that this citizen science exercise can simultaneously transform our ways of studying and teaching the LL through (i) the integration of innovative learning processes with participatory action research and (ii) the provision of specific tools, such as the *Street Languages* workshop and the guide that orients its execution, to mobilize changes from within the educational institutions and communities where it is implemented. Thus, we affirm that our work and commitment as sociolinguists are not limited to observing and systematizing knowledge of the situations of inequality that we detect around us, but to actively aspire to change them, moving towards a sociolinguistic justice that can only work if speakers become involved and agents of change in their contexts.

Notes

1 This chapter is the outcome of the R&D project 'Towards a New Linguistic Citizenship' (ref. PID2019-105676RB-C41/AEI/10.13039/501100011033), funded by the Spanish Ministry of Science and Innovation. For more information, visit https://www.equiling.eu/en/. The chapter benefited from theoretical and methodological debates at the MIRCo-UAM Research Center for Interdisciplinary Research in Multilingualism, Discourse, and Communication.

References

Alonso, Lara, and Luisa Martín Rojo. 2023. "Madrid/Nueva York: la transformación de dos ciudades a través del paisaje lingüístico: una herramienta de acción educativa." In *Superdiversidad lingüística en los nuevos contextos multilingües: Una mirada etnográfica y multidisciplinar*, edited by Gabriela Prego Vázquez, and Luz Zas Varela, 157–182. Frankfurt/Madrid: Vervuert Verlagsgesellschaft.

Blommaert, Jan. 2013. *Ethnography, Superdiversity and Linguistic Landscapes: Chronicles of Complexity*. Bristol: Multilingual Matters. 127 pp.

Bourdieu, Pierre. 1982. *Ce que parler veut dire. L'économie des échanges linguistiques*. Paris: Fayard.

Bourdieu, Pierre. 1999. *Meditaciones pascalianas*. Translated by Thomas Kauf. Barcelona: Anagrama.

Freire, Paulo. 1970. *Pedagogía del oprimido*. Translated by Jorge Mellado. Montevideo: Tierra Nueva.

Freire, Paulo. 2004. "On the Right and Duty to Change the World." In *Pedagogy of Indignation*, edited by Donaldo Macedo, 31–43. London: Paradigm Publishers.

Hyltenstam, Kenneth, and Caroline Kerfoot. 2022. "Foreword: Linguistic Citizenship: Unlabeled Forerunners and Recent Trajectories." In *Struggles for Multilingualism and Linguistic Citizenship*, edited by Quentin Williams, Ana Deumert, and Tommaso Milani, vii–xxv. Bristol: Multilingual Matters.

Irwin, Alan. 1995. *Citizen Science: A Study of People, Expertise and Sustainable Development*. London/New York: Routledge.

Lefebvre, Henri. 1974. *Le production de l'espace*. Paris: Éditions Anthropos.

Martín Rojo, Luisa. (2016 [2014]). "Occupy: The Spatial Dynamics of Discourse in Global Protest Movements." *Journal of Language and Politics* 13, no. 4: 583–598.

Martín Rojo, Luisa, ed. 2020. "Sujetos hablantes." In *Claves para entender el multilingüismo contemporáneo*, edited by Luisa Martín Rojo, and Joan Pujolar Cos, 9–30. Zaragoza: Prensas de la Universidad de Zaragoza.

Martín Rojo, Luisa. (forthcoming). "Landscapes of Protest Movements: Spaces and Discourses That Prefigure and Perform Other Possible Worlds." In *Sociolinguistics of Protesting*, edited by Ashraf Abdelhay, Christine Severo, and Sinfree Makoni. Berlin: De Gruyter.

Martín Rojo, Luisa, Camila Cárdenas-Neira, and Clara Molina. 2024. *Lenguas callejeras: paisajes colectivos de las lenguas que nos rodean. Guía para fomentar la conciencia sociolingüística crítica*. Barcelona: Octaedro. Available at https://octaedro.com/producto/lenguas-callejeras-paisajes-colectivos-de-las-lenguas-que-nos-rodean/. Version in English available at https://octaedro.com/libro/street-languages-collective-landscapes-of-the-languages-that-surround-us/

Portal Estadístico. 2023. Available at https://portalestadistico.com/municipioencifras/?pn=madrid&pc=ZTV21

Rymes, Betsy. 2020. *How We Talk about Language: Exploring Citizen Sociolinguistics*. Cambridge: Cambridge University Press.

Sabaté-Dalmau, Maria. 2022. "*'Localizing English in Town'*: A Linguistic Landscape Project for a Critical Linguistics Education on Multilingualism." *International Journal of Bilingual Education and Bilingualism* 25, no. 10: 3580–3596.

Stroud, Christopher. 2023. "Linguistic Citizenship." In *The Routledge Handbook of Multilingualism*, edited by Carolyn McKinney, Pinky Makoe, and Virginia Zavala, 144–159, 2nd ed. London/New York, NY: Routledge.

Svendsen, Bente A., and Samantha Goodchild. 2024. "Citizen (Socio)Linguistics: What We Can Learn from Engaging Young People as Language Researchers." In *The Routledge Handbook of Language and Youth Culture*, edited by Bente A. Svendsen, and Rickard Jonsson, 407–420. London/New York, NY: Routledge.

9 Ideologies around "Galicianness" commodification in the multilingual linguistic landscapes of marketplaces in Galicia

A participatory action research with high school students

Gabriela Prego Vázquez, Luz Zas Varela, Pablo Montaña Prieto and Celtia Rey Brandón

Introduction

The research approach known as Linguistic Landscape (LL) emerged in the late twentieth century to address the "visibility and salience of languages on public and commercial signs in a given territory or region" (Landry and Bourhis 1997, 23).[1] In Galician sociolinguistics, this approach garnered significant interest from its inception and has since undergone substantial development. Early studies on the Linguistic Landscape in Galicia particularly focused on the vitality of the Galician language by examining its visibility and symbolic values in signage, public notices, and other elements of public space. This ongoing line of research allows us to assess the success of the Linguistic Normalization process and understand how Galicia's bilingualism is reflected in public written signage, as well as the tension and conflict between its two official languages, Galician and Spanish, and their speakers. To date, notable works include those by Dunlevy (2020), Järlehed (2020), Lago Caamaño, Silva Hervella and Gómez Martínez (2020), López Docampo (2011), Regueira Fernández, López Docampo and Wellings (2013), Rodríguez Barcia and Fernando Ramallo (2015), Sobocinska (2019), among others.

Another significant direction in Linguistic Landscape research has focused on analyzing multilingualism in relation to migration, globalization, and touristification. In recent decades, Galicia has been enriched by the linguistic repertoires of its migrants. However, not all the resources or languages that make up these repertoires crystallize in the linguistic landscape (Ben Rafael et al. 2006; Blommaert 2010, 2013; Cenoz and Gorter 2009; Landry and Bourhis 1997; Prego 2023), and those that do acquire different symbolic values in the language market (Bourdieu 1977). This has been demonstrated in various studies conducted in Galicia (Järlehed 2020; Regueira et al. 2013; Zas and Prego 2016; Zas and Prego 2018). Despite the low number of English-speaking migrants in Galicia, the use of

DOI: 10.4324/9781032687087-10

English in commercial signs has increased considerably due to the impact of globalization and touristification (Castro, Gómez and Montaña 2021; Montaña Prieto 2020; Prego and Zas 2018; Prego 2020; Zas and Prego 2018). These studies have examined the polycentric distribution and the hierarchization of emerging multilingual ecologies.

In our study, we specifically focus on the linguistic landscape of traditional food markets, an area that remains underexplored to date in Galicia. Due to their influence on the socioeconomic organization of the territory, Galician markets have been the subject of various studies from anthropological, geographical, and economic perspectives (e.g., Carré 1964; Fraguas 1968). Within the framework of interactional sociolinguistics, the oral communicative practices of buyers and sellers have also been examined (Prego Vázquez 1998; Rodríguez Yáñez 1994). However, written manifestations, that is, the linguistic landscape of markets and fairs, have received little attention (Montaña 2020; Prego Vázquez and Zas 2016; Prego Vázquez 2020).

Additionally, there are several reasons that justify the suitability of these spaces as a framework for research on linguistic landscapes. First, they are indoor spaces with well-defined boundaries, facilitating a thorough analysis. Second, these markets clearly reveal the symbolic power of many of the languages present in the Galician linguistic landscape and the motivations behind their use. In these settings, the conflicting relationship between Galicia's co-official languages (Galician and Spanish) becomes evident, as well as the presence of other languages driven by factors such as migration, touristification, or globalization. This is because traditional markets, as key centers of social and commercial interaction in Galicia's towns and cities, represent spaces that allow us to address the communicative repertoires circulating in the community and shaping the linguistic landscape (Montaña Prieto 2020). Also, as strategic meeting points for people from diverse backgrounds and social groups (Prego Vázquez 1998; Prego Vázquez 2020), they become important sites for the negotiation of linguistic identities and ideologies. This social and linguistic diversity is supported by the transformation that traditional markets have been undergoing in recent years to remain relevant and adapt to changes in the current socioeconomic context. This transformation does not break with the local and traditional character of the markets, but rather combines this dimension with a process of opening up to new customers, which involves gentrification and touristification of the space. These changes are primarily aesthetic[2] but ultimately affect the institution's communication policies, the languages used, and even the types of businesses within the market.

Considering this transformation of traditional markets into glocal spaces, in this chapter, we focus on a specific aspect of their linguistic landscape: not only which languages are present, but also how they are commodified. This phenomenon, commodification, refers to the process by which goods, services, ideas, or even aspects of social and cultural life are transformed into commodities that can be bought and sold. This implies that something originally without commercial value, or not intended to be commercialized, becomes an object of economic exchange. Commodification is a complex process involving the commercialization of goods

Ideologies around "Galicianness" commodification 219

and aspects of life previously not considered within the market sphere, leading to various economic, social, and ethical consequences. Specifically, the commodification of language (Heller 2003) constitutes a type of commodification through which languages and linguistic competencies, traditionally seen as a means of communication and an integral part of cultural identity, become economic resources or, as Pujolar (2020) notes, economic assets.

As we mentioned, our objective is to analyze how the discursive commodification of the linguistic landscape occurs in Galician markets, while also observing how the ideologies that mediate this commodification process are (mis)recognized, reproduced, contested, or interpreted by the people. To achieve this, our approach to the linguistic landscape is conducted within the framework of participatory action research (Lassiter 2005; Leyva and Speed 2008; Unamuno 2019). This research was carried out with high school students from a school in Tomiño, a rural-urban municipality on the border between Galicia and Portugal, and a school in the center of Vigo, one of the most important cities in Galicia. These students focused their research on the linguistic and semiotic landscape of the municipal market in Tomiño and the Berbés market in the city of Vigo. In this chapter, we develop our analysis of the linguistic reality of the markets based on the photographs taken by the students. Additionally, we contrast our analysis with their reflections on the linguistic landscape, the languages, and their uses.

Methodological aspects: Participatory action research within the educational context

This research is situated within a multimethodological framework that combines the Language Landscape approach (Landry and Bourhis 1997; Leeman and Modan 2009), Sociolinguistic Ethnography (Heller, Pietikäinen and Pujolar 2018), and the Critical Language Awareness Approach (Fairclough 2013). The data analyzed comes from participatory action research that incorporated co-labor research (Lassiter 2005; Leyva and Speed 2008; Martín Rojo, Cárdenas and Molina 2023; Unamuno 2019) to involve high school students as co-researchers in an ethnographic process to collect and analyze the linguistic landscape of the Municipal Market of Tomiño and the Berbés Municipal Market of Vigo. The selection of the markets was based on their proximity to the educational centers, but we also ensured that each had unique characteristics compared to the other. In this regard, the Tomiño market is crucial for supplying essential goods in the municipality. Recently, the town council carried out a renovation, modernizing the space not only for the sale of local products but also for hosting social events. Its location in the town's main square, the limited presence of supermarkets, and its status as the only market in Tomiño (apart from the Goián market, which is reserved exclusively for residents of that area) further enhance its relevance and dynamism in the community. In contrast, the Berbés market holds less significance. Vigo is a city filled with supermarkets and shopping centers, and within this context, the Berbés market competes with more prominent ones, such as the one in Calvario. The facility has not been updated for years and its offerings have gradually diminished. However, it remains operational due to its specialization in seafood, given its proximity to the port and the fish market, and because it is located in an area of Vigo where one must travel some distance to reach a supermarket.

An important remark is that Critical Linguistic Awareness was the vertebrae of the whole ethnographic process (Fairclough 2013). The conscientization process took place through critical observation of language presence/absence in the public space and specifically within the municipal market. An analysis of the linguistic landscape in this market allowed the young people to transition between different phases and to participate in proposing solutions to the linguistic inequalities observed in the analyzed space. The research was carried out in a secondary school in Tomiño from 2019 to 2022, and in a secondary school in Vigo in 2022. In Tomiño, the participants were 50 secondary school students (second- and third-year groups in secondary education), a Galician Language and Literature teacher, and two researchers from the Universidade de Santiago de Compostela; in Vigo, the research took place during the 2021–2022 academic year with 25 fourth-year students in a secondary school. A Spanish Language and Literature teacher and two researchers from the Universidade de Santiago de Compostela also participated. In both cases, the research was used to work on specific curriculum content related to sociolinguistics, as well as to develop oral and written production skills.

The participatory research process was carried out in the following phases:

1. Work in the regular classroom of the teachers. These sessions involved reflecting on the sociolinguistic landscape of the Galician language, including its representation or absence in signage across the educational institution, town, and municipal market.
2. Collaborative work between students, the teachers, and University of Santiago de Compostela researchers. Through telecommunication, students share knowledge and methodological tools to develop their research.
3. Visit to the local market, where materials were collected, and the linguistic landscape was analyzed with the aid of MAVEL, an application developed by the USC researchers for geolocating linguistic features (https://mavel.avel.cesga.es/).
4. Preparation of findings in the school classroom for public presentations.
5. In Tomiño, presentation at the market to the community with the presence of the Councilor for Social Welfare, Equality, and Education and the representative from the Municipal School Council. In the case of Vigo, the results were presented to the academic community at the Faculty of Philology at USC.

Discoursive Commodification: Enregisterment and ideologies in LL

The new sociolinguistic order of the linguistic landscape in both markets: Multilingualism and glocality

In previous research, we have observed how markets, in addition to being places of buying and selling, become points of tourist and cultural interest, transforming

Ideologies around "Galicianness" commodification 221

into cultural commodities and forming as sociospatial constructs laden with ideologies (Lefebvre 1974; Leeman and Modan 2009). Firstly, the linguistic landscape of the markets, being of municipal character, becomes subject to public normalization policies that influence the language choices of various public bodies in Galicia. Therefore, we identify Galician as the vehicular language in the different linguistic signs attributable to the market as an entity, and in those bearing the seal of public administrations such as the town council. In this regard, it is indifferent whether these are signs with an informational function or those with an advertising function. This language choice does not reflect the preferences of the market's buyers and sellers, as it aligns with the requirements of the *Galician Language Normalization Law,* which aims to promote the vitality of Galician and expand its functions in contexts where Spanish was traditionally considered more prestigious (see Figures 9.1 and 9.2).

Although the communication policy of both markets mandates the predominance of monolingual Galician signs in the corporate linguistic landscape, specific demands, such as ensuring the establishment's health and safety, sometimes require the inclusion of information in other languages, such as Spanish or English. This presence of other languages is more evident in the Vigo market, which attracts a larger Spanish-speaking audience and where the influence of the town council is less significant. The complexity in the corporate linguistic landscape is already evident in the following example, based on the analysis by the students from Tomiño in their presentation to the academic community at the Faculty of Philology at

Figure 9.1 Poster from an advertising campaign at the Berbés Market.

222 *Ethnographic Landscapes and Language Ideologies in the Spanish State*

Figure 9.2 Poster with information near the Tomiño Market.

University of Santiago de Compostela, where the linguistic characteristics of the market's linguistic landscape are examined from both quantitative and qualitative perspectives:

Case 1: Languages in the linguistic landscape of Tomiño

E2: (…) cales son as linguas máis empregadas no mercado de Tomiño / aquí tedes unha gráfica que como vedes a lingua máis empregada é o galego aínda que temos outros carteis que saen en galego e en castelán / que son os de normativa covid //

E1: nos soportes podemos ver que as placas pegatinas e carteis son os máis utilizados / despois están menos normalizados fotocopias e posters e possits // se usan menos no mercado / e isto son algúnsexemplos //

E3: a continuación vamos a falar das funcións que encontramos na lingua / primeiramente temos o galego que a función que empregan este mercado é a de normalización / ou sexa o de facer máis común a lingua galega neste mercado como comprobamos na presentación // pero / sempre e é bo que haia máis galego do que ten que estar // na segunda temos aínda castelá / que é pa- por se por exemplo temos ó lado / por exemplo / ó lado entre moitas comillas castela / que / ao mellor / temos familiares eu en México teño familiares que veñen aquí / e / e ter o protocolo covid ou outras eh/ outros carteis en castelán lles axuda moito porque non entenden o galego tan ben // e por último temos inglés que / e pra turistas ou ou xente que vén doutros lados do mundo / como o inglés é unha lengua case fundamental no mundo pois axuda muito pa entender o que temos no mercado e o que vendemos //

S2: (…) what are the most used languages in the Tomiño market / here you have a graph that as you can see the most used language is Galician although we have other signs that appear in both Galician and Spanish / which are the covid regulations ones //

S1: on the supports we can see that plates stickers and signs are the most used / then less standardized are photocopies and posters and post-its // they are used less in the market / and here are some examples //

S3: next we are going to talk about the functions we found in the language / firstly we have Galician which the function it serves in this market is normalization / that is making the Galician language more common in this market as we checked in the presentation // but / it's always good to have more Galician than just what needs to be there // secondly we still have Spanish / which is for- in case for example we have beside / for example / beside in quotes Castilian / which / maybe / we have relatives I have relatives in Mexico who come here / and / and having the covid protocol or other uh/ other signs in Spanish helps them a lot because they don't understand Galician so well // and lastly we have English which / and for tourists or or people who come from other parts of the world / since English is an almost fundamental language in the world it helps a lot to understand what we have in the market and what we sell //

The predominance of Galician monolingualism in the institutional linguistic landscape contrasts with the multilingualism observed in the written language displays of the different stalls in both markets. In the private linguistic landscape, authored by the vendors, also Galician and Spanish are the most commonly used languages. However, many stalls prefer Spanish over Galician as the vehicular language. In fact, there are several stalls where Galician is minimally present or entirely absent. Furthermore, the presence of foreign languages is also more prominent in the stalls' linguistic landscape than in the corporate one.

As we could already infer from the final reflection in *Case 1*, globalization and neoliberal practices have penetrated both the Tomiño Market and the Berbés Market, affecting their sociolinguistic order. In recent decades, these traditional spaces, essential for trading local products, have faced new challenges. On one hand, the markets have had to adapt to expand their clientele. One of the strategies adopted has been to leverage the increase in tourism to attract non-local customers. As seen in the following example from two students in Vigo, they are aware of the influence of the touristification process affecting their city, and even see adapting the linguistic landscape to visitors from other countries as a gesture of hospitality.

Case 2: Multilingualism and tourism in the market

E16: e ademais a inclusión doutras linguas que non sexan o castelán ou o galego pode dar un sentimento de benvida a outros //

E3: <palabra_inintelixible> //

E16: a outras persoas que poidan querer visitar o Mercado do Berbés ou incluso mercar algo / algún recordo ou souvenir / produto // pode dar un sentimento / o uso doutras linguas / como xaponés, italiano, ou mesmo inglés // un sentimento

224 *Ethnographic Landscapes and Language Ideologies in the Spanish State*

de benvida / de respecto por outras culturas, outras nacións, etcétera, e non só usando as linguas que só se falan neste país //
S16: and besides the inclusion of languages other than Spanish or Galician can give a feeling of welcome to others //
S3: <unintelligible_word> //
S16: to other people who might want to visit the Berbés Market or even buy something / some souvenir or memento / product //it can give a feeling / the use of other languages / like Japanese, Italian, or even English // a feeling of welcome / of respect for other cultures, other nations, etcetera, and not just using the languages that are only spoken in this country //

On the other hand, the reality of both markets contrasts with the idealized notion of markets as places where only local products from small producers are sold. In fact, in both markets, a customer might choose to buy Moroccan octopus because it is cheaper than that from the Ría de Vigo, or they might even seek out Golden or Pink Lady apples instead of the less attractive but equally delicious Camoesa apples, native to Galicia (see Figure 9.3). Ultimately, while the markets aim to promote local products, they also embrace diversification and inevitably find themselves within a global market. This global market is one where diets are becoming increasingly similar across regions, local and exotic products are both valued,

Figure 9.3 Counter of Frutería Maty.

Ideologies around "Galicianness" commodification 225

international and transnational brands are established, and cost reduction often involves importing foreign goods and cultivating foreign varieties and breeds in all territories. Thus, both markets have diversified their offerings, combining a wide variety of foreign and local products, and this diversity is reflected in the linguistic landscape. As a result, we can find languages such as English, French, German, Japanese, or Chinese, alongside Galician and Spanish, on the signage (Martín Rojo 2023). Note how the multilingual nature of a fruit stand is connected to the different origins and denominations of its products:

In their analysis, the students also observe this multilingual nature of the linguistic landscape connected to the diverse origins of the products, as seen in the following commentary by students from IES de Vigo about the Berbés Market:

Case 3: The multilingual nature of the linguistic landscape in the Berbésmarket

E13: comenzando xa con algunhas gráficas que fixemos eh clasificando en multilingües e monolingües / na gráfica podemos ver e atopamos eh umm / umm vinte e tres monolingües e / eh once multilingües // e aquí podemos ver o todo tipo de idiomas que vimos eh que / vemos nos carteis // vimos eh no primeiro español con inglés en Pink Lady / vemos o inglés en pera Ercolini / atopamos tamén o italiano en judías / o español e manzana Fuji atopamos o xaponés // e vendo todo isto fixemo sunha gráfica na que eh umm / vemos / dentro dos monolingües / vemos só vinte e un / en español / e dentro dos multilingües / hai varias combinacións / o español co inglés temos / oito.

S13: starting now with some graphs that we made uh classifying them as multilingual and monolingual / in the graph we can see and we found uh umm / umm twenty-three monolingual and / uh eleven multilingual // and here we can see all the types of languages that we saw eh that / we see on the signs // we saw eh first Spanish with English on *manzana Pink Lady* / we see English / on *pera Ercolini* we also found Italian / *judías* in Spanish and *manzana Fuji* we found Japanese // and seeing all this we made a graph where uh umm / we see / in / within the monolingual / we only see twenty-one / in Spanish / and within the multilingual / there are various combinations / Spanish with English we have / eight.

Enregisterment in the linguistic landscape: A discursive commodification strategy in both markets

The results of our analysis also show how discursive commodification of the linguistic landscape, whereby languages become an essential part of the goods and products, that is, they become commodities, gains special relevance in both markets. Following the line indicated by Leeman and Modan (2009, 337), the commodified repertoires in the linguistic and semiotic landscape acquire new ideological values and become part of the symbolic economy, that is, the union of cultural symbols and entrepreneurial capital. The analyzed data show that the discursive commodification of the linguistic landscape in these markets is carried out through the process of enregisterment (Agha 2007, 55), which consists of "processes whereby diverse behavioral signs (whether linguistic, non-linguistic, or both) are functionally reanalyzed as cultural models of action, as behaviors capable of indexing stereotypic characteristics of incumbents of particular interactional roles, and relations among them."The data show that the resources that are enregistered are recognizable as specific to English and local linguistic and semiotic registers. In this process of enregisterment, local social actors, the authors of this signage, reinterpret and reproduce the symbolic values assigned to these languages within the framework of a glocal culture, reifying them to become an essential part of the establishments and/or products they name. Discursive commodification based on the enregisterment strategy is a metadiscursive process through which the social actors responsible for the linguistic landscape, that is, the shop owners, reproduce and reinforce the ideological values attached to these languages in postmodernity. The results show that the linguistic ideologies of anonymity and authenticity (Gal and Woolard 2001;Woolard 2007) support and naturalize these new symbolic values conveyed by the languages.

Global English enregisterment and commodification

As discussed above, the use of English is enregistered in the signage of both markets to convey the ideologies of anonymity, which intersect with local ideologies, indexed by Galician and Spanish. In this way, the products are presented as "universal, non-localized, and global" within local frameworks, thus projecting a glocal space. Note how in the sign of the "peixería"(fish shop) in Galician, the name of a well-known dolphin protagonist from an American TV series, Flipper, is enregistered in a sign in Galician. The owners of this fish shop, through this denomination, reinterpret and reposition their products in a glocal space (see Figure 9.4).

Often, in the process of enregisterment, a single letter, such as the "y"in the name of an establishment, proves to be sufficiently significant and identifiable with English to associate the establishment with the values of modernity and cosmopolitanism attributed to this language.

Note this example from the Berbés Market, where English is commodified through the enregisterment of the letter "y"in the Spanish sign for "Frutería Maty"(see Figure 9.5).This association with modernity and global values is anchored in a metadiscursive process, through which the meanings associated with English that circulate in society are reproduced and reinforced, sustained by the ideological system of anonymity. The students' analysis recognizes the symbolic value of the "y"associated with English and, therefore, with modernity, and how this language is capable of permeating the names of local stalls:

Case 4: Frutería Maty

E14: neste negocio, Frutería Maty, a lingua vehicular é o español xa que é a máis empregada nos signos lingüísticos. Tendo en conta que a maioría das pizarras do establecemento co nome dos eh produtos conteñen e usan español, poderíamos supoñer que tanto o emisor como eh receptor…eh, o dono do establecemento

Ideologies around "Galicianness" commodification 227

Figure 9.4 Sign of Peixería Flipper.

Figure 9.5 Sign of Frutería Maty.

e os clientes son hispanofalantes... .e o inglés tamén se ve reflexadoao estar presente no propio título do establecemento, Frutería Maty, con i grego (...) Como podedes observar eh a mestura do español co inglés, unha lingua globalizada e moderna. Apela a un público mozo, e da mesma maneira emprega as pizarras para presentar o nome dos produtos con cor, aportando dinamismo e mesmo ummm un efecto atractivo. Por outro lado, tamén se presentan outras linguas como o galego, o italiano e incluso o xaponés.

S14: in this business, Frutería Maty, the vehicular language is Spanish since it is the most used in the linguistic signs. Considering that most of the boards in the establishment with the names of the uh products contain and use Spanish, we could assume that both the sender and uh receiver...uh, the owner of the establishment and the customers are Spanish speakers ... .and English is also reflected by being present in the establishment's own name, Frutería Maty, with a "y" (...) As you can see uh the mixture of **Spanish** with **English,** a **globalized and modern language**. It **appeals to a young audience**, and in the same way, it uses the boards to present the names of the products with color, adding **dynamism** and even ummm **an attractive effect**. On the other hand, other languages such as Galician, Italian, and even Japanese are also presented.

In this analysis where students examine the functions of different languages, we observe that, in addition to highlighting the multilingual nature of the linguistic landscape, the relevance of English is emphasized. In bold, we have marked how the students define English: as a globalized and modern language that connects with a young audience in a stall where the products have colorful signs, with dynamism and attractiveness. Underlying their analysis of English are the ideologies of anonymity. The students have naturalized the hegemonic value of English as the "common voice"of modernity, which is not identified with any particular place, and as a symbol of cosmopolitanism and youth. We observe how the students reproduce, in conclusion, the values around English, present in the global linguistic landscape, as noted in the works of Ben Rafael et al. (2006) and Cenoz and Gorter (2009).

The students themselves, after associating English with young people, reflect on the effect it might have on older people:

Case 5: Names in English

E11: eu penso que para a xente maior pois o ven como algo novo xa que agora o mundo está máis globalizado e hai produtos en inglés // Veno como algo exótico, e xa que teñen produtos en inglés, tal vez poñer os nomes en inglés no mercado é unha boa idea //

S11: I think that for older people, they see it as something new because the world is more globalized now and there are English products // They see it as something exotic, and since they have products in English, maybe putting the names in English in the market is a good idea //

Ideologies around "Galicianness" commodification 229

Figure 9.6 Sign of Pescadería Fashion Fish.

From the previous case, it is evident how the students see a continuity between the use of English in product names and, as a consequence of touristification, its presence in names or advertising to connote this idea of modernity. Although they use terms like "exotic," we did not find negative opinions about this strong presence of the English language in the markets, nor do they consider it a real problem for older people. The idea of English as a global brand would then combine both this symbolic use of the language and its presence due to a global market and the presence of tourists. In our corpus, it is very common for students' analyses to link the uses and motivations of the English language, leading to the emergence of the idea of internationalization. In the following example, the students highlight the relationship of English with tourists and with modernization (see Figure 9.6).

Case 6: Modernization and tourism

E11: e xa pensan que / eh umm o han modernizado / eh pois / lle dálle dá un toque moderno //

E15: si o sea / eh por exemplo na miña última presentación podíamos ver a Pescadería Fashion Fish, non? Ninguén esperaría / encontrar Fashion Fish / nunha pescadería en Galicia //

Participante externo[3] 3: si //

Participante externo 3: s si //

E15: pero resulta que si porque / ao estar preto do porto / donde veñen moitos turistas a Vigo / pois eh / é máis sinxelo que eh os <pausa/> turistas síntanse atraídos a estes comercios / se eh len / títulos en inglés //

Participante externo 3: en inglés //
Participante externo 3: pola globalización //
E15: pola globalización / hum //
S11: and they think that / uh um it has modernized /uh well / it gives it a modern touch //
S15: yes, I mean /uh for example in my last presentation we could see the fish shop Fashion Fish, right? no one would expect /to find Fashion Fish /in a fish shop in Galicia //
ExternalParticipant 3: yes //
ExternalParticipant 3: y yes /
S15: but it turns out yes because /being close to the port /where many tourists come to Vigo /well uh /it is easier for uh the / tourists to be attracted to these shops /if uh they read /titles in English //
External Participant 3: in English //
External Participant 3: because of globalization //
S15: because of globalization /hum //

In this episode, English is conceived as a global language, an "anonymous" language not tied to any specific place. It is perceived as depersonalized and delocalized. English is established as a hegemonic language, acting as a lingua franca. The analysis of the data shows how the students accept its authority and legitimize its role in social communication to project a new conception of the markets as "modern." In their discourse, we observe how this hegemony is naturalized. Furthermore, the students also recognize multilingualism and the predominance of English in their linguistic landscape as a symbol of global values, as seen in the last part of the previous excerpt and the following fragments.

Additionally, in all four examples, the symbolic function of this language is evident in indexing the transformations of these spaces. As Leeman and Modan (2009) point out, the symbolic function of languages in the linguistic landscape contributes to transforming physical spaces, and in this case, the symbolic function of English plays a significant role in creating new translocal social spaces in the markets. In the transformation process that these spaces are undergoing, the global and the local intertwine in the linguistic landscape, resignifying it as a glocal linguistic landscape. The linguistic landscape is an ideological and scalar representation (Prego 2020) of the transformations occurring in both markets and shows the extent to which neoliberal practices influence the linguistic landscape. Thus, the observation of the students' analyses reveals how hegemonic linguistic ideologies around English have been naturalized in this new sociolinguistic order of the markets.

Galicianness enregisterment: Authenticity commodification in PL markets

In these new globalized markets, we observe how local products gain added value and enter neoliberal dynamics by being offered as authentic and quality products. Specifically, in our analysis, we discovered how in this new multilingual

Ideologies around "Galicianness" commodification 231

sociolinguistic order of the linguistic landscape, local products are also commodified through the construction of "Galicianness." This commodification sells an identity of utopian authenticity linked to the values of a desired natural and sustainable space, connected to the sea, the land, and its traditions. Thus, we have observed that what we have termed "Galicianness enregisterment"gains special relevance in this process.

The results of the analysis reveal how, in addition to the linguistic resources typical of the local and everyday Galician register, lexical items in Galician or Spanish that index references from the traditional Galician universe or semiotic resources that evoke traditional Galicia are enregistered in the linguistic landscape of the markets. This constitutes a discursive commodification strategy to sell an authentic product rooted in a place, as addressed by Remlinger (2018). By mobilizing the ideologies of authenticity (Gal and Woolard 2001; Woolard 2007) through these linguistic and semiotic resources, the local and authentic value of the product or establishment is enhanced, repositioning it in a global space where sustainable products acquire special relevance. Let us observe the following examples:

Enregisterment of resources from the local and colloquial register of Galician: -iña (see Figure 9.7)

In the name of this establishment, the diminutive morpheme *-iña* is enregistered, which is used in spontaneous interaction with connotations of affection and

Figure 9.7 Sign of A Tendiña.

closeness as strategies of positive politeness (Prego 2010). The diminutive employed is a recognizable resource of the colloquial Galician register, associated with traditional local cultural values. Moreover, this morpheme *–iña* is an identifiable resource with what Gumperz (1982) would call the Galician "we code." In fact, it is a stereotype to represent Galicians speaking with diminutive endings and also call them *galleguiños*.

As we noted in the previous analysis, the enregisterment of *–iña*, following Remlinger (2018), constitutes a metadiscursive practice. Its strategic use stems from the reflection and reinterpretation of the meaning of *–iña*. In this process, the morpheme also transforms into an authentic asset that becomes part of the establishment's name, which in turn becomes a shop offering merchandise with local and authentic values. In this discursive commodification, *-iña* transforms this establishment into a valuable authentic commodity (Remlinger 2018, 264). Finally, other elements such as the type of lettering or the wood in the exterior decoration of the shop, a material widely used in traditional Galician construction, reinforce this authenticity.

Enregisterment of lexicon and/or images that evoke the universe of Galicianness

In other instances, the construction of authenticity is achieved through the enregisterment of a lexicon that evokes traditional Galicia, both agrarian and maritime. We observe that this strategy can occur in signage in both Spanish and Galician (for example, see Figure 9.8).

In this first example from a fruit shop in Tomiño, not only is the choice of Galician important for the name and slogan, but also the lexical selection. "Horta" refers to a traditional garden, "vella" refers to an elderly woman who traditionally cultivates products. Similarly, the phrase "da terra" ("of the land") reinforces the idea of natural and local produce. Additionally, this is a clear example of a multimodal message, as the central part of the sign features an image of a Galician field, reinforcing the idea connoted by the written text. In the following signs, although the statement is in Spanish, the lexicon points to the Galician universe. Note: "mariscos de la ría" (seafood from the stuary, which can only refer to the Galician estuary), or "bolla del país" (bread of the country, which can only be Galician bread) (see Figures 9.9 and 9.10).

And finally, observe the following example: "Pescadería Narcisa." Although it is written in Spanish, authenticity is constructed through the enregisterment of the image of a traditional fish seller and the name "Narcisa," a typical Galician name now out of use. Additionally, the attire, footwear, and hairstyle of the woman in the drawing evoke an authentic fish seller from the past. The sign also explicitly states the establishment's founding date, aiming to evoke a long tradition (see Figure 9.11).

In summary, what was once rural and marginalized in Galicia is now repurposed to become a tourist and commercial attraction offering authentic experiences. Features of the minority language, historically marginalized, are commodified to market local products associated with a traditional place. In this analysis, we see

Ideologies around "Galicianness" commodification 233

Figure 9.8 Sign of A Horta da Vella.

Figure 9.9 Mariscos Victoria Sticker.

234 *Ethnographic Landscapes and Language Ideologies in the Spanish State*

Figure 9.10 Informational sign about a Rustic Bread.

Figure 9.11 Sign of Pescadería Narcisa.

how the discourse of authenticity is transformed into a form of marketing. The products named with the analyzed resources, along with the linguistic and semiotic forms, are transformed into goods for a new market aimed at a global audience that consumes authentic cultural goods (Prego Vázquez 2012).

The students' analysis recognizes these values in traditional products and observes the role of discursive commodification in "selling the authenticity" of a product. Note their analysis of "queixo fresco" (soft cheese) in Galician versus "queso fresco" in Spanish:

Case 7: Un queixo fresco and a queso fresco

E15: segurame eh o sea seguramente se nós imos / agora a un supermercado e lemos "queixo fresco" o preferimos a / "queso fresco" porque sentimos que é máis noso / e seguramente mellor //

S15: surely, I mean, surely if we go / now to a supermarket and we read **"queixo fresco"** we would **prefer it to / "queso fresco"** because we feel that it is **more ours** / and **surely better** //

The "queixo fresco" in Galician refers to a specific type of local cheese and, therefore, "ours" and "better." The quality and authenticity are identified with the Galician language designation of the product.

Galician language as pride or benefit in the new sociolinguistic order of the markets: Reimagining the discursive space with transformative linguistic landscape practices

The findings of this research also show how the students analyze the position and values of the Galician language in these new glocal scenarios. Galician is a minority language experiencing an intergenerational break, leading to a significant loss of speakers among young people. Thus, in the students' analysis, we observe how they navigate the concept of the language as "pride" or "benefit" (Duchene and Heller 2012), and how languages are valued in different sociopolitical and economic contexts. The concept of language as "pride" focuses on languages as a community's unique form of communication, bearing identity and heritage. The language is linked to the history and traditions of a community. This concept of language as "pride" is particularly relevant for minority languages like Galician, which must resist homogenizing globalization. Conversely, the concept of language as "benefit" refers to its economic value, whereby languages are seen as resources that can generate economic benefits or job opportunities. In new global scenarios, these two dimensions coexist in tension, as the commodified uses of a minority language do not always correspond to its sociolinguistic promotion.

Thus, in the analysis of the market's linguistic landscape, we observe that the commodification of Galician does not ensure the linguistic normalization of this language in this context. In their analyses, the students, on one hand, consider the value of the Galician language as a "good," that is, "benefit," a resource to characterize authentic products. However, on the other hand, they point out that a greater commitment to Galician in the linguistic landscape is necessary and propose transformations addressing the linguistic inequalities identified in the market spaces. In this sense, both the students from Vigo and Tomiño discursively reimagine the public space of both markets through their proposals. For example, in the following fragment, the students from Vigo navigate between revitalizing Galician in the market (Galician as pride) and the "no linguistic intervention" in the market (Galician as benefit). Contrast the interventions, for example, of students 3 and 17 with the intervention of student 16.

Case 8: Different opinions

Investigadora 2: e o que dicía eh / que se ti tiverades que facer un informe / para o concello //

Investigadora 2: e facer propostas / para as linguas do mercado que faríades? / que lles / diríades? / pausa longa //

E15: eh pois seguramente / eh poñer as etiquetas os carteis os eslóganes / bueno os eslóganes e os nomes dos comercios é máis complicado porque é algo máis persoal para a persoa que ten ese comercio //

E15: pero as etiquetas os carteis informativos as decoracións poderían estar en / en galego e castelán ao mesmo tempo / sen ningún problema para que / todas as persoas que frecuentan o mercado poidan sentirse identificadas //

E15: coa lingua na que están os seus / eh comercios habituais / pausa longa //

E3: e tamén non só oficial porque parece que / a publicidade ten que ser en galego para quedar ben //

E3: e ao final / eh no mercado ves que está case todo en castelán / que se equilibre un pouco a balanza porque vemos que non hai case galego / pausa longa //

E17: e nos aspectos informativos / tamén eh / eh nunha carnicería por exemplo todos os / eh símbolos lingüísticos que atopamos estaban en castelán //

Researcher 2: and what I was saying uh / that if you had to make a report / for the town council //

Researcher 2: and make proposals / for the languages of the market what would you do? / what would you / say to them? / long pause //

S15: uh well surely / uh put the labels the signs the slogans / well the slogans and the names of the businesses are more complicated because it's something more personal for the person who has that business //

S15: but the labels the informational signs the decorations could be in / in Galician and Spanish at the same time / without any problem so that / all the people who frequent the market can feel identified //

S15: with the language in which their / uh regular businesses are / long pause //

S3: and also not just official because it seems that / the advertising has to be in Galician to look good //

S3: and in the end / uh in the market you see that almost everything is in Spanish / that the balance is a bit equalized because we see that there is hardly any Galician / long pause //

Ideologies around "Galicianness" commodification 237

S17: and in informational aspects / also uh / uh in a butcher shop for example all the / uh linguistic symbols we found were in Spanish //
S17: and also in the seafood shop that my group commented on / well the majority were also in Spanish //
S17: so maybe / uh um / uh //
S17: end that imbalance in the information / uh so even though the majority is in Spanish / well / uh vary or / have them in both uh languages / long pause //
S16: I honestly / uh would leave the market / with a / small free will that is not intervening not intervene much //
S16: in the current order that the market has / but yes / uh maybe some uh //
S16: make some decision or something like that so that the / the balance that they mentioned / between Galician and Spanish //
S16: is more balanced / and thus Galician has more importance and weight in the products in the information in the / in the decoration even in the rules / of the place //
S16: but that's what I said at the beginning that / it shouldn't be intervened much / because uh / after all the market is //
S16: something / important / and it has a lot of vitality from Galicia / and it has a lot of its spirit inside //
S16: and the Xunta or the government or whoever can make changes in it / uh shouldn't meddle much and change its personal spirit that O Berbés has //

Similarly, following the example of students 3 and 17 from Vigo, the students from Tomiño proposed specific changes to the market signage based on their analyses. They examined the languages used in the signage, the mediums on which they were printed, and the functions of the languages. They presented specific proposals to normalize the Galician language to the Social Welfare, Equality, and Education city councilor and the representative of the city council on the municipal school board. Their analysis concluded that while Galician is present in about 50% of the signage, Spanish also occupies a significant percentage, and English is increasingly being introduced. They declared that "it is necessary to ask businesses to use signage in Galician." The following example shows how students in Galicia designed a series of recommendations for the city council to change the language policy of the market and thereby transform its linguistic landscape. The specific proposals aimed at normalizing the Galician language on the market signs. For instance, for the bakery and fish sections, students proposed placing colored post-its with all the product names in Galician to make it easier for buyers to request them in this language and, hence, for Galician oral linguistic practices to increase.

Case 9: In the bakery

E: As linguas que atopamos foron o castelán / galego / inglés / e italiano // Carteis (...) normativos con frases (...) dose / doces e salgados (...) En conclusión / ademais do galego / hai moita diversidade / moitas máis linguas diversas (...) Como normalizar o galego? A nosa proposta sería publicar unha senda con postits para que a xente vexa o galego e así normalizalo / e tamén para que o dono da tenda fale en galego porque iso anima a outras persoas a intentar falar máis galego //

S: The languages we found were Spanish / Galician / English / and Italian // Signs (...) normative with phrases (...) dose / sweets, and savory items (...) In conclusion / besides Galician / there is a lot of diversity / many more diverse languages (...) How to normalize Galician? Our proposal would be to publish a path with post-it notes so that people can see Galician and thus normalize it / and also for the store owner to speak in Galician because that encourages other people to try to speak more Galician //

Case 10: In the fish shop

E: É preciso que todos os nomes tamén estean en galego para así ampliar o vocabulario //

S: It is necessary for all the names to also be in Galician in order to expand the vocabulary//

Once the presentation of all the proposals was finished, the councilor took the floor to publicly express the following:

Concelleira (en galego): parece que queredes rexistrar [as miñas palabras] porque queredes que o concello se comprometa coas propostas que presentastes como resultado do voso traballo / O noso compromiso [como concelleira] é aceptar as propostas viables para a normalización do galego neste mercado. Entendo que é a nosa lingua / que non debemos perdela / e / polo que a nós respecta / podedes contar conosco compromiso para que isto suceda //

Councilor (in Galician): it seems that you want to record [my words] because you want the city council to commit to the proposals that you have presented as a result of your work / Our commitment [as a councilor] is to accept the feasible proposals for the normalization of Galician in this market. I understand that it is our language / that we should not lose it / and / as for us / you can count on our commitment for this to happen //

The young students became aware of the unequal distribution between Spanish and Galician in both personal and public (market) domains. Within the framework of Galician as "pride" they proposed, as we have seen in the previous examples, a series of visual transformations in the linguistic landscape of the markets to contribute to the normalization of the language. The various interventions by the students from Vigo and Tomiño show how they designed a series of recommendations for the city council to change the language policy of the market and transform the linguistic landscape of both the Vigo and Tomiño markets. The critical sociolinguistic consciousness activities carried out in the classroom allowed them to critically analyze a public space shared by different social agents (Prego Vázquez and Zas Varela 2018). Additionally, the collaborative research work fostered collective action on this space. In this sense, aligning with Lefebvre (1974), they understood the dynamism of space and became aware of its symbolic value. They mobilized their collective agency with a proposal for transformative action, demonstrating clear social and political intent (Freire 1970; Pennycook 2001), in line with Freire's critical pedagogy proposals (1970, 1975). Their efforts aimed not only at transforming the market space but also at reversing the hegemonic sociolinguistic order.

Conclusions

In this research, we have analyzed globalization in the line indicated by Fairclough (1993), that is, we have observed how globalization processes are managed in local contexts. Specifically, this study shows the results of research developed within the framework of participatory action research, which was carried out with high school students from a high school in Tomiño (a rural-urban municipality located on the border between Galicia and Portugal) and from a high school in the center of Vigo (one of the most important cities in Galicia) about the linguistic landscape of markets. The results of the research show that the multilingual sociolinguistic order of the linguistic landscape of both markets is a consequence of the transformations connected with globalization and the introduction of neoliberal practices in these local spaces. In the section "Discursive Commodification: enregisterment and ideologies in LL," we also demonstrated the special relevance that discursive commodification has in the linguistic landscape of the market. The analysis reveals how the different languages and semiotic resources involved in this sociodiscursive commodification (Galician, Spanish, English, and multilingual practices) are connected to different values and ideologies: authenticity, anonymity, and internationalization through the metadiscursive processes of linguistic and semiotic enregisterment.

We also observe how this linguistic and semiotic enregisterment in the linguistic landscape is the result of a process of strategic circulation in which new linguistic ideologies are re-signified and renegotiated to sustain and naturalize the construction of the commodification of languages as goods and essential parts of the products they represent. Additionally, we observe how this process rides between the local and the global to construct and indexicalize a glocal symbolic space. In stores, discursive commodification based on the strategy of enregisterment is a metadiscursive process through which the social actors responsible for the linguistic landscape, that is, business owners, reproduce and reinforce the ideological values attached to these languages in postmodernity. As we have observed, the use of English is enregistered in the signage of both markets to convey the ideologies of anonymity (Gal and Woolard 2001; Woolard 2007) that intersect with local ideologies, indexed by Galician and Spanish. In this way, the products are presented as "universal, non-localized, and global" within local frameworks, thus projecting a glocal space.

Moreover, Galicianness enregisterment is particularly important in both markets. The study shows how "Galicianness" is commodified (Järlehed 2020) to construct an identity of utopian authenticity linked to the values of a desired natural and sustainable space, connected to the sea, the land, and its traditions. The introduction of the trope of a utopian Galicia into the linguistic landscape constitutes a metadiscursive practice, a reification of authenticity that transforms into what Marx (1867) would call a commodity fetish. In a postmodern society, where products resulting from the industrialization of agriculture and live stock dominate the market, a new discourse emerges that celebrates the consumption of local and natural products. In this new scenario, the use of linguistic resources from the colloquial register of Galician, as well as lexical or semiotic resources that evoke the local, serves a strategic function. The results of the analysis reveal that the naturalization of the discursive commodification process in the linguistic landscape is based on the management of the ideologies of anonymity and authenticity, underlying the mobilization of various linguistic and semiotic resources. Additionally, they show how students, in their analyses, navigate between the conceptions of Galician as pride or benefit (Duchene and Heller 2012). This ideological management of the linguistic landscape allows for the discursive projection and reimagining of various conceptions of translocal space. It also addresses the symbolic values and ideologies on which these identities (global and local) are based and how these are (mis)recognized, reproduced, or contested by the young students in sociodiscursive processes that renegotiate and reimagine market spaces where Galician language is positioned in a tension between pride or benefit in the multilingual landscape. Ultimately, the linguistic landscape is an ideological and scalar representation (Prego 2020; Leeman and Modan) of the transformations occurring in both markets.

Notes

1 This study has been conducted within the framework of the I+D+I projects Espacios de transformación sociolingüística en el contexto educativo gallego: agencia de los hablantes, repertorios multilingües y prácticas (meta) comunicativas (Plan nacional I+D+I FEDER/ Ministerio de Ciencia, Innovación y Universidades – Agencia Estatal de Investigación PID2019-105676RB-C44/AEI/10.13039/501100011033.), Universidade de Santiago de Compostela).
2 Markets are becoming a site for hipster restaurants too.
3 External participants are researchers, university professors, and university students who participate as audiences in the high school students' presentation.

References

Agha, Asif. 2007. *Language and Social Relations*. Cambridge: Cambridge University Press.
Bem Rafael, Eliezer, Elana Shohamy, Muhammad Hasan Amara, and Nira Trumper Hecht. 2006. "Linguistic Landscape as Symbolic Construction of the Public Space: The Case of Israel." In *Linguistic Landscape: A New Approach to Multilingualism*, edited by Durk Gorter, 7–30. Bristol, Blue Ridge Summit: Multilingual Matters. https://doi.org/10.21832/9781853599170-002
Blommaert, Jan. 2010. *The Sociolinguistics of Globalization*. Cambridge: Cambridge University Press.
Blommaert, Jan. 2013. *Ethnography, Superdiversity and Linguistic Landscapes: Chronicles of Complexity*. Bristol, Blue Ridge Summit: Multilingual Matters. https://doi.org/10.21832/9781783090419

Bourdieu, Pierre. 1977. *Outline of a Theory of Practice*. Cambridge: Cambridge University Press.
Carré, Leandro. 1964. "As feiras na Galiza."*Revista de Etnografía* 2 (1): 97–124.
Castro, Carlota Gómez, Fátima and Montaña, Pablo. 2021. "A Rúa do Franco: Entre a Turistificación e a Glocalización."*Cadernos CIPCCE sobre Emerxencia Cultural* 6: 55–67.
Cenoz, Jasone, and Durk Gorter. 2009. "Language Economy and Linguistic Landscape." In *Linguistic Landscape: Expanding the Scenery*, edited by Elana Shohamy and Durk Gorter, 63–77. New York: Routledge.
Duchêne, Alexandre, and Monica Heller. 2012. "Pride and Profit: Changing Discourses of Language, Capital and Nation-State." In *Language in Late Capitalism*, edited by Alexandre Duchêne and Monica Heller, 1–21. New York: Routledge.
Dunlevy, Deirdre A. 2020. "Blurred Lines: The Effect of Regional Borders on the LL in Northern Spain." In *Reterritorializing Linguistic Landscapes: Questioning Boundaries and Opening Spaces*, edited by David Malinowski and Stefania Tufi, 236–261.London: Bloomsbury Academic.
Fairclough, Norman. 1993. "Critical Discourse Analysis and the Marketization of Public Discourse: The Universities.". *Discourse & Society* 4 (2): 133–168.
Fraguas, Antonio. 1968. "Emplazamiento de ferias en Galicia a fines del siglo XVIII."*Cuadernos de Estudios Gallegos* 23 (70): 200–223.
Freire, Paulo. 1970. *Pedagogía del oprimido*. Montevideo: Tierra Nueva.
Freire, Paulo. 1975. *Acción Cultural para la Libertad*. Buenos Aires: Tierra Nueva.
Gal, Susan, and Kathryn Woolard. 2001. *Languages and Publics: The Making of Authority*. New York: Routledge.
Gumperz, John J. 1982. *Discourse Strategies*. Cambridge: Cambridge University Press.
Heller, Monica. 2003. "Globalization, the New Economy, and the Commodification of Language and Identity." *Journal of Sociolinguistics* 7: 473–492.
Heller, Monica, Sari Pietikäinen, and Joan Pujolar, eds. 2018. *Critical Sociolinguistic Research Methods: Studying Language Issues That Matter*. London/New York: Routledge. https://doi.org/10.4324/9781003394259
Järlehed, Johan. 2020. "Pride and Profit: Naming and Branding Galicianness and Basqueness in Public Space."In *Namniskrift. Names in Writing*, edited by Maria Löfdahl, Michelle Waldispühl, and Lena Wenner, 147–175. Gothenburg: MeijerbergsInstitut.
Lago Caamaño, Clara, Irma Silva Hervella, and Lidia Gómez Martínez. 2020. "An Analysis of the Compostelian Linguistic Landscape: The Centrality of the Cathedral of Santiago De Compostela."*RiCOGNIZIONI. Rivista Di Lingue E Letterature Straniere E Culture Moderne* 7 (13), 93–104. https://doi.org/10.13135/2384-8987/4383
Landry, Rodrigue, and Richard Y. Bourhis. 1997. "Linguistic Landscape and Ethnolinguistic Vitality: An Empirical Study." *Journal of Language and Social Psychology* 16 (1): 23–49. https://doi.org/10.1177/0261927X970161002.
Lassiter, Luke Eric. 2005. *Collaborative Ethnography*. Chicago: University of Chicago Press.
Leeman, Jennifer, and Gabriella Modan. 2009. "Commodified language in Chinatown: A contextualized approach to linguistic landscape." *Journal of Sociolinguistics* 13 (3): 332–362.
Lefebvre, Henry. 1974. *La production de l'espace*. Paris: Anthropos.
Leyva Solano, Xochitl, and Shannon Speed. 2008. "Hacia la investigacióndescolonizada: nuestraexperiencia de co-labor. In *Gobernar (en) la diversidad: experiencias indígenas desde América Latina. Hacia la investigación de co-labor*, edited by Xochitl Leyva Solano, Araceli Burguete, and Shannon Speed, 65–107. Mexico City: CIESAS/FLACSO.

López Docampo, Miguel. 2011. "A paixase lingüística: unha análise dun espazo público galego". *Cadernos de Lingua*, 33, 5–35. A Coruña: Real Academia Galega.

Martín Rojo, Luisa. 2023. "Multilingualism, the New Economy and the Neoliberal Governance of Speakers." In *The Routledge Handbook of Multilingualism*, edited by Carolyn McKinney, Pinky Makoe, and Virginia Zavala, 286–299. New York: Routledge.

Martín Rojo, Luisa, Camila F. Cárdenas Neira, and Clara Molina Ávila. 2023. *Lenguas callejeras: Paisajes colectivos de las lenguas que nos rodean. Guía para fomentar la conciencia sociolingüística crítica*. Barcelona: Octaedro.

Marx, Karl. 2000 [1867]. *El capital*. Madrid: Akal.

Montaña Prieto, Pablo. 2020. A PL de Catro Mercados Galegos. *Master'sthesis*, Universidade de Santiago de Compostela.

Pennycook, Alastair. 2001. "The Politics of Pedagogy." In *Critical Applied Linguistics: A Critical Introduction*, 114–140. Mahwah: Lawrence Erlbaum Associates.

Prego Vázquez, Gabriela. 1998. *Negociando precios e identidades en los mercados gallegos. Una aproximación socio-interaccional al género discursive de los regateos*. Valencia: University of Valencia.

Prego Vázquez, Gabriela. 2010. "Communicative Styles of Code-Switching in Service Encounters: The Frames Manipulation and Ideologies of 'Authenticity' in Institutional Discourse." *Sociolinguistic Studies* 4 (2): 371–412.

Prego Vázquez, Gabriela. 2012. "Identidades en las regueifas gallegas: La reconstrucción de la etnicidad en el espacio global." *Spanish in Context* 9 (2): 244–267.

Prego Vázquez, Gabriela. 2020. "Escalas sociolingüísticas." In *Claves para entender el multilingüismo contemporáneo*, edited by Luisa Martín Rojo and Joan Pujolar, 91–129. Zaragoza: Editorial UOC/Prensas de la Universidad de Zaragoza.

Prego Vázquez, Gabriela. 2023. "(Des)reconocimiento sociolingüístico y escalaridad en los nuevos repertorios glocales de los jóvenes en Galicia." In *Superdiversidad linguistic en los nuevos contextos multilingües: una mirada etnográfica y multidisciplinar,* edited by Gabriela Prego and Luz Zas, 85–118. Madrid: Iberoamericana Vervuert.

Prego Vázquez, Gabriela, and Zas Varela, Luz. 2018. "Paisaje lingüístico. Un recurso TIC-TAC-TEP para el aula". *Lingue e Linguaggi* 25: 277–295. https://doi.org/10.1285/I2239 0359V25P277

Pujolar, Joan, 2020. "La mercantilización de las lenguas (commodification)." In *Claves para entender el multilingüismo contemporáneo*, edited by Luisa Martín Rojo and Joan Pujolar, 131–164. Zaragoza: Editorial UOC/Prensas de la Universidad de Zaragoza.

Regueira, Xosé Luís, Miguel López Docampo, and Matthew Wellings. 2013. "El paisaje lingüístico en Galicia." *Revista Internacional de Lingüística Iberoamericana* 11 (1): 39–62.

Remlinger, Kathryn. 2018. "Yooperisms in Tourism: Commodified Enregistered Features in Michigan's Upper Peninsula's Linguistic Landscape." In *The Sociolinguistics of Pace and Belonging: Perspectives from the Margins*, edited by Leonie Cornips and Vicent de Rooij, 261–286. Amsterdam: John Benjamins.

Rodríguez Barcia, Susana, and Fernando Ramallo. 2015. "Graffiti y conflicto lingüístico: el paisaje urbano como espacio ideológico." *Revista Internacional de Lingüística Iberoamericana* 13 (25): 129–154.

Rodríguez Yáñez, Xoan Paulo. 1994. *Estratexias de Comunicación nas Interacccións Cliente-Vendedor no Mercado da Cidade de Lugo: As Alternancias de Lingua Galego/Castelán e a Negociación da Escolla de Lingua (Estudio Etnográfico e Sociolingüístico da Interacción Campo-Cidade nun Espazo Urbano)*. Unpublished Ph Dissertartion: Universidade da Coruña.

Sobocińska, Marta. 2019. "La (in)visibilidad de las lenguas regionales en el paisaje linguistico de Asturias y Galicia of Regional Languages in the Linguistic Landscape of Asturias and Galicia." *Lletres Asturianes* 120: 117–143.

Unamuno, Virginia. 2019. "N'kuIfweln'uhu: etnografía en co-labor y la producción colectiva de la educación bilingüe intercultural desde la lengua y la cultura wichi (Chaco, Argentina)." *Foro de Educación Musical, Artes y Pedagogía* 17–27: 125–146.

Woolard, Kathryn. 2007. "La autoridad lingüística del español y las ideologías de la autenticidad y el anominato." In *La lengua, ¿patria común?*, edited by José del Valle, 129–142. Madrid: Vervuert.

Zas Varela, Luz, and Gabriela Prego Vázquez. 2016. "Las escalas del paisaje linguistico en los márgenes de la superdiversidad" *CesContexto. Debates* 15: 6–25.

Zas Varela, Luz, and Gabriela PregoVázquez. 2018. "A View of Linguistic Landscapes for an Ethical and Critical Education." In *Galician Migrations: A Case Study of Emerging Super-Diversity*, edited by Renée Depalma and Antía Pérez Caramés, 249–264. New York: Springer.

Index

Note: Page locators in **bold** and *italics* represents tables and figures, respectively. Endnotes are indicated by the page number followed by "n" and the note number e.g., 111n5 refers to note 5 on page 111.

agency 4, 41, 50, 147–8, 162–3, 163n1, 165, 189n1, 195, 198–202, 212, 239
Albayzín Neighbourhood 5, 67, 70, 72, 75, 83–5, 86n1
Alhambra 65, 70–1, 75, 78–9, *80*, 81
Andalusia 5, 64, 94–6, 108–10, 114, 117n14
Asturian 2, 3, 5, 14, 17, 21, 22, 26–39, 88n8, 243
Asturias 4, 16, *17–18*, 19, 21, 26–38, *28–30*, **31**, 243
asynchronous dialogue 16, 20, 22, 27, 34–6
authenticity 1, 5, 10, 41, 46, 47, 49, 58, 157, 226, 230–42
awareness-raising 166, 197, 198

Bakhtin 121, 147, 149, 157, 158, 164
Bangladeshi: Bangladeshi Diaspora 167–91, *173*, *174*, *184*, 208; Bangladeshi identity 175–80
Basque 2, 4, 6, 17, 19, 21–38, *23–5*, 64, 70, 74, 79–80, 87, 146–66, 168, 241
Bengali language 166–70, 174–6, 178–89
Benimaclet Neighbourhood 54–5, 59, 60, **46**
Ben-Rafael, Eliezer 4, 11, 13, 14, 44, 73, 89, 94, 116, 189, 190
bilingualism 2, 5, 13, 34, 40–60, 140, 160, 183, 192, 216, 217
Blackwood, Robert 1, 3, 4, 11, 15, 19, 21, 37, 41, 168, 190
Blommaert, Jan 2–5, 10, 11, 41, 44, 45, 72–4, 81, 89, 93, 95, 116, 123, 125, 131, 141, 147, 149, 150, 152, 164, 167, 168, 170, 190, 191, 198, 215, 217, 240
Bourhis, Richard 1, 13, 73, 90, 217, 219, 241

Camino de Santiago 4, 5, 16–39, *17*, *29*, *30*, **31**, 67
Cánovas Neighbourhood 59n2
carnival 6, 117, 117n13, 146–64
Castilian 48, 214, 223
Catalan 2, 3, 5, 6, 11, 20, 37, 42, 59n1, 60n3, 70, 74, 80, *81*, 81, 87, 90, 127, 129, 140, 143n8
Cenoz, Jasone 2, 11, 12, 17, 19, 20, 22, 24, 28, 30, 32, 37, 74, 89, 92, 93, 115–18, 166–8, 190, 217, 228, 241
citizen science 7, 8, 195, 201, 203, 214, 216
collaborative research 167, 238
commodified Arabic *83*
conscientization 10, 196, 197, 201–5, 212, 220
corporate identity 129, 143
critical language/linguistic awareness 9–10, 166, 170, 189, 197, 205, 219–20
critical language/linguistic education 9, 10, 166, 194
critical pedagogies 6, 196, 201, 204, 239
critical sociolinguistic ethnography 10, 238

didactics 201
diglossia 42, 55–9
discourse analysis 89, 124, 126, 150, 165, 241

Index

8M 92, 96–108, 117
emplacement (of signs) 22, 45, 151
English 2, 4–6, 20–39, *29*, 43, 50–1, 64–91, *82*, 64, 95–118, *104–9*, 123, 133, 140, 161, 170, *172*, 175, *176*, 177, *177*, 180, 190, 195, 197, 201, 207, 210, 211, 214, 216–18, 221, 223–32, 237–9
enregisterment 10, 220–40
ethnic area/community 74, 83, 215
ethnographic linguistic landscape analysis (ELLA) 5, 72–3, 81, 191
ethnography 11, 40–63, 73, 74, 89, 149, 164, 168, 190, 215, 219, 240, 241

feminisms/feminist 5, 55, 92–8, 101, 103, 105, 107–11, 112–15, 117n13, 118n21
Freire, P. 10, 12, 196, 197, 212, 215, 239, 241

Galicia 4, 10, 14, 17, 21, 28–39, *29*, **31**, *32*, 217–24
Galician 2–4, 10, 12, 15, 17, 30–8, 70, 74, 80, 164, 217–43
Galicianness 10, 38, 164, 217–43
geosemiotics 20, 22, 41, 151
globalization 3–5, 9, 11, 71, 94, 95, 106–7, 113, 117n11, 197, 168, 190, 210, 217, 218, 230, 235
glocal scenarios 235
Gorter, Durk 2, 4, 6, 11, 12, 15, 17, 19, 20, 22, 24, 26, 30, 32, 37, 38, 44, 74, 89, 92, 93, 115–18, 123, 165–8, 170, 189–91, 193, 217, 228, 240, 241
graffiti: campus graffiti 124, 125; toilet graffiti 125, 133, 140–2
Granada 4, 5, 12, 64–91, **66**, *67*, **70**, *82*, 97
grotesque realism 153

habitus 147, 150, 196
Heller, Monica 1, 12, 13, 157, 164, 219, 235, 240, 241

indexicality 40, 102, 162, 163, 167, 168, 182, 188
institutional voice 6, 126, 127, 129, 135, 139–42
intersectionality 4, 17, 95
(in)visibility 4, 9, 16–39, 166–93

Jaworski, Adam 4, 13, 38, 116, 126, 150, 164

Kress, Gunther 6, 13, 126, 136, 139, 143, 150, 165

Landry, Rodrigue 1, 13, 73, 90, 217, 219, 241
landscape: linguistic landscape 10, 40–60, 64–91, 92–118, 166–93, 194–216, 217–43; semiotic landscape 4, 6, 13, 38, 124, 140–1, 146–65, 197, 219, 225; silent landscape 74; urban landscape 5, 7, 40, 58, 65, 71, 152, 167, 188–9, 201–2, 206
language: (co) official language 2, 3, 5, 33, 42, 50, 59, 74, 127, 128, 174, 213, 217, 218; hegemonic language 2, 5, 40, 230; language choice 6, 123–42, 221; language/linguistic ideologies 1–2, 7, 10, 40, 42, 57, 65, 95, 206, 218–21, 226, 230–1, 239–40, 242; language/linguistic practices 4, 9, 40, 56, 93, 163n2, 188, 191, 195, 203, 235, 237, 239; language planning 2, 3, 41, 42; language policy 5, 14, 32, 33, 39, 40–60, 123, 168, 190, 192, 203, 237, 238; language processes 38; migrant language 2, 3, 5, 74–5, 86, 87, 166, 168, 211; minoritized language 3, 40, 60n4, 191; minority language 2, 4, 11, 17, 20–2, 27, 30, 32, 37–8, 41, 44, 74, 75, 86, 87, 140, 161, 167, 168, 190–1, 211, 214, 232, 235; regional language: 19–20, 24, 28, 31–4, 36, 40, 44, 243
Lavapiés neighborhood 9, 14, 167–93, *176*, *177*, *182*, *184*, *200*, 208, *209*, 210, 211, 214
Leeman, Jennifer 3, 13, 64, 65, 81–2, 89, 219, 225, 225, 230, 240, 241
Lefebvre, Henri 1, 13, 210, 216, 221, 238, 241
linguistic commodification 1, 13, 64; linguistic conflict 2, 40, 42; linguistic ethnography 10, 219; linguistic identity 40, 42, 58, 117; linguistic (mis)recognition 27, 33, 39, 168, 195, 196, 198, 202, 214, 230; linguistic normalization 3, 5, 42, 43, 59, 217, 221, 223, 235, 238; linguistic repertoires 1, 3, 4, 194, 217; linguistic self spaces 151, 151, 163, 165; linguistic underrepresentation 20, 21

Madrid 3, 4, 7–11, 13, 42, 65, 72, 74, 79, 83, 84, 88–91, 97, 109, 128, 166–93, 194, 195, 197, 207–16
Málaga 3, 5, 88n13, 92–118, *98–115*
Malinowski, David 13, 41, 90, 166, 189, 191, 241
Maly, Ico 3–5, 11, 41, 44, 72, 73, 89, 93, 116, 123, 125, 131, 141, 168, 170, 190, 191

Index

markets 9, 10, 182, 217–43, *221–34*
migration 3, 65, 68, 72, 81, 94, 172, 175, 197, *200*, 214, 217, 218
misrecognition 196
Modan, Gabriella 3, 13, 64, 65, 81–2, 89, 219, 225, 225, 230, 240, 241
multilingual (in)equality 20, 22, 32, 190
multilingualism 3, 5, 7–9, 40, 43, 44, 60–2, 64–91, 95, 97, 125, 126, 165, 166, 168, 173, 175, 188–92, *200*, 206, 207, 215n1, 216, 217, 220, 223, 230, 240, 242
multimodality 12, 14, 165, 190
Muslim community/identity 64, 65, 67, 70–2, 86, 174, 180–2

Nasrid kingdom 70, 71, 91

Old Town Neighbourhood 75, 151, 152, 162, 163

Pamplona 6, 16, 146–65
parody 6, 146, 151, 155, 157, 159
participatory action research 10, 163n2, 165, 201, 212, 215, 217–43
Patraix Neighbourhood **46**, 50–4, *51*, 59, 59n2, 60n9
performance 6, 148–63
pilgrimage 16, 180
popular education 10, 201, 202, 204
prestige planning 58–9
problematization 196
protest banners 96, 99, *104*, 105, 113, 150

Realejo Neighbourhood 75, 79
reflective journaling 21–5, 28–9, 32–5
reification 240
reterritorialization 13, 198, 209, 211, 241

satire 6, 146, 147, 149, 152, 155, 159, 162
scale/scalar 8, 22, 167–70, 188, 194, 230, 240
Scollon, Ron 4, 14, 20, 22, 38, 44, 73, 91, 148, 150, 151, 165, 168, 180, 192
Scollon, Suzie Wong 4, 14, 20, 22, 38, 44, 73, 91, 148, 150, 151, 165, 168, 180, 192
semiotic analysis 4, 18, 44, 55, 157; (re)semiotization of space 124, 147, 151–2, 162; semiotic artifacts 175, 183; semiotic landscape 4, 6, 13, 38, 124, 140, 146–65, 197, 219, 225; semiotic space 133, 141–2, 168, 177
semiotics 6, 20, 22, 41, 126, 147, 148, 151, 163, 179

Shohamy, Elana 3, 4, 6, 11, 13–15, 37, 89, 94, 147, 149, 165, 168, 188, 189, 192, 193, 240, 241
signage 3, 5–6, 15, 19–20, 22, 25, 32–7, 40–1, 43, 45, 52–3, 55–7, 60, 75–6, 86, 124, 127, 129–30, 140, 212, 217, 220, 225–6, 232, 239; signage choices 127, 129, *130*, 140, 141, 143
social networks 86, 203
sociocultural processes 198, 207, 210, 212
sociolinguistic (in)equality; sociolinguistic (in)justice 196, 214; sociolinguistic order 195, 196, 207, 209, 220, 223, 230, 231, 235, 239; sociolinguistic stratification 168
sociolinguistics 1, 4, 11, 13, 38, 40, 146, 190, 195, 216–18, 220, 240–2
Spanish language 2–6, 17, 23–31, 33–4, 40, 43–5, 47–57, 59–60, 64–5, 68, 71, 73–9, 81–3, 85–7, 94, 95, 97–9, 101–7, 114–18, 127–9, 139–40, 146, 151, 160–1, 177, 179–80, 183–6, 194–5, 207–10, 212–14, 217–18, 221, 223–6, 228, 231–2, 235–9
Spanish varieties 3, 107–13
students 5–10, 19, 65, 68, 70, 71, 78, 84, 87, 117, 124–42, 166, 169, 195, 197, 199, *200*, *208*, *211*, 212–14, 217–43; international students 6, 68, 78, 124, 126, 127, 140; secondary students 217, 219–21, 223, 225, 226, 228–30, 235–40; university students 7, 68, 124, 125, 133, 166, 195, 196, 240n3

temporality 9, 73, 183, 188
Thurlow, Crispin 4, 13, 38, 126, 150, 164
tourism 11, 13, 20, 21, 33, 37, 64, 68, 71, 75, 88, 175, 210, 211, *211*, 223, 229, 242
touristification 167, 170, 210, 211, 215, 217, 218, 223, 229
transgression 147–60
translocality 191
Tufi, Stefania 4, 13, 41, 44, 241
typography 6, 129–30, *131*, 135, 140–3

universcapes 6, 123–42
University of Salamanca 128
university semiotic landscape 6, 124, 140
urban processes 10, 197–9, 203, 240, 210, 213

Valencian 3, 5, 13, 40–63, **43**, **58**, 59n1, 59–60n3, 60n7
Van Leeuwen, Theo 6, 13, 126, 136, 139, 143, 150, 165
Vítores 129–42, *131*, *132*